PREHISTORIC and ROMAN ESSEX

PREHISTORIC and ROMAN ESSEX

(including Gazetteers for Essex and South Suffolk)

JAMES KEMBLE

The
History
Press

First published in 2001

This edition first published in 2009

The History Press
The Mill, Brimscombe Port
Stroud, Gloucestershire, GL5 2QG
www.thehistorypress.co.uk

© James Kemble, 2001, 2009

The right of James Kemble to be identified as the Author
of this work has been asserted in accordance with the
Copyrights, Designs and Patents Act 1988.

British Library Cataloguing in Publication Data.
A catalogue record for this book is available from the British Library.

ISBN 978 0 7524 5032 2

Typesetting and origination by The History Press
Printed in Great Britain

Contents

List of illustrations

Text figures

Colour plates

Acknowledgements

Grateful acknowledgement is given to the following for kind permission to use illustrations and sources:

Essex Society for Archaeology & History and Essex County Council: **1-4, 11, 13, 14-17, 19, 23-5, 29, 33-6, 41-7, 55, 56, 58, 59**. Essex County Council: **5, 6, 9, 10, 12, 18, 20-2, 27, 30-2, 38-40, 53, 54, 57, front cover, back cover, colour plate 2**, 3, 7, 8, 10, 19, 21-2, 25-8, 32. Butser Ancient Farm: **colour plate 12-13, 16, 18, 29, 31**. Chelmsford Museum: **28, colour plate 6, 15, 30**. Peter Froste: **colour plate 23**. Royal Anthropological Institute: **8**. Suffolk Institute of Archaeology & History: **49-51**. Valence House Museum, Barking, and Essex Record Office: **26**.

Quotations from classical authors are from *Roman Britain, a Sourcebook* by S. Ireland, Routledge, 1986.

Foreword

Essex has a diverse and rich landscape which has been appreciated from the time of the earliest farming communities. Clearance and settlement was a continuous process throughout prehistory and by the time of the Roman conquest virtually all of the region was being farmed and managed. This has given an outstanding archaeological heritage which is reflected in the existence of many surviving features such as Bronze Age burial mounds, Iron Age banks and ditches, and Roman sites ranging from waste dumps of salt-production around the coast to the impressive walls around Roman Colchester. However these represent only a small part of the available evidence which embraces extensive areas of preserved prehistoric land surface with associated occupation sites in the coastal intertidal zone. Thousands of sites of all periods have been identified from aerial photographs.

Knowledge and understanding of this heritage has increased hugely over recent years. Our museums have exceptional collections of finds, details of all sites are contained within the respective Sites and Monuments Records, and reports of excavations are published in national and local journals. However while this information is accessible to the specialist, it is not so readily available to the interested lay person. This book aims to put this right. It explores the nature of the archaeological evidence in a non-technical way, considers the kinds of site which can be identified at different periods of time and the functions which they fulfilled, and provides an extensive gazetteer of sites and places. The media, especially through popular television programmes, helped to generate a considerable interest in archaeology and particularly a desire on the part of many people to know more about their local area. For those with an interest in the past of Essex and south Suffolk, this book provides an informative read, a reference resource and a valuable guide to places to visit.

David Buckley
Essex Heritage Conservation Branch Manager and County Archaeologist

Introduction

Over the north door of Sir Christopher Wren's St Paul's Cathedral are the words 'If you need a monument, look around you' ('*Si monumentum requiris, circumspice*'). The entreaty applies equally to our archaeological heritage. Looking for evidence of our prehistory may require use of imagination to recreate it in the mind's eye, but is no less satisfying. This book results from an awareness from teaching at Further and Adult Education courses of the increasing desire for an accessible source of information about our regional heritage which does not, at least initially, require search in the more specialist journals and monographs. While the book stands on its own, it also provides an easy guide as to where to find information on a particular topic or locality. The region covered includes Essex and part of Suffolk. The geology of these counties is similar in so far that the Anglian ice age boulder clay covers much of both. Hence the landscapes and human land use are likely to have been similar. The influence of the Trinovantian tribe for which there is evidence from the latter part of the first millennium BC included Essex and south Suffolk. This region is one, both in prehistory and historically prior to the Saxon period. Colchester has been relatively well served by publications so this book concentrates on the wider context.

Much has been achieved by local Archaeological Groups of which several remain active. Much too will be learned by going outdoors to appreciate the nature of the landscape, the siting of a monument in relation to its surroundings, even if the monument is no longer visible. Such approaches may suggest the reasons why one area was favoured for settlement rather than another.

Within 10 miles of almost every town and village in our region at least one piece, and often many more, of archaeological evidence of earlier human activity has been recorded. The gazetteers provide references to books, journals and monographs for the monuments and sites. They include a small selection from the Sites and Monuments Records of Essex and Suffolk, both available to the public, a database of tens of thousands of the known historical and archaeological sites. The criteria for entry in the gazetteers are partly one of fullness and accessibility of published record, partly one of archaeological or historical significance, and partly in order to give as even a coverage as possible across the region, though, without doubt, lack of space has necessitated omission of many sites.

Pre-Roman and Roman roads in Essex and Suffolk are a relatively under-researched subject. Stane Street from Colchester through Great Dunmow, the A12 from London to Colchester, and the road from Chelmsford to Braintree are comparatively well known but there must be many lanes and byways which have a very long history awaiting investigation. Wary observation — sometimes purposeful, sometimes chance — by non-professional informed archaeologists and historians has brought to light many sites otherwise overlooked.

Metal detectionists and walkers are increasingly reporting finds under the National Portable Antiquities Scheme which encourages reporting for identification and recording to museum curators. 'Finds' are now being placed for public viewing on the web at www.finds.org.uk and www.essexcc.gov.org/ero. In the past, much important evidence about sites which are later excavated methodically has been found to have been lost through previous piecemeal removal, especially of metal and coin. Coins remain one of the most useful ways of dating a site that loss of even one, perhaps the only one present, can render a potentially close-dateable site undateable to any closer than several decades or even centuries. Every observer contributes by reporting finds to the museum so they can be added to the body of knowledge.

The draft text has been read by Nigel Brown of Essex Heritage Conservation, Paul Sealey of Colchester Museum and Scott Martin of the Essex Field Archaeology Unit, to whom I am extremely indebted for their constructive and helpful comments. David Buckley, Head of Heritage Conservation of Essex County Council, has been most supportive throughout the project in giving me access to material, as have Owen Bedwin, Ken Crowe, Richard Havis, Trevor Anderson, Teresa O'Connor, Paul Gilman and the staff of the Essex Sites and Monuments Record. The Essex Society for Archaeology & History, The Suffolk Institute of Archaeology & History, Mark Atkinson, Peter Froste, Roger Massey-Ryan, Peter Reynolds, Susan Tyler, Phillip Wise, Nick Wickenden and John Wymer have generously provided me access to illustrations. The Essex Record Office staff has without fail helped with the tracing of reports and documents. Peter Kemmis Betty of Tempus Publishing has steered the publication with sensitivity and enthusiasm.

The book aims to give a better impression of the wealth of our prehistoric and Roman heritage. The monuments, settlements, landscapes, their siting and the evidence are there to be found. Without a proper appreciation of our past we can scarcely evaluate our present.

James Kemble

Preface to the second edition

In the past nine years there have been significant further archaeological discoveries and publications, such as of the Neolithic causewayed enclosure at St. Osyth (Germany, 2007), the circus at Colchester (Crummy, 2008), evidence for prehistoric and Roman landscapes along the A130 and A120 bypass corridors (Dale, 2005; Timby, 2007), the prehistoric settlement at Maldon Elms Farm (Atkinson, 2001), and work at Hoxne (Tolan-Smith, 2000). The concentration by the Ancient Human Occupation of Britain Group since 2001 on the coast of Suffolk and Norfolk and associated research, and particularly work at Pakefield, have pushed back the evidence for human activity in Britain a further 200,000 years (Parfitt, 2006; Wymer, 2006). The opportunity has been taken to carry out a modest updating of this edition, and, where appropriate, the relevant references have been incorporated to enable readers to identify them.

1 The nature of the evidence

In Essex and Suffolk, ancient monuments standing above ground level are less numerous than in some parts of the country. This is because both counties have been intensively occupied for the past 3000 years, and because large building stone is scarce. Ploughing has destroyed many earthen burial mounds, enclosure banks, ditches and field boundaries. Robbed stone, brick and tile have been reused in later buildings, of which church walls and towers are beneficiaries. In Suffolk, prehistoric monuments such as barrows have survived better. In recent years several important monuments such as the Chelmsford cursus have been built over. Many monuments originally made of wood survive now only as postholes and ditches.

While these losses may be regretted, building development and gravel extraction have, at least recently, provided funding for evaluations and excavations which otherwise might not have occurred. Such evaluations incorporated into the planning permission process allow archaeologists to assess the likely importance of a site and to take appropriate action before building or destruction is allowed.

Sites and Monuments Records

The Sites and Monuments Records for Essex and Suffolk, held respectively at County Hall Chelmsford and Bury St Edmunds, and available by appointment to the public, have been compiled from a variety of sources, documentary and archaeological. They provide a valuable reference to actual or potential sites. As the name implies they include both above- and below-ground sites, and historic buildings are being added to the database. The Victoria County Histories of Essex and of Suffolk contain details of archaeological and historical places of interest, though do not yet cover the whole region in the same uniform depth. The majority of archaeological excavations of significance are published in the annual *Essex Archaeology & History Transactions*, *Proceedings of the Suffolk Institute of Archaeology & History* and *East Anglian Archaeology* monographs. Some local societies such as the Colchester Archaeological Trust publish their own journals with reports and articles on local excavations. The Victoria County Histories, *Essex Archaeology & History*, and the *Proceedings* are available at the Record Offices, Wharf Road, Chelmsford, and Raingate Street, Bury St Edmunds, the Essex Archaeology and History Society library at Essex University and in some public libraries. Reports on a few sites of national importance appear additionally in journals such as *Britannia* and *Proceedings of the Prehistoric Society*.

Documentary sources

The 6in Ordnance Survey first edition maps (about 1875) show sufficient detail to trace property and land boundaries. Unexplained deviations in boundaries or roads seen on the ground now may be explained by consulting such maps. At Asheldham the road deviates northwards to run outside the bank of the Iron Age hillfort (Bedwin, 1991). It is suggested that the double bend in the High Street at the south end of Kelvedon High Street is the result of the blocking of the original north-south street by a Roman enclosure (Eddy, 1982; Rodwell, 1988; Ennis, 2002).

By plotting field boundaries and roads from early estate and tithe (about 1840) maps, prehistoric field systems have been claimed to be identified. The fields to the north of Little Waltham and to the south of Braintree are aligned with relation to the River Brain which runs north-south (**1**). They are crossed diagonally by the Roman road to Braintree (**A**), suggesting that the fields pre-date the road and were therefore set out or developed in the Iron Age (or earlier) (Laver, 1889; Drury, 1976, 1978). Rodwell (1993) noted how the Roman road at Witham ignored the Iron Age enclosure at Witham Lodge, Hatfield Road, on which the adjacent fields were orientated, running straight across the ditch and bank at an angle to the fields, the road therefore post-dating the enclosure and field system.

The tithe and enclosure maps and awards and estate maps are more selective in the detail recorded but often give field names which may give clues to earlier land use. Thus two earth mounds, one partly ploughed out, the other standing to 4ft high near Fryerning church could be identified as mill mounds from the field name Mill Hill Field in which they stand; they may of course have older origins as prehistoric barrows (**colour plate 1**).

In a field 'Fen & Loews' — derived from Old English 'hlaw', a tumulus or hill — in Rivenhall End, Buckley and others (1988) excavated a crop mark which proved to have been a Neolithic burial mound (see Gazetteer). In Shardlows (Cressing), Old English meaning 'mutilated mound', is an enigmatic circular ploughed-out crop mark (Hope, 1978; Kemble, 1999, 2003). For Essex the $2\frac{1}{2}$ inch map surveyed in 1774 by Chapman and André shows settlements and roads, grazing marsh and wood (the last not always accurately), but does not delineate field or estate boundaries (Hunter, 1999).

Earlier documents such as surveys may be available for the area of interest. They may mention fishponds now visible only as a dry earthwork, or woods which have since been converted to arable. More rarely, documentation of pre-Domesday landholdings is available in the form of bounds in Anglo-Saxon charters. These boundaries sometimes still exist in the form of banks and ditches often delineating part of a parish. The charter bounds of Upminster documented in 1062 record a long extant field boundary from Tylers Common westwards across Nags Head Lane to the River Ingrebourne, still representing the county and parish boundary (Dr Hart, pers. comm.). Such boundaries may predate the Saxon holding (Aston, 1985; Rodwell, 1978). Hunter (1993) using a combination of early maps, field survey and archaeology postulates a Roman or pre-Roman origin for parallel field boundaries south and east of Cressing Temple into Rivenhall where there is known a high-status villa (Rodwell & Rodwell, 1985, 1990).

The determination of the origin of landscapes and how they have evolved requires a multidisciplinary approach, involving documents (including maps), place names, field

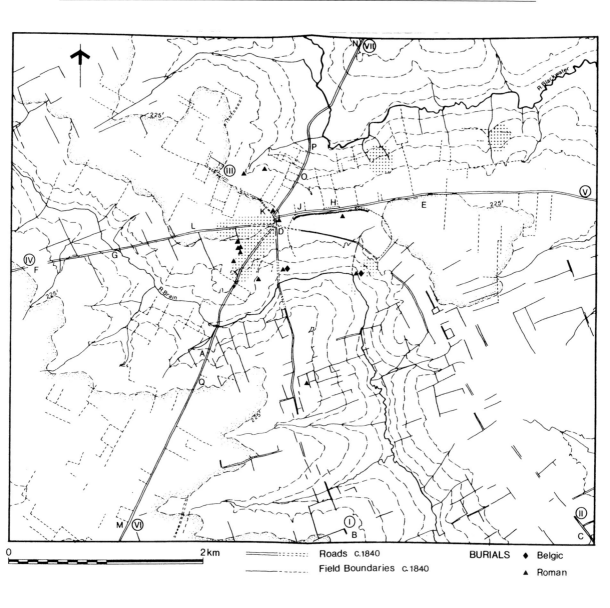

1   Braintree field systems (after Drury, 1976)

19

survey, settlement history (often revealed by archaeology), topography and field morphology (Williamson, 1987). In south-east and east Essex a late prehistoric date was suggested for the regular field pattern of the Dengie and Asheldham area (Drury, Rodwell, 1978; Rackham, 1986), though subsequently challenged as being too early. For the Southend area particularly around Orsett, there is some evidence for Roman influence on the subsequent development of the field pattern, though most is probably Saxon and later (Rodwell, 1978; Rippon, 1991).

Archaeological evaluation

Although the counties have a dearth of large boulders and significant amounts of stone for building which might be expected to survive for long periods, they have the advantage of long reaches of marine and estuarine silts (Thames, Crouch, Blackwater, Stour, Orwell, Deben and Alde) which have been shown to be capable of remarkable conservation of organic matter such as wood. The oak paddle found at Canewdon is some 3000 years old; the alder, oak, yew and ash forests exposed at low tides date from 4000 years ago (**colour plate 2**) (Wilkinson, Murphy, 1995). Erosion by rivers and the sea of ancient land has revealed the 350,000-year-old yew hunting spear at Clacton, one of the oldest wooden implements known in Europe, and 200,000-year-old bones of elephant, rhino and bison at Aveley.

Sites of archaeological significance have been found by chance observation of surface finds after ploughing, or the recording and reporting by a metal detectionist of a buried artefact. The hoard of 15,000 gold and silver coins, spoons, jewellery and silver pepper pots of the early fifth century AD was so detected from Hoxne, Suffolk (Johns, 1993). Occasionally unusual weather conditions can throw slight earthworks into emphasis; a light sprinkling of snow may accumulate in furrows, showing up low banks which are normally invisible. Careful observation on activities such as pipe-laying, turf-stripping and road-building have detected the Iron Age settlement at Wendens Ambo (Hodder, 1982) and the vicinity of a Roman villa farm at Rayne (Smoothy. 1989).

More structured approaches include field-walking. This involves the systematic collection of surface artefacts from recently ploughed land which has been sectored or gridded by marker poles. The collection includes pottery, flint, tile, implements, bone and glass, encountered on the traverses. The artefacts may provide evidence as to the age of the underlying archaeology and what type of site it is. Places where artefacts are concentrated are more carefully examined and may reveal an under-surface structure. Extensive areas have been subjected to field-walking evaluations in Essex, and standardisation of the method allows comparability between sites geographically separate (Medlycott, 2005).

In 1150ha field-walked before 1994, 54 prehistoric and 29 Romano-British sites were identified. In 300ha of the proposed Stansted airport development 30 sites were located where only four had been known previously. At Fox Hall, Southend (now the Leisure Park), field-walking revealed a prehistoric site, and in Crondon Park, Stock, an Iron Age site and a Roman farmstead were identified (Ecclestone, 1995; Medlycott, Germany, 1994). Field-walking at Boreham located a Roman building, subsequently excavated (see Glossary) (**2**). In an area of 28km^2 around Great Chesterford 28 probable Iron Age and 35 Romano-British settlement sites were located (Williamson, 1986).

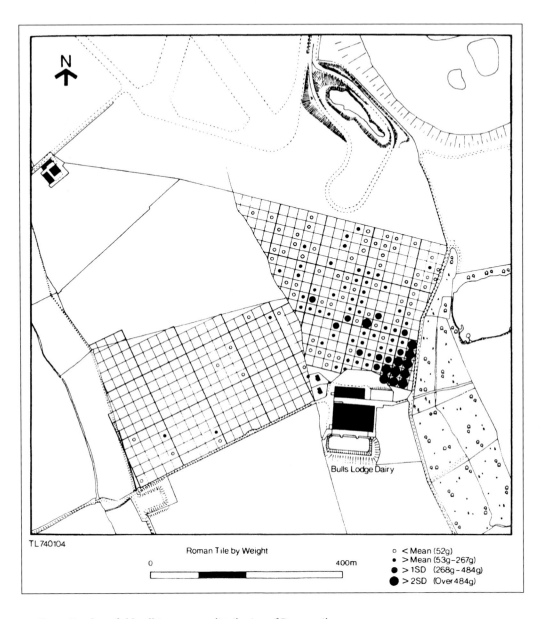

Roman Tile by Weight

0   400m

TL 740104

Bulls Lodge Dairy

o   < Mean (52g)
•   > Mean (53g–267g)
●   > 1SD   (268g–484g)
⬤   > 2SD   (Over 484g)

2   Boreham fieldwalking survey; distribution of Roman tile

3   *Rectangular cropmark, Great Bentley*

Aerial photography

The use of the camera and aeroplane has revealed many features which cannot so readily be appreciated from ground level (**back cover**). Features may show up only at certain times of year or in certain weathers. Some of the photographs by the German Luftwaffe during the Second World War, taken before the extensive wartime ploughing occurred, have contributed to the archaeology of Essex. Some of the vertical photographs taken by the Royal Air Force in 1946-7 are held at the National Monuments Record at Swindon; Cambridge University has also undertaken a very large photographic survey; and The Essex and Suffolk Sites & Monuments Records hold oblique photographs (**3**). In favourable slanting (morning or evening) light archaeological sites may be revealed better than when viewed in high sunlight. The overall wide panoramic view that aerial observation provides allows appreciation of field and boundary patterns and shapes of settlements (Strachan, 1995; Brown, 2002).

Grass and crop growth may show patterns of underlying ditches or walls. In dry weather lines of crops may thrive, growing faster and remaining greener longer above a buried ditch where moisture is preserved, or wilt above a stone wall where moisture is lacking. Extensive features dating from Bronze Age to modern showed as crop marks at Mucking (**4**). The Roman villa complex at Chignall St James has been so clearly outlined by differential grass growth that a plan of the building can be made without the need for excavation or geophysical survey (see Gazetteer).

4 *Cropmarks at Mucking (after Jones, 1973)*

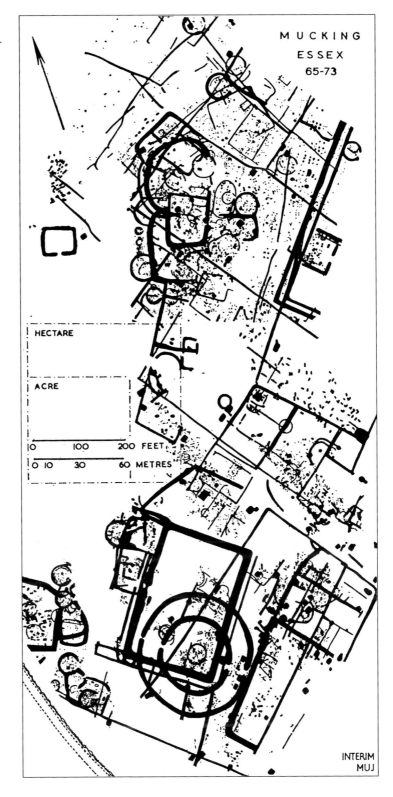

MUCKING
ESSEX
65-73

HECTARE

ACRE

| 0 | 100 | 200 FEET |
| 0 10 | 30 | 60 METRES |

INTERIM
MUJ

These 'crop marks' need to be differentiated from marks made by the plough when its share scrapes and brings to the surface part of a buried feature such as a wall, or surface soil colour differences due to different rates of drying from underground walls or silted ditches; these are better termed 'soil marks'. The Chelmsford Springfield Neolithic cursus, the Iron Age enclosure at Orsett Cock, the Roman fort at Gosbecks, the first-century AD graves at Colchester Stanway and the hengiform monument at Stratford St Mary were first recognised from aerial photography as crop and soil marks. At Colchester Gosbecks, a pattern of wild flower growth outlined the buried rubble walls of the Romano-British temple, the better drainage contributing to the selective growth at a particular time of year (Brown & Germany, 2002).

Mucking

From 1960s' air photographs, a landscape full of ancient occupation evidence was recognised and a start made on the surveying and excavation before gravel quarrying destroyed much of it. The main concentration was at that part of the Thames terrace where the river took an S-shaped turn first north then east, by Chadwell St Mary, Mucking, Tilbury and Linford. In this area alone were found an Iron Age hillfort, pre-Roman fields defined by ditches, Roman pottery kilns, Iron Age, Romano-British and Saxon houses, Bronze Age to Romano-British and Saxon burials. The late Bronze/early Iron Age mini-hillfort was about 80m in diameter, defended by a bank and double ditch. Later the area was used for sheep and cattle raising, confining the animals within ditched fields. Postholes interpreted as granaries attest to agriculture. In the Roman period long ditched enclosures suggest a new field system possibly worked from a villa farmhouse from which window glass, tile and wall daub have been recovered. Close by were two Roman cemeteries.

Prehistoric monuments standing above ground are, in this region for reasons already discussed, mainly earthworks. The large Iron Age defended enclosures would be called 'hillforts' in other parts of the country when sited on an elevated defendable position. Ambresbury Banks (Epping), Loughton Camp and Ring Hill (Littlebury) have been more appropriately termed 'plateau forts'. Several smaller banked and ditched enclosures, such as that at Writtle, represent what must have been a common settlement site in the Bronze and Iron Ages. There remain several round barrows, such as that at Sturmer, Risby Poor's Heath and Bartlow/Ashdon (**colour plates 4 & 20**). They date from the Neolithic to Saxon (and, in other parts of the country, Viking) periods and have often been found to contain cremation or inhumation burials (Lawson et al., 1981).

Less obvious, but nevertheless still in some instances existing as raised earthen mounds, are the salt-working sites named 'Red Hills' from the colour of the earth found in them. Their position along the former shoreline in Bronze Age to Roman periods helps to identify them. All these mounds need to be differentiated from mill mounds raised from the thirteenth/fourteenth centuries and onwards to support windmills. Earth mounds may be Second World War battery and observation sites, garden ornamental features, beacons or boundary markers.

Requiring perhaps a little greater degree of caution is interpretation of the evidence of current street or road patterns which result from Roman or earlier structures or workings. Deviation of the road round the fort at Great Hallingbury is apparent as part of the Iron Age bank is still present. Roads round a circular graveyard may indicate that the site has been a ritual one from prehistoric times.

Archaeological techniques

Excavation is, by definition, a destructive exercise. Increasingly, non- and minimally-invasive techniques are being used to preserve archaeology *in situ*. Auguring uses a long corkscrew which is twisted into the ground and a ream of the probe-hole extracted. The soil sample may contain mortar, pottery, charcoal or other archaeological material. Several drill-holes over a site may provide clues as to the density and type of the underlying archaeology. The method located the limestone causeway across the ditch of the prehistoric hillfort at Wandlebury (Trump, 1993). It was used also at Pound Wood, Thundersley to investigate a pond formed by an artificial dam at least 500 years old (Delderfield, 1996). A similar technique uses a hollow-core soil-borer. The extracted core is examined for seed, pollen, macro- and micro-fossils and soil samples. Samples from the Crouch and Blackwater estuaries have produced evidence of Palaeolithic and Mesolithic environments and activity.

Probing into the ground with a T-shaped metal rod to detect buried walls or voids such as vaults has been used successfully to map a site. The method is inexpensive, fairly quick and can lead to detection of areas which may need more intensive and sophisticated survey.

Geophysics

Several geophysical methods require special apparatus and some expertise to operate and interpret. Two techniques in particular have been extensively used. Resistivity survey involves setting out a sector or grid over the survey area. The resistance of the soil to an electrical current across the site is then measured and plotted onto a ground plan. Since an electrical current passes more readily through a moist medium than a dry one, high resistance occurs across buried stone walls, low over moist silted ditches. The effective depth of penetration into the soil is of the order of 1.5m. The condition of the soil may be critical to the obtaining of satisfactory results. A soil which contains many stones or rocks is less amenable to a satisfactory survey than one which is homogeneous, for example of sand. In Essex the method is therefore often successful in the estuaries in muds, silt and clay, but less so in areas of flinty limestone. Resistivity survey detected the Iron Age enclosure and burials at the Fairlop Quarry, Ilford (Meddens, 1995) and the Iron Age and Roman field ditches and pits at Great Sampford (Garwood, 1998).

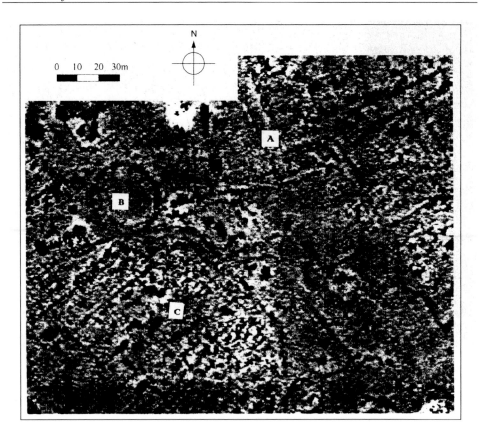

5   *Magnetometer survey, Great Chesterford Roman town*

Magnetometer survey is a means of detecting buried walls, pits, silted ditches, hearths and kilns. Disturbances in the magnetic field produced in the iron-bearing particles in the soil can be detected with a magnetometer and plotted onto a ground plan to produce a map of buried features. The method is most effective on soils with a high iron content, but may also be useful when the contrast between the buried feature and the soil is large, even when the soil iron content is low. Walls and roads tend to show a weaker magnetic field than the surroundings because the subsoil from which they are made has a lower magnetism than the nearby topsoil (Clark, 1996). Magnetometry was used at Great Chesterford to plot the road entering the Roman fort from the north (**5, A**) possible temple (**B**) and gridded streets (**C**) (Wardill, 1997). It was successful in plotting the position and dimensions of the portico and temple ditch at Gosbecks, Colchester, and showed that neither were quite square. A large complex of Neolithic and Bronze Age ring-ditches and enclosures was mapped prior to flooding for a reservoir at Langford, and allowed a limited excavation to be targeted to key areas (Cooper-Reade, 1996).

A Magnetic Susceptibility Meter detects alterations in the magnetism of soil caused by burning or from organic matter, by measuring the magnetic properties of the ground around which the meter is placed. The depth of measurement is not

0   50mm

6   *Gold torcs from Woodham Walter*

usually much greater than the topsoil which has been ploughed to the surface, so the method is often of use to define areas which merit more detailed investigation by other means.

Metal detectors emit an alternating magnetic field which is distorted by metal objects, walls, kilns, pits and ditches containing iron particles. The method has the advantage of speed and, used in conjunction with the readiness to investigate further when a significant find is made, can be most useful in identifying archaeological sites which can then be subjected to appropriate assessment. Unfortunately an isolated coin or metal object extracted from its context in the soil loses its value for dating any other material which might have been found associated with it unless the precise location and depth is marked when it is removed. The immediate declaration by the finders of the spectacular Bronze Age gold *torcs* at Woodham Walter allowed a proper archaeological investigation of the site (**6**) (Meeks, 1994). The huge hoard of Roman coins, jewellery and table ware buried in a wooden box in the fifth century AD was initially found by a metal detector at Hoxne in 1992 and is now in the British Museum (Jones et al, 1994).

The Standing Wave technique employs the principle of variable resonances from a buried void (such as a burial chamber) or wall on a quantifiable basis. The speed of passage of waves down to 70m below the surface produced by striking the ground can be measured by detectors; rapid waves suggest solid buried materials, slow ones soft materials. Sonar, seismic and ground radar devices use similar principles measuring the reflection of waves off a buried surface. The last is especially appropriate for dry sandy soils and can read down to 3m or so. It failed to locate St Runwald's church in Colchester but did detect a burial chamber under a mound at Sutton Hoo. In especially favourable conditions it has been effective down to 20m.

Increasing understanding of the past climate and appearance of the land is being culled through environmental analysis. The former concept of deep forest is now known to be incorrect, though certainly there was greater tree cover than at present. Samples of buried soils taken at excavation, quarrying and core sampling have been examined for pollen and seeds which may survive intact and be recognisable for many thousands of years. An increasing number of sites sampled in Essex have widened the understanding of how humans have affected the landscape, particularly since the Neolithic period. Cereal pollen first appears in environmental samples as elm tree pollen diminishes around 5000 years ago. The elm decline has been attributed to Neolithic man clearing land for cereal planting, but could be due to other factors (such as elm disease) (Brown, Germany, 2002).

Dowsing, the 'spontaneous' deflection of two metal rods held in the hands of the operator, remains a controversial technique amongst many mainstream archaeologists because of the lack of a satisfactory scientific explanation for its efficacy. Practitioners claim its usefulness to detect flowing underground water and mineral veins. One possible scientific explanation is the response of the dowser to changes in the soil magnetism. Claims have been made for the detection of underground steel pipes, wells, electricity cables, chromite ores and graves. Dr Trump (1993), a sceptical enthusiast, having apparently used the technique to good effect in detecting the Roman road near Burwell (Cambs) and the entrance to Wandlebury hillfort, dowsed the detailed outline of old Mistley church which proved on excavation to be a figment of imagination.

Lasar scanning of landscape from a plane or of individual objects records the surface contour in 3D and allows virtual replicas to be produced. One application LIDAR (Light Detecting and Ranging) will penetrate through trees which may cover earthworks and allows contours of now wooded areas to be accurately mapped (Miles, 2008).

Sites of burials where no skeletal or other visible evidence remains have been plotted by geochemical analysis of the concentrations of soil phosphate. A grid laid over the site is soil-sampled at regular intervals and a map of phosphate levels is built up. High phosphate levels of soil may indicate where organic matter has been concentrated such as where animals have been stalled, corralled and deposited manure, or where bone has decayed. A concentration of growth by plants such as nettles nourished by the phosphate may indicate the site of ground disturbed by human activity.

So far little exploited for Essex and Suffolk, but potentially appropriate for such seaboard counties, are techniques for underwater exploration and mapping. The preservation in these marine environments of organic matter has already been appreciated. Side scan sonar and magnetometry have been specifically adapted for underwater use.

No one method may in itself be adequate to map an archaeological site, but the accumulation of evidence from several sources, often over several years, may be compounded to provide information about the probable age, nature and extent of a site without recourse to destructive excavation.

Palaeolithic Essex and Suffolk

Stage	Climate	Years bp	Oxygen isotope stage	Geology	Sites
Flandrian	Warmer		1	Thames terraces	Mesolithic: Crouch Epping, South Benfleet, Burnham-on-Sea
		——— 13000 ———			
	Glacial maximum	19000	2		
Devensian			3,4		White Colne, Ipswich, Barham leaf points
			5a-d	Tilbury marshes	Tilbury
		——— 110000 ———			
Ipswichian	Warmer		5e		Bobbitshole Ipswich, Trafalgar Square London
		——— 130000 ———			
	Colder		6	Mucking	
		200000			
(Ilfordian)	Warmer		7		Brundon, Aveley, Purfleet, Levalloisian
Wolstonian		260000			
	Colder		8		
		330000			
	Warmer		9	Corbets Tey	Belhus Park, Acheulian handaxes, Purfleet, Acheulian, Levalloisian
	Colder		10		Little Thurrock, Clactonian
		——— 380000 ———			
Hoxnian	Warmer		11	Orsett Heath	Hoxne, Acheulian Barnham, Clactonian, Clacton-on-Sea, Clactonian, Swanscombe Acheulian/Clactonian
		——— 425000 ———			
Anglian	Major glaciation		12	Boulder clays	Thames diverted from central Essex to present course
		——— 475000 ———			
Cromerian	Warmer		13	Kesgrave gravels Tendring plateau terraces	Britain joined to continent. Mildenhall, High Lodge, Suffolk Boxgrove Man, Sussex
			14,15,16		
complex	Warmer		17	Forest beds	Pakefield

(After Wymer, 1996, 1999 and 2006; Stringer, 2008. All dates are approximate.)

2 Hunters and knappers
The Palaeolithic and Mesolithic Periods (700000 to 4000 BC)

The time interval between the first record of human presence in Essex and Suffolk, and the end of the last (Devensian) Ice Age about 12,000 years ago spans the order of 700,000 years. To encompass this period it is proposed to adhere to the traditional divisions of three cold (glacial) periods — Anglian, Wolstonian and Devensian (see Glossary) — and the intervening warmer periods — Hoxnian, Ipswichian and the present Flandrian. It is now recognised that each cold stage contained within it warmer phases (interglacials and interstadials) during which parts of Britain were reoccupied by humans from the mainland (Bridgland, 1994; White 2000).

As each of three glacial stages came to an end and a warmer climate returned, the ice and tundra landscape was replaced. Evidence for the appearance of the changing landscape comes from soil samples analysed for pollen and seed remains. These have been obtained from such places as the Mardyke (south Essex), Marks Tey (mid-Essex), Bradwell and Clacton (east), Enfield and Mildenhall (west and north-west). These show that after the end of the cold periods there was open grassland with birch and pine trees which was gradually replaced by hazel, elm, alder and, at the warmest, oak, hornbeam and lime forest.

The Pre-Anglian Interglacial and Anglian Ice Age

Before the Anglian Glacial, Britain was joined to the continent (Wymer, 2006). The Bytham river flowed south-eastwards from the Midlands to Norfolk, future Bury St Edmunds and Great Yarmouth, and gave access to the interior along it from the Rhine region. Human activity has been found near Coventry so it is reasonable to suppose *Homo* moved either from the south-west or through Suffolk along the Bytham river north-westwards (Lang, 2005) (7).

Evidence for human activity in the region prior to the Anglian glacial period over 475,000 years ago is at Mildenhall High Lodge (see Gazetteer). A human tibia and two incisors found at Boxgrove near Chichester are contemporary (Roberts, 1994, 1997). These may belong to an antecedent of *Homo sapiens*, either *Homo erectus* or *Homo heidelbergensis*, who was butchering giant deer, rhinoceros and horse with flint tools, leaving cut-marks on the bones. At High Lodge remains of extinct rhinoceros, *Dicerorhinus etruscus*, were found in the 1960s. It is likely that the High Lodge artefacts have been brought to the site by glacial movement, having originated further upstream in the Bytham valley. Some of these tools were sharp cutters, or the flakes struck from the core flint were modified

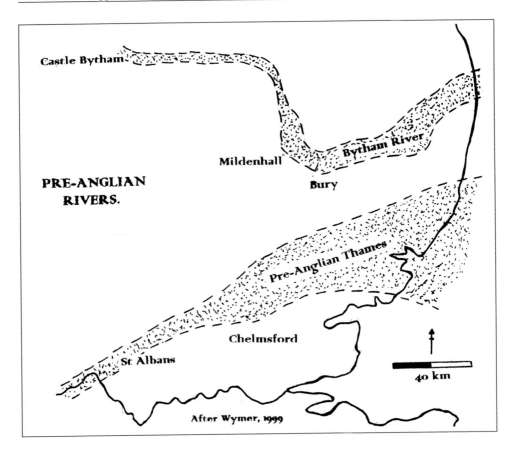

7   *Pre-Anglian rivers*

into hide-scrapers and wood-whittlers. Choppers and, at nearby Mildenhall Warren Hill, handaxes similar to those found at Boxgrove are probably of a similar date (Cook, 1991; Roe, 1968). From the coastal cliffs at Pakefield have been removed earlier worked flints in sediments dated to before 680,000 BP (Parfitt, 2005; Wymer, 2006).

Homo species

Homo erectus has been described as a hominid from which both *Homo sapiens* and *Homo neandertalensis* have evolved. Fossil remains of *Homo erectus* have been found in Africa, the Far East, Asia, the Middle East and Europe, dating from 1.6 million years until 300,000 years ago. Anatomically the species has a long low skull squared at the back (occiput), a thick bony keel for attachment of neck muscles running across the back of the skull, a strong continuous bony brow ridge above the eye sockets, and a brain size smaller than or at the lower end of the normal range of *Homo sapiens*. Probably closely associated but of which few examples are known is *Homo heidelbergensis*. The type specimen, a lower jaw only, was found at Mauer in West Germany, but specimens from Zambia, Atapuerca

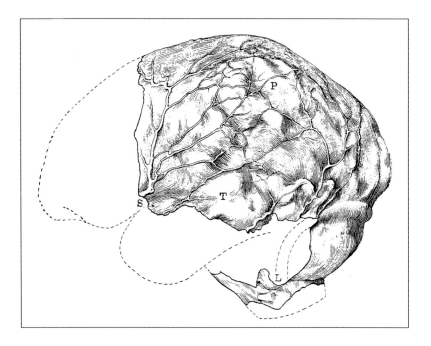

8   Endocranial cast of the Swanscombe skull bones

(Spain) and Swanscombe, Kent have also been tentatively ascribed to similar species. The bones are robust with strong muscle attachment marks, and the chin is absent. Both species are associated with tools of Acheulian industry (see Glossary) (Day, 1986).

No skeletal remains of *Homo* of this period have been found in Essex or Suffolk, but just south of the Thames at Barnfield Pit, Craylands Lane, at Swanscombe near Dartford, part of the skull of a young woman was excavated in 1935/6. Another piece was found 20 years later and found to fit with the earlier pieces (Swanscombe Committee, 1937, 1938; Bridgland, 1994). This is an archaic form of *Homo* probably ancestral to the Neanderthals (Wymer, 1996). Thermoluminescence dating suggests about 225,000 years (see Glossary) (Day, 1986). If this date is correct it would put it near to the mid-Wolstonian Stage (see below), though on evolutionary and depositional criteria this seems too late a date and the Hoxnian interglacial around 380,000 years ago is generally preferred. The implements found with the skull were handaxes and flake tools of Acheulian industry. Wolf, lion, straight-tusked elephant, rhinoceros, giant deer and giant ox were found in the same stratum.

The Swanscombe skull

The Swanscombe skull has a brain capacity of about 1325cc; this compares with that of modern humans whose skull capacity is about 1150-1700cc (**8**) (Overy, 1964; Tobias, 1971). A similar, more complete but distorted skull was found in Steinheim 12 miles north of Stuttgart in 1933. The cranial capacity of several skulls of *Homo erectus* discovered varies between about 800cc and 1200cc, but '*Archaic Homo sapiens*' to which the Swanscombe skull might reasonably be included and *Homo neandertalensis* average from 1100cc to 1750cc. Cro-Magnon Man (see Glossary) which is '*Early modern Homo sapiens*' has an estimated cranial capacity of about 1600cc (Day, 1986; Aiello, Dean, 1990).

Some observers have pointed out the features of the Swanscombe skull which resemble Neanderthals, others *Homo erectus*. There are also some similarities with *Homo sapiens*. Consequently it has been proposed that the Swanscombe skeleton was at the evolutionary split from *Homo erectus* between Neandertal from *Homo sapiens*. Some DNA evidence suggests sapiens and neanderthal lines began to diverge around 700,000 years ago, possibly *Homo heidelbergensis* being a common ancestor (Stringer, 2006). More recent finds dating from 100,000 years ago, including in Zambia (Kabwe, Broken Hill), South Africa, Eritrea and Ethiopia (Omo Valley), suggest that *Homo sapiens* evolved in Africa separately, and migrated into Europe from where it displaced *Homo neandertalensis* finally about 30,000 BC (Barham, 1994; Abbeto, 1998).

Homo neandertalensis

Evidence of Neanderthal skeletons from St Césaire north of Bordeaux, La Ferrassie and La Chapelle-aux-Saints in the Dordogne, the Neander valley near Dusseldorf, Shanidar north of Baghdad and elsewhere show they generally had prominent brow-ridges above the eyes, receding forehead, wide nose and projecting middle face. The St Césaire skeleton has been dated by thermoluminescence of associated flints to about 32,000 years ago, making it one of the most recent Neanderthal skeletons (Mercer, 1991).

Compared to *Homo sapiens*, the Neanderthal hand is very similar, but it differs in three main features: its size, the joint at the base of the thumb, and the thumb length. The Neanderthal hand bones are larger, thicker and stronger. The basal thumb joint is relatively flat rather than shaped like a saddle. The two bones (phalanges) of the Neanderthal thumb are of about equal length but the terminal bone (distal phalanx) of *Homo sapiens* is only two-thirds the length of the proximal phalanx. These differences have been interpreted as Neanderthal being less dextrous but stronger in pinch and grasp.

Evidence from the skull, spine, pelvis, leg and foot bones confirm that *Homo erectus* and *neandertalensis* were fully upright walkers. Neanderthal arm and leg bones tend to be shorter and thicker than those of *Homo sapiens*, though are within the modern average ranges. They compare well with modern human populations of cold climates such as the Inuit. The shorter stature has the effect of reducing body skin surface relative to body mass, a heat-conservation mechanism. In short, Neanderthal Man dressed in today's clothing would appear shortish, stockily-built and not wholly out of place in modern society (Trinkaus, Shipman, 1993; Stringer, 2001; Boismier, 2002; Mellars, 2004).

Climate change

During the Anglian glaciation (about 470,000-420,000 years ago) the ice sheet extended as far south as an approximate line linking the following: Chigwell, Hornchurch, Brentwood,

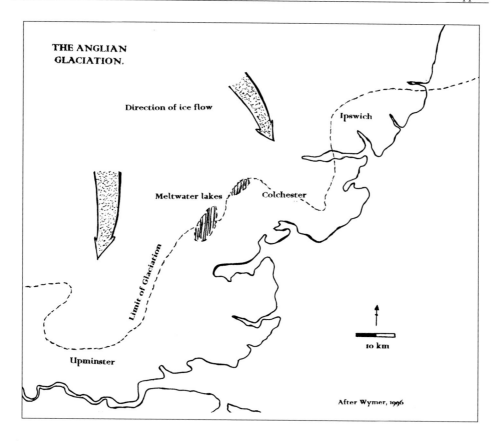

THE ANGLIAN
GLACIATION.

Direction of ice flow

Ipswich

Meltwater lakes

Colchester

Limit of Glaciation

10 km

Upminster

After Wymer, 1996

9   Maximum extent of the Anglian glaciation

Danbury, west of Colchester, Tendring peninsula, Stutton, Ipswich and Aldeborough (**9**). The landscape of East Anglia would have been tundra, similar to that of present Siberia. For much of these periods, the southern parts of what is now the North Sea and English Channel were low-lying marsh or permafrost because water locked up as ice resulted in low sea levels. The Goodwin Sands and Dogger Bank were low hills or islands. Land continuous with the continent allowed hunter-gatherers as well as animal herds to live on what is now the North Sea and English Channel (from where bones and artefacts are sometimes dredged) and to cross into Britain, until warmer periods resulted in the land link being submerged. A fall in sea level of less than 50m (170ft, 28 fathoms) is sufficient to connect Britain with the mainland (White, 2000; Gaffney, 2007).

The clay, flints, chalky rocks and boulders from further west and north deposited on Essex and Suffolk by the Anglian ice sheet as it thawed had a profound effect on the region. Glacial action is responsible for dumping the boulder clay on north-west Essex and much of Suffolk. The boulder clay obliterated the Bytham river so that pre-Anglian sites are now buried beneath it. Before the Anglian glacial stage the Thames flowed across Essex from Harlow through Chelmsford and Braintree to the Tendring peninsula, Ipswich and south-east Suffolk in a broad flood plain. This course has left the sands and gravels of mid-Essex and Suffolk (known as Kesgrave, after the village in Suffolk where similar gravels have been exposed) which lie beneath the boulder clay.

The river systems

The Anglian ice sheet blocked the course of the Thames in the Vale of St Albans at Marlow causing a massive lake which eventually overflowed to empty into the more southerly course it now occupies. The newly diverted Thames was joined by the River Medway at Southend, both flowing together northwards to the Tendring peninsula and Clacton when sea levels were lower than now, and depositing across the Dengie peninsula gravels which originate both from Kent and from the west of Britain. At the end of the Anglian Stage, the Gipping, Stour, Blackwater and Crouch rivers had their approximate present courses flowing to a coast far east of what is the present North Sea shoreline. At Hoxne, lakes filled with glacial meltwater drained into the Waveney valley. A meltwater lake at Marks Tey and Copford beside which lived elephant, bison, giant beaver and giant ox drained into the Roman river valley. The lake at Kelvedon, Rivenhall and Witham was fed at first by fast-running rivers from the icefields in the Blackwater and Brain valleys. The lakes slowly silted up and disappeared, leaving only the deposited silt and gravel as evidence for their existence (Bridgland, 1994; Gibbard, 1994; Lucy, 1999).

The Hoxnian Interglacial

Following the retreat of the Anglian ice sheet, evidence of human activity, probably at a temporary camp, has been found at Clacton on the banks of the former course of the Thames/Medway (Singer, 1973). The tools are mostly flint cores and flakes for cutting, meat butchery, scraping hides and wood-working (Clactonian industry). Here, at Lion Point Jaywick, bones of wild boar, straight-tusked elephant and wild ox were excavated. These were accompanied by one of the oldest wooden implements in Britain, 350,000 years old, a thrusting spear, sharpened to a point, made of yew which had been preserved in the wet mud (Oakley, 1977).

The Clactonian tools were relatively crudely fashioned by striking a flint nodule with a hammer stone or on an anvil to produce largish flakes which could be used as choppers (**10**). Chronologically, this industry overlaps with the Acheulian which itself contains chopper tools but has a more sophisticated kit in addition. That at Clacton, beside the former Thames, was a flint-knapper's 'working floor' shown by fitting together flakes to reform the flint core from which they had been struck. Were those humans who made Clactonian tools of a different species from those who knapped Acheulian tools? Certainly microscopic study of the cutting and scraping surfaces of the two types of tool suggest that both types of tool were used on bone, animal hide and wood. Clacton was the first Palaeolithic site to have a pollen sequence analysed, and shown to date to the Hoxnian Stage.

Clactonian tools have been found also at Barnham St Gregory and Little Thurrock, both beside rivers. At Barnham, a lake fed by the River Lark provided *Homo* opportunities

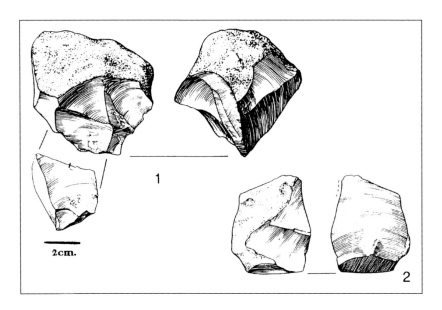

10   Clactonian flints: 1 Core with conjoinable flake; 2 wood whittler

for fishing. Amino-acid dating of mollusc shells suggests they date to about 400,000 years ago, broadly contemporary with that at Swanscombe, Kent (Wymer, 1999).

The site at Hoxne on the Suffolk-Norfolk border is one of the classic sites for Palaeolithic archaeology, dating also from about 400,000 years ago. The climate during the Hoxnian interglacial was mild and moist. Mixed woodland was interspersed with open grassland and there were plentiful numbers of large herbivores, lion, bear, giant deer, horse and wolf. Also present were macaque monkey, fallow deer, now-extinct water vole and giant beaver. Britain was linked to continental Europe throughout the period (Evans, 1975).

Acheulian industry

Hoxne, then a lake as at Marks Tey in Essex, produced flint handaxes, cleavers and flakes of Acheulian industry during excavations in the 1970s (**11**). The tools were finished by flaking, using a soft bone or antler hammer, which resulted in a more regular surface than Clactonian tools. Cut marks on bones showed that animals were being butchered. Here was found the earliest evidence in Britain of a human 'construction', a stone cluster emplacement, perhaps a shelter floor (Wymer, 1999).

The relatively large number of find-spots for Acheulian industries and the long period of time over which these tools were produced (even into the Last (Devensian) Ice Age) suggests that innovation was extremely conservative. Small differences in groups of tools between one find-spot and another suggest a degree of isolation between 'family' groups. The population presumably consisted of bands of people, extended families, working

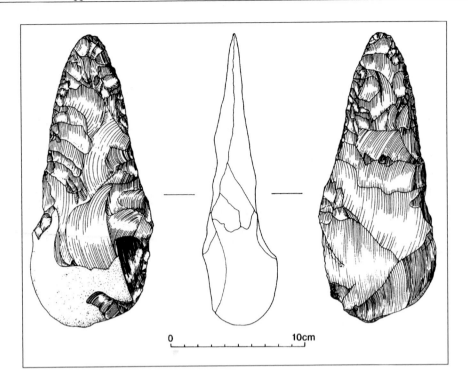

11   Acheulian handaxe from Aveley

together and moving from one temporary camp to another, living in hide and brushwood shelters or caves, hunting, scavenging, fishing and collecting edible plant-produce. Though the surviving evidence is sparse, these people perhaps undertook wood and leather working, using bone and antler for needles and bodkins. Burned wood at sites such as Marks Tey and Hoxne suggest the deliberate use of fire (Evans, 1975; Wymer, 1984).

Wolstonian glacial and warm periods

From the start and during warmer periods of the next cold stage, the Wolstonian glaciation (which lasted from about 380,000 to 130,000 years ago), tools including handaxes have been found at Orsett, South Ockendon, Dovercourt (Pounds Farm) and Brundon. At Woodford during construction of the M11/North Circular Road junction, were found handaxes and cleavers on a knapping site, probably about 350,000 years old.

Several sites along the north Thames valley and estuary between Leytonstone and the coast have yielded evidence of human activity between about 320,000 years and 200,000 years ago (Middle Palaeolithic period). These include Wanstead, Ilford, Purfleet, Thurrock, Tilbury, South Ockendon and Stanford le Hope (Roe, 1968; Wymer, 1985, 1999). The important Purfleet sites have yielded the earliest evidence of Levallois industry in the Thames valley and it seems clear that this part of the Thames was well-exploited during this time, partly because of the outcropping of workable flint.

Levallois industry

The technique of tool-making, called Levallois, involved preparing the core of flint into a 'tortoise' shape before beginning to strike the flakes from it. This produces a predictably-shaped flake (**12**). The industry was practised as part of and at the same time as the Acheulian but seems to have begun after the earliest Acheulian, possibly in the mid-Wolstonian about 250,000 years ago. The Levallois flakes and new types of handaxes (flattened at the base, flat-butt or bout-coupé, rather than rounded) are associated with *Homo neandertalensis* and the industry is termed Mousterian (see Glossary). It is possible that new arrivals had brought the technique from the continent as warmer weather allowed reoccupation. This implies that the preceding glacial period had lowered the sea level sufficiently to re-establish a land connection, or, at least, only a narrow intervening channel. There are detectable differences between

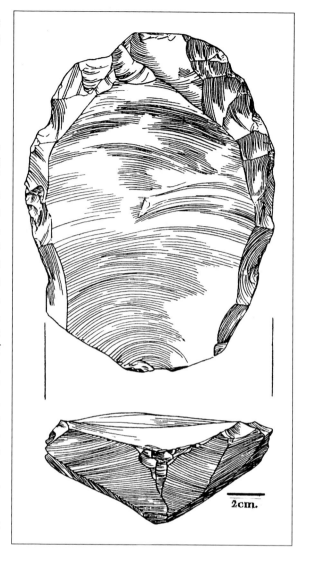

12   Levallois 'tortoise' flint core from South Woodford

the Mousterian of France from that of Britain. In France there is a greater variety of forms of tool. This suggests a degree of isolation of the two communities.

The only known skeletal remains in Britain of the Middle Palaeolithic are from the cave at Pontnewydd in Clwyd, North Wales, uranium- and fluorescence-dated to about 225,000 years old. Here parts of a human jaw, a spinal vertebra and teeth with the Neanderthal characteristic of fused roots were recovered, together with handaxes and Levallois-type flakes (Day, 1986; Green, 1981; White, 2002, 2003).

During the Wolstonian Stage about 210,000 years ago, there was a warm stage tentatively labelled the Aveley or Ilfordian interglacial, from finds at Sandy Lane Pit near the Thames in 1997. These included a jungle cat, lion, straight-tusked elephant, rhinoceros, auroch, bison and mammoth. A contemporary site is at Brundon near Sudbury.

From the same or a similar interglacial were excavated in 1863 remains of the complete skull and tusks of a woolly mammoth from Uphall brickearth pit to the west of Ilford Lane, Ilford. This is now in the Natural History Museum (Davies, 1874). More recently in 1984 during the construction of the Ilford southern relief road mammoth, rhinoceros and giant ox bones were found.

This warmer interglacial stage (about 200,000 years ago) has been explored at Stoke Tunnel and Maidenhall in Ipswich, Harkstead in Suffolk where there were pond tortoises, and in south Essex from where have been found Acheulian handaxes (Layard, 1920; Buckley, 1977). Animals here included the giant ox (*Bos primigenius*), rhinoceros, giant elk (*Megaceros*) and elephant. The interglacial was followed by another cold period (corresponding to Oxygen Isotope phase 6 beginning 185,000 years ago lasting over 50,000 years) which may have caused the extinction of the human population here (Bridgland, 1994).

Ipswichian interglacial

There is a scarcity of sites with evidence of human activity from this warm period about 120,000 years ago, perhaps because repopulation of Britain was impossible as it was cut off from the mainland by the sea. Animal remains of hippopotamus, straight-tusked elephant, rhinoceros, giant ox and bison, as well as (appropriately) lions found at Trafalgar Square, London, give an indication of the landscape at this time, uninterrupted by humans. The type site is Ipswich, Bobbitshole (see Glossary).

From about 110,000 years ago the climate again started to deteriorate into the Devensian glaciation. Tools associated with *Homo neanderthalensis* which include flat-butted cordate (heart-shaped) forms of handaxe of the later phases of the Ipswichian interglacial period or of the early Devensian stage called 'Mousterian of Acheulian tradition, MAT' have been found at Tilbury.

The Devensian glacial

Evidence for human habitation is rare, even during warmer phases of the last ice age, the Devensian (about 110,000 to 12,000 years ago), when the ice sheet reached north Norfolk at its maximum around 19,000 years ago. At the height of the glaciation the southern North Sea was permafrost or ice. The coastline may have extended from Perth to Denmark, the English Channel was tundra and the Scilly Isles were part of the Cornish peninsula (Evans, 1975; Coles, 1998). Bones of rhinoceros, reindeer and mammoth dating to the Devensian have been found at Great Totham and in the Lea Valley.

Modern humans, *Homo sapiens sapiens*, arrived in north-west Europe about 40,000 years ago during the Devensian. Rare human presence in a warm interstadial is attested by a leaf-point flint tool, hearths, burnt and crazed stones (pot-boilers) from White Colne together with a mammoth tusk, and remains of wild ox and ibex (Layard, 1927). Leaf-points (indicating their leaf shape) are usually about 5in long, sharpened by striking flakes off both sides of the edge (bifacial). They may have been bound to a wooden shaft to form a spear, harpoon or arrow, or used as a knife blade. If leaf-points were technology only of *Homo sapiens*, the White Colne leaf-point is evidence that *Homo sapiens* was already in Britain at a time at the extreme latest limit survival of *Homo neandertalensis* in Europe.

Evidence as to whether *Homo neandertalensis* and *Homo sapiens* were in Britain simultaneously is very tenuous (Mellars, 1998). At Ipswich Bramford Pit, Levallois flakes (interpreted as Neandertal) have been found with *sapiens* leaf-points. Had two communities merged their technologies, cooperated or learned from one another? Canewdon, Creeksea, Burnham-on-Crouch, Rochford, Shoebury and Prittlewell on the Thames-Crouch peninsula have produced handaxes probably of the Early Devensian period 100,000 years ago, presumably of Neanderthal origin. But further north in the Lark valley there is little evidence that there was any human presence (except perhaps at Barnham) from about 200,000 years ago until the later Devensian period, then *Homo sapiens* (MacLeod, 1971). Handaxes made for 500,000 years seem no longer to have been made after around 30-40,000 years ago (Wymer, 1999). Does this mark the end of the Neanderthals? (Aston, 2003).

The two species lived concurrently for perhaps 40,000 years. Recent DNA analyses of the Neander Valley humerus and of the infant from Mesmaiskaya Cave, North Caucasus, suggest *Homo neandertalensis* constitutes a separate evolutionary line from *Homo sapiens sapiens* (Krings et al, 1997; Ovchinnikov et al, 2000). But from Largar Velho, Portugal the discovery of a four-year-old child with both Neanderthal and modern human features suggests the two species interbred before 25,000 BC incorporating some of the Neanderthal gene pool into *Homo sapiens* (Ward, Stringer, 1997; Pettitt, 1999).

If evidence for human presence in Britain during much of the the Devensian ice age is scanty, *Homo sapiens* was occupying southern Europe where cultures called Aurignacian, Solutrean and Magdalenian (see Glossary) have been found. Tools were finely fashioned for particular purposes. The technique of controlling the removal of a small flake was developed by pressure (probably with a piece of antler) rather than striking the flint core. Arrowheads with barbs and tangs were made.

From the Palaeolithic evidence available emerges a picture of the intermittent presence of groups of perhaps not less than 25 persons (enough to maintain a reproductive community) entering Britain from the mainland. These may have been seasonal migrations following herds, as do the Laplanders now. They lived probably in hide and brushwood shelters by scavenging, fishing and hunting and by collecting fruits, fungi, nuts, plants, roots, berries, mussels, shellfish and eggs. While almost the only artefacts which have survived are of stone, they will have made use of a large range of materials including bone, antler, hide, hair, sinew, wood, grass, fire and probably many of the plant materials such as flax. Their knowledge of the biological world would have been handed down over thousands of generations.

Evidence for ritual burial has been found at La Ferrassie, Dordogne, where four Neanderthal graves were occupied by two adults and two children, and at Paviland Cave in Glamorgan, where a modern human was found. Here the left half of a male skeleton buried with bracelet and ivory rods was found sprinkled with red ochre, dated to about 29,000 BP (Aldhouse-Green, 1998; 2001; Higham, 2008). The Devensian glaciation reached its maximum about 18,000-16,000 BC. As the ice sheet reached north Norfolk it would be remarkable if humans were able to continue occupation in Britain, though reindeer and horse both appear to have survived into the post-glacial period.

Towards the end of the Devensian glaciation, occupation by *Homo sapiens* was re-established in Britain, radiocarbon dated to about 12,500 bc (Jacobi, 2004). There were rapid fluctuations in climate resulting in alternating growth of pine and birch forests, with hazel and elm. Late Upper Palaeolithic tools and barbed spear points of antler and bone of the industry termed 'Creswellian' with horse and reindeer have been found at Sproughton about 11,000 years old, a blade from Shoeburyness, and a shouldered blade from Mildenhall (Jacobi, 1980, 1996) (see Glossary). The four flints described by Martingell and Jacobi (1978) from Walton-on-Naze have points at either end of tools about 7cm longx1.25cm wide (bi-points); similar found elsewhere in Britain are dated around 9000 bc (**13**) (Richards, 2000; Bahn, 2003; Ripoll, 2004; Pettitt, 2006).

The Flandrian warm period (present interglacial)

Temporary camps were being occupied by hunter groups who were making tools at the end of the last glacial. Shouldered blades and tanged points are known from Manningtree, Widford and Ipswich. By 8500 BC all of the large mammals such as mammoth, rhinoceros and hippopotamus were extinct in Britain. While the climatic changes will have influenced these extinctions, hunting is likely to have contributed though to what extent is difficult to determine. The nineteenth- and twentieth-century experience of colonists and ivory poachers with North American bison and African elephant demonstrates how relatively few hunters can virtually exterminate large herds of herbivores within a few decades.

When sea levels were low at the start of the Mesolithic period, the Crouch and Blackwater rivers flowed into the Thames to form one estuary east of Foulness, the course of which, now silted, has been traced into the North Sea (Murphy, 1996). As sea levels rose, this common estuary was drowned. Previously occupied land sites on which Mesolithic flints have been found are exposed at low tide and have been explored at South Woodham Ferrers, Maylandsea, Crouch estuary and elsewhere along the Hullbridge estuary and coast (Warren, 1909; Wilkinson, 1995). The land link with the mainland was last broken about 7500 BC as sea levels rose in the southern North Sea. Around 7000 BC sea level in the Thames estuary was about 14m (45ft) below that of today, and because of the gently sloping terrain large areas of now-drowned land were then dry or marshy (Hunter, 1999). Sea levels continued to rise until about 4000 BC. Initially isolation of the population in Britain would not have been absolute since there will have been some successful sea crossings but as the English Channel widened year on year the passage became increasingly dangerous, and land-animal migrations ceased (Coles, 1998; Gaffney, 2007).

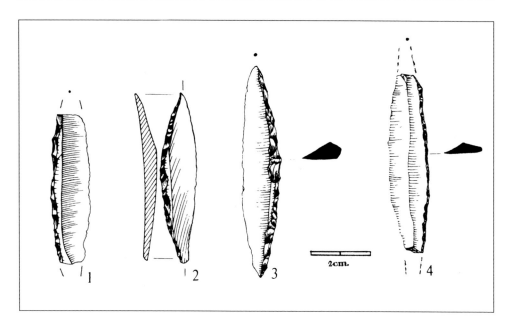

13   *Late Devensian bi-point flints from Walton-on-Naze*

By about 8000 BC the Lea Valley landscape was dominated by an open countryside with sedge, some birch and willow. Following the retreat of the ice sheet northwards, the climate was improving markedly by 7000 BC. The tundra was replaced by sallow, birch and aspen, then by hazel and pine. Continuing warming allowed alder and oak then elm, lime, holly, ash, beech and maple in thickening forest. During the Mesolithic, lime (*Tilia*) was a dominant species in Lowland Britain (Rackham, 1987). By 6500 BC samples from Bradwell show a woodscape of lime trees and by 5500 BC oak, lime, hazel and alder were predominant around Purfleet and Grays when forestation was at its maximum.

Elk became extinct about 6000 BC, but wild cattle (auroch), roe and red deer and boar roamed widely. Packs of wolves could pose a danger to a lone person, but the tamer wild dogs found food easily available for scavenging at human settlement sites and some were becoming domesticated. At a lakeside settlement site at Thatcham, Berkshire, were excavated horse, beaver, pine martin, elk, roe and red deer, wild ox, pig and cat.

The Mesolithic tool kit

About 8000 BC new types of flint technologies developed. The Mesolithic toolkit contained small flints (microliths) and core axes/adzes. The mode of life would initially not have been greatly different from the Upper Palaeolithic. Smaller game was hunted with flint arrow tips and fish caught with slivers of antler barbed as 'hooks'. Antlers were used also as mattocks. Wood was being worked with stone adzes and notched flints (saws). The tranchet axe, transversely sharpened, an elongated core tool with an edge sharpened by removal of flakes from one end, could be resharpened by the subsequent removal of further flakes. Good examples have been found at Ingatestone (see Gazetteer), Walton-on-Naze, Ongar, Ardleigh, Lackford and Mildenhall West Row (Martingell, 1986; Jacobi, 1996; Austin, 1996). A flint-working site has been excavated at Basildon.

The large collection of Mesolithic artefacts found at High Beach, Epping before 1913 contains burins, scrapers, awls and punches (Jacobi et al., 1978). Further excavations in 1959 and 1961 produced 1704 flint pieces, of which microliths with obliquely blunted points figured prominently amongst the 'essential tools' category. The site seems to have been in use throughout a major part of the Mesolithic period.

A much smaller but nevertheless interesting group has been collected over a period of years by members of the public at South Benfleet on the Thames estuary. The tools consisted of flint axes, blades, scrapers and cores from which they had been struck (Crowe, 1992). Clearly the site had been a flint-knapper's 'working floor' near a suitable source of flint on the Claygate/Bagshot ridge at which other Mesolithic production sites are also known.

At Hullbridge on the Crouch estuary was a preponderance of finds such as scrapers, burins and knives, dating to the later Mesolithic around 5000 bc. There may have been a temporary occupation site here which, at that time, would have been inland. A 'working floor' is strongly suggested by the finding of a flake near a core to which it fits. A radiocarbon date of 5880 bc±520 can be given to peat immediately underneath Mesolithic microtriangles (?points, arrowheads) at Broxbourne in the Lea valley (Jacobi, 1980). The distribution of find-spots makes it apparent that river- or lake-side locations were preferred, particularly if workable flint was at hand.

Population estimates are difficult to arrive at but a figure between 3000 and 20,000 has been postulated for the country as a whole (Jacobi, 1978; Darvill, 1987). The numbers of people were not enough to cause significant conflicts for space. By the end of the Mesolithic period between 5500 and 4000 BC temperatures were 2-3°C higher than now. Climatic conditions had reached the optimum making frequent and long migrations unnecessary, and a smaller area of occupation could be worked all year round by a group of hunter-gatherers. Forestation was much more widespread. Pollen data from Bradwell, then well inland, and from south Essex at the Mar Dyke have shown extensive oak and lime (Murphy, 1984; Murphy, Brown, 1999).

Encampments settled for parts of the year of increasing lengths would have become practicable. Riverside sites seem to have been favoured, no doubt for their convenience and access to fishing (Wymer, 1991). From these, hunting and collecting sorties would have been made, and then returned to at the end of the day. Circular depressions in the soil up to 4ft deep and 8ft across have been interpreted as house sites, probably covered with hides or brushwood (Jacobi, 1980).

The conditions were appropriate for replacing the migratory way of existence by settlement, the planting of crops, the baking of pottery and the introduction of farming. The peoples who had migrated from the continent while the landbridge existed developed closer links with sites favourable for permanent occupation. A recognisable pottery style such as 'carinated' vessels (see Glossary) and distinctive types of 'monument' mark the beginning of the Neolithic period.

Chronological periods in Essex and Suffolk

Period	Years BC/AD	Event
Norman		Anglo-Norman landlords
	1066	William I (Duke of Normandy, King of England)
	c.855	Viking incursions
	c.625	Raedwald, king of the Angles
Anglo-Saxon	604	Mellitus bishop of London
	c.580	Kingdom of East Saxons emerges.
		Anglo-Saxon incursions from Holland, Germany, Scandinavia
	410	Romano-British organise their own defence
	313	Christianity adopted in Roman Empire
	c.280	Saxon shore fortifications (Othona, Walton).
	c.250	St Alban martyred at Verulamium
Roman		
	c.120	Hadrian's wall built
	60/61	Boudican revolt. Colchester, London burned
	AD 43	Invasion by Emperor Claudius
	c.AD 5-40	Cunobelin, King of Trinovantes/Catuvellauni
	c.15 BC	Death of Addedomaros, ?Lexden tumulus
Late Iron Age	55/54 BC	Expeditions by Julius Caesar to southern Britain
		Increasing contact with Gaul
		La Tène type of decoration
Middle Iron Age	c.350 BC	
		Defended hillforts
Early Iron Age		
	c.700 BC	Introduction of iron technology
		Deposit of broken bronze implements
Bronze Age		Deverel-Rimbury pottery
		Copper alloy technology
	c.2200 BC	
Neolithic		Cursus monuments (eg Chelmsford Springfield)
		Settlements, farming
	c.4000 BC	
Mesolithic		Microlith flint technology
		Hunter-gatherers
	c.8000 BC	
		End of Devensian (last) Ice Age c.10,000 BC
Upper Palaeolithic		*Homo sapiens* in Europe

3 Settlement and monuments

c.4000 to 1000 BC

By the beginning of the Neolithic Period, around 4000 BC, the climate had passed the optimum of the Mesolithic. Temperatures were beginning to fall and by the middle of the fifth millennium there had been a rise in sea levels, swamping coastal regions and estuaries and turning other low-lying land into marsh (Wilkinson, 1988; Coles, 1998). The Early Neolithic high water mark was approximately at the present low water mark. This allowed access to and exploitation of land, now mudflat and marsh, in and around estuaries; these are large areas, the extent of which can be appreciated in the estuaries at low tide. Perhaps the warmer temperatures earlier in the fifth millennium and the loss of former coastal land encouraged groups to concentrate efforts into growing crops rather than to rely on gathering food, to domesticate herds rather than to hunt. As is evident from a large area of submerged Neolithic land surface at The Stumble in the Blackwater estuary, foraging for food, hunter-gatherer style, continued into the Neolithic period. Here collections of hazelnuts, sloes and other wild plant foods are at least as plentiful as cultivated crops. At Purfleet, butchery cuts on the bone of a wild ox suggest a continuation of hunting or scavenging. 'Mesolithic' practices were clearly continuing (Murphy, 1996; Murphy, Brown, 1999).

Charred emmer wheat grains from the Blackwater estuary dated 3605-3370 BC are the earliest evidence in Essex for cereal production (Wilkinson, Murphy, 1995). Pollen sampling from the Mar Dyke in south Essex has shown that around 2600 BC cereals were present (Scaife, 1988). Crops being grown included einkorn, emmer and bread wheat, naked barley and flax (Wilkinson, Murphy, 1995). That land was being cleared of trees has been suggested by the discovery of declining amounts of elm and lime pollen in the Thames estuary, though at other locations such as the Blackwater, close to known Neolithic sites, woodland cover was extensive (Brown, 1997). Explanations of causes other than human activity, such as elm disease, for woodland loss are clearly feasible (Murphy, 1996). The evidence from the Blackwater estuary suggests clearance was small-scale and short-lived (a few years perhaps), indicative of a shifting pattern of occupation allowing regeneration. Here and in the Crouch estuary there continued to be a dense cover of oak and alder into the later Neolithic period (**colour plate 2**) (Wilkinson, Murphy, 1995; Murphy, Brown, 1999).

After a period of relatively stable sea levels, the coasts were again being encroached on by the sea around 2000 BC, submerging forests whose oaks are now eroding out of the estuarine mud of the Thames, Crouch and Blackwater (Wilkinson, Murphy, 1995;

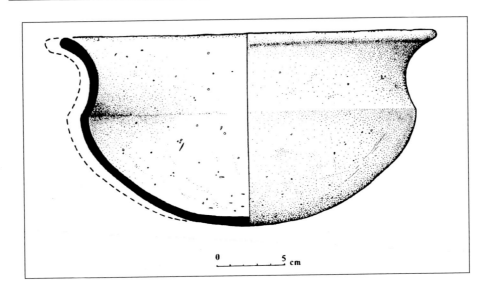

14   *Neolithic bowl, Layer de la Haye*

Murphy, Brown, 1999). An expansion of woodland, elm, ash and lime near the Thames at
Mar Dyke was accompanied by a decline in cereal production, but elsewhere growing of
crops continued (Whittle, 1978, 1985).

Settlement

Neolithic settlement sites have been recognised from characteristic pottery and flints,
often recovered from pits. At Great Totham, temporary Neolithic occupation carried
on on a more permanent basis into the Bronze Age. River terraces seem to have
been favourite occupation sites. Others are found, better preserved, at The Stumble
(River Blackwater), where emmer wheat, pottery, flints and refuse middens have been
recovered. Carinate Grimston-style bowls (see Glossary), squat with a wide opening,
have been found at Layer de la Haye and Shoebury (**14**) (Hedges, 1982; Holgate, 1996;
Brown, 1998). At Lawford, the area enclosed by a bank measured about 40x36ft, with
the internal bank retained by a wattle fence. At the centre was found a layer of ash, late
Neolithic (Grooved ware) pottery, bone pins, pig and cattle bones and tranchet flint
arrowheads (Hedges, 1980). Some sites seem to have had specialised functions, perhaps
remaining inhabited for several years. A site dating to about 2500 BC has been excavated
at Mildenhall, Hurst Fen. There was here a flint-knapping site. The presence also of
bone and antler bodkins and chisels suggests a leather, wood, cloth and hide industry
(Clarke, 1960).

Evidence of buildings and dwellings in the form of postholes is rare in Essex/Suffolk,
much having been destroyed by erosion, ploughing and subsequent human activity. Such
as there is, as at The Stumble (Blackwater) and Chigborough, is of timber post structures.

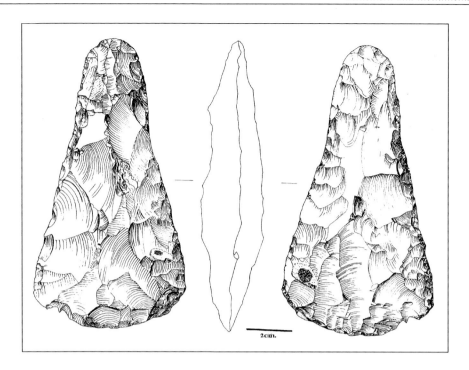

15   Neolithic handaxe from Southend

At Chigborough, a structure about 8x8m square with an internal partition contained Mildenhall pottery, affirming an early to mid-Neolithic date (Wilkinson, Murphy, 1995; Wallis, Waughman, 1988). At Mildenhall Hurst Fen, rectangular timber houses are suggested by postholes (Clarke, 1963). Though information is meagre, a pastoral and agricultural economy is likely to have been coupled with hide, wood and cloth industries. By comparing excavations elsewhere in southern England, it can be inferred that fields were delineated by ditches by the end of the period. Pottery styles and the density of Neolithic find-spots make it likely that a south and east Essex social group was distinct from another based on the north-west chalk uplands and Chilterns, the central boulder clay area being relatively sparsely populated.

Trading was conducted along routes which may have been long-established. The Icknield Way, which runs across the north-west of Essex through Suffolk, linked East Anglia with Wessex (Cleal, 2002). Routes crossing the Thames, one of which has been recognised at Vauxhall dating at least from the Bronze Age and possibly earlier (Orton, 1998; Denison, 1999), linked Essex with Sussex, where flint was mined at places such as Angmering and Cissbury near Worthing. Tools such as axes, knives and chisels made from flint mined in Sussex have been found at Chelmsford, Canewdon and Stratford. Igneous stone tools from Cornwall and from Italy were harder wearing and therefore perhaps highly sought after (Holgate, 1996). Axes from Great Langdale in the Lake District have been found at Mildenhall. Surface nodules of flint occurring on the boulder clay would have been used in local flint-tool industries (**15**).

The flint mines at Grimes Graves near Thetford and close by at Lynford, of which 350 funnel-shaped shafts have been identified, were dug through the more superficial boulder clay and top-stone courses of flint to the better-quality floor-stone flint at about 15m depth (**colour plate 5**). From the bottom of the shafts the miners dug radiating horizontal galleries up to 7ft (2m) wide and 5ft (1.5m) high along the line of the floorstone, mining it as they went, leaving intervening pillars of chalk as roof props. Mining over an area of 16 acres has been recognised. The flint must have been carried on ladders or hoisted by ropes to the surface. Graffiti over a gallery have been interpreted as a tally of loads. Flint tool waste shows that tools were fashioned on site. The proximity of these large mining centres makes it likely that they produced flints used in Suffolk and Essex.

The hard chalk was prised and hacked out using red deer antler, stone axes, ox bone and (at least in one instance) a human thigh bone. Underground light was provided by chalk cups containing grease and a wick. Radiocarbon dates obtained from a number of the shafts show the mines were in use between about 2330-1740 BC. Carvings on the walls suggest a ritual cult, perhaps a supplication for a successful mining season (HMSO; Russell, 2000; Topping, 2003).

Hafted axes of the Neolithic period had a surface polished by another stone (**16**; **colour plate 6**). The edge could be re-sharpened on a rubber stone of quartzite such as that found at Lound (Clarke, 1963). Such axes are likely to have been used for woodworking but may also have been gifts and ritual offerings. Sickles, perhaps better described as reaping knives, have been shown to have their cutting edge glossed with silica from repeated cutting of straw or reeds. Gloss has not been found on Mesolithic sickles (Pitts, 1980). Though some of the axes and other tools recovered by excavation or by chance may represent artefacts accidentally lost or deliberately discarded at the end of their useful life, many occur in situations strongly suggesting deliberate deposition, perhaps offerings to the Earth, goods for an afterlife. Axes found in rivers and streams may have been votive offerings (Holgate, 1996). A clearer idea of the rituals practised in Neolithic Essex is still due, but the wooden 'Dagenham Idol', a statuette possibly of ithy-phallic rite and carbon-dated to 2351-2139 bc, provides tantalising evidence of rituals and belief (see Gazetteer) (Wright, 1923; Coles, 1990).

The monuments

New to the early Neolithic landscape from the beginning of the third millennium BC were large earthen structures which would have required significant co-operative effort to build (Bradley, 1993; Chadburn, 2008). Some degree of central organisation would seem likely. Whether co-operation was voluntary or forced and indicative of a class structure is unclear. At least some of these 'monuments' seem to relate to one another and to the landscape in the vicinity, and to mark a transition of territory from the lower river gravel to the higher boulder clay areas (Brown, 1997).

Circular causewayed enclosures were surrounded by a ditch and crossed at several places by earthen balks. Examples are at St. Osyth (Germany, 2007), Orsett and Chelmsford Springfield Lyons (Buckley, 1987; Brown, 1997). At Orsett there were three concentric

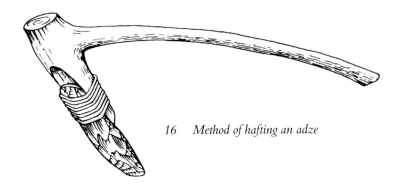

16   Method of hafting an adze

ditches, about 90m across the inner diameter, with causeways across them. Between the inner and middle ditches was an interval of about 30m, and one of 10m between middle and outermost (**colour plate 7**). A timber palisade lay inside the middle of the three ditches and, at least within the outer bank, there was a rampart bank. This was the first Neolithic causewayed enclosure shown to have been palisaded. An oval posthole structure 11x8m of uncertain purpose had a pit at its centre. Radiocarbon dates concentrated around 2600 bc (Hedges, Buckley, 1978).

At Springfield Lyons a curved causewayed ditch separated off a spur of land between two streams. Pits and ditches contained large quantities of Mildenhall-style mid-Neolithic pottery and a polished axe flake. At least some of these appear to have been deliberately (ritually?) deposited (Brown, 1997).

There often seem to have been few buildings within these enclosures, but important activities clearly went on around the monuments. Possible functions for such monuments include tribal meeting sites for trade, weddings, decision-making, ceremonials and delineation of territory for a particular purpose. Of course, similar-appearing enclosures may have had a differing meaning and purpose.

Cursus monuments

Rare but significant in the landscape were the Cursus monuments, such as those at Bures St Mary, Chelmsford Springfield, Fornham All Saints (1580m long) and Stratford St Mary (McMaster, 1982; St Joseph, 1964; Clarke, 1963; Buckley, Hedges, Brown, 2001). These monuments are often set in gravel terraces in mid-valley landscapes with associated monuments nearby. The Springfield cursus and the probable long barrow or enclosure with which it aligned to its north-east isolate a spur of land in a bend of the River Chelmer, just above the floodplain. The 10km long cursus in Dorset is similarly aligned with a long barrow (Bradley, 1993). In the absence of intervening woodland the Springfield cursus would have been easily visible from the Springfield Lyons enclosure only 1.25km away. The siting of the cursus monument just above the Chelmer valley floodplain and that of the ditched enclosure at Springfield Lyons between two streams seems to infer a separation of territories (**colour plate 28**).

Cursus monuments consist of a long (in the case of Springfield 690m long) rectangular ditch, square- or round-ended, usually surrounding a continuous bank. The side-ditches at Springfield were about 49m apart at the western end, narrowing to 37m apart towards the eastern end. The Essex and Suffolk examples cited above were ploughed out and recognised from crop marks, but standing earthworks remain near Stonehenge, at Gussage in Dorset and elsewhere. The Springfield cursus was unique at the time of excavation in being shown to have had a timber post structure (of which a semicircle 26m in diameter was excavated) at one end. Near the centre was a large pit which could have contained a tree-stump such as was revealed at Seahenge in Norfolk, an object of ritual significance (Brennard, Taylor, 2000). Radiocarbon analysis and pottery styles suggest a construction date about 3000 BC, but activity lasted long into the Bronze Age (Hedges, Buckley, 1981; Buckley, Hedges, Brown, 2001).

Springfield cursus, Chelmsford

Discovered by aerial photography, this Neolithic cursus was excavated prior to the building of houses and stores in 1979. The cursus is about 690m long, running from south-west to north-east. The long earth mound was flanked on either side by ditches about 40m apart, which ran round the ends of the mound. At intervals the ditches had gaps along their length. About 300m to the north-east was an oval-shaped enclosure which may have been a small long-barrow but was destroyed by housing development before it could be excavated. An area of 50x35m at the eastern end of the cursus was excavated. The ditch was 2.75m wide by 1m deep and contained pottery and flint-working debris. Within the end of the enclosure was a semicircle of 14 postholes (the western half had been destroyed by a sewer trench). These may have supported a roof or been part of an unroofed structure, about 26m in diameter. Pits contained burnt cattle, sheep and pig bones, saddle-shaped flour-grinding querns and Neolithic pottery of the Peterborough style (see Glossary). The excavated eastern-end structure might therefore be interpreted as a ritual temple. Other possible cursus monuments in East Anglia are known or suspected from Stratford St Mary, Bures St Mary, Fornham All Saints and Kedington in Suffolk, Kempston, Barnack and Maxey in Cambridgeshire, Lawford and Rivenhall in Essex (**colour plate 28**).

The role of cursus monuments has been the subject of debate; possibilities include processional ways, alignments of an astronomical, physical or topographical nature, linkage of significant places, demarcation of ritual or physical significance (Barclay, Maxwell, 1998), formalistion of pre-existing pathways (Last, 1999) or symbolic rivers (Brophy, 1999). The finding of a pit containing Neolithic flints in the ring-ditch at Springfield, which could indicate a burial, may associate the monument with mortuary practices. It may be that the very long examples, hundreds or thousands of metres from end to end, such as Fornham All Saints and Springfield, had a different function from those tens of metres long such as at Stratford St Mary.

Barrows and long mortuary enclosures

Evidence for barrows and long mortuary enclosures in this region is mainly in river valleys, though this may be due to the selective survival of the crop marks in these soils rather than being a true reflection of the original distribution of these monuments (Buckley et al, 1988; Brown, Germany, 2002).

To the east of the Springfield cursus, at Rivenhall and elsewhere are crop marks of long barrows and long mortuary enclosures. In Essex, shapes vary from oblong to (approximately) oval (**17**) (Tyler, 1984). A ditch surrounded an elongated mound or bank. If the East Anglian and Essex representatives had similar structures to standing Wessex examples, these monuments contained at (usually) the eastern end a wooden structure in which were placed the dead, sometimes over several generations.

At Haddenham, ten miles north of Cambridge, the burial chamber was of split oak planks supported by posts and was divided into two by an internal partition with evidence of burning. The larger part contained the bones of at least five partially articulated individuals with grave goods of a leaf arrowhead, jet pin and a jet bangle. As in some of the Wessex megalithic tombs (West Kennet for example), there was a screen (at Haddenham, of timber posts) to the east of the chamber and timber post horn-work forming a forecourt with a gravelled floor. A timber-revetted soil and turf mound 50m long by 16m wide extended westwards. Dendrochronology and radiocarbon dating suggest construction around 4000-3500 BC (Shand, Hodder, 1990).

Some evidence of an internal mortuary chamber remained at Lawford and Great Braxted. The Lawford barrow (50m long) remained a recognisable mound until after 1971 (Erith, 1971). Others such as at Birch (45m long), Thorrington (50m long), Feering (over 80m long), Great Braxtead (50m long), Ashen (40m long) and Tollesbury (35m long) are recognisable from crop marks (Tyler, 1984). Alignment is usually north-east to south-west, but east to west is also found. Other monuments of Neolithic date are often in the vicinity. The example at Great Totham was rectangular, about 27m long and 12m wide, and had pottery shards, suggesting a late Neolithic date, at the east end (Wallis, 1989). That at Rivenhall End, about 49x16m, had a continuous enclosing ditch, an internal bank and contained Mildenhall-type pottery (Buckley et al, 1988). The Neolithic and Bronze Age Swale's tumulus at Worlington contained within it charred oak, possibly a coffin, cremated bone, and part of a polished flint axe (Clarke, 1963). Because inhumations, when they are found, are often incomplete or jumbled, it has been suggested that the rite of excarnation (exposure of the body to the elements) had been practised prior to burial.

Several examples of circular ditches containing a burial, often a cremation, at the centre, off-centre or near the periphery are known. It is likely in some instances that a mound thrown up from the soil dug from the ditch originally occupied the middle, forming a round barrow where now only a ring-ditch remains. While most have been dated to the Bronze Age and later, some are Neolithic. The barrow at Brightlingsea contained large quantities of mid-Neolithic pottery. Here within the 23m diameter ditch were broken bowls of Mildenhall-style and charcoal. An earth causeway across the ditch allowed access to the centre from the east (Lavender, 1996). A ring ditch at Rainham contained a central pit and several Mildenhall and Beaker pottery shards

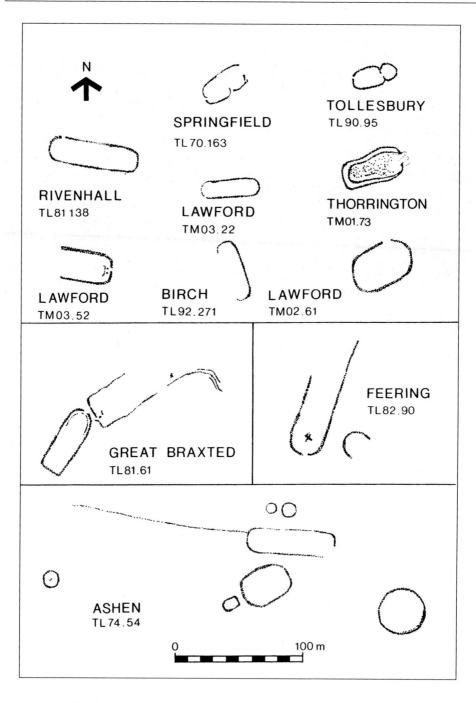

N

SPRINGFIELD
TL 70.163

TOLLESBURY
TL 90.95

RIVENHALL
TL 81 138

LAWFORD
TM 03.22

THORRINGTON
TM 01.73

LAWFORD
TM 03.52

BIRCH
TL 92.271

LAWFORD
TM 02.61

GREAT BRAXTED
TL 81.61

FEERING
TL 82.90

ASHEN
TL 74.54

0   100 m

17   *Cropmarks of Long Enclosures*

18   Ring ditch and cremation pit at Langford

(Hedges, 1980). Another at Langford dated to the Late Neolithic/early Bronze Age had an entrance causeway and post holes (?a burial chamber) around a cremation pit without urns (**18**) (Cooper-Reade, 1996).

Clusters of crop marks of circular ditches occur in north Essex and along the Stour valley. Some suggest barrow cemeteries (McMaster, 1982). Neolithic worked flint including a scraper and borer has been collected at Wormingford (Priddy, 1982) but although clusters of smaller ring-ditches may reasonably be interpreted as barrow cemeteries, caution is needed with a similar interpretation for double-ditched and larger rings (Brown, Germany, 2002).

Henge monuments

The great henge monuments of Wessex such as Avebury, Durrington and Knowlton seem hardly to be echoed in Essex/Suffolk. They may be represented at Little Bromley and Stratford St Mary, where ones with a diameter of 89ft (30m) are recognisable from crop marks (Hedges, 1980). A circular bank *outside* an encircling ditch distinguishes these from defensive earthworks, and a ceremonial purpose is ascribed to them. At Knowlton, Dorset, a Norman church occupies the middle of the henge, perhaps expressing a continuation or re-establishment of ritual/religious practice over three millennia.

Though the full role or purpose of these monuments is unclear, they were often the focal points of round barrow building in the Late Neolithic and Early Bronze Age, and seem to have superseded the focus of the Neolithic long barrows (Burl, 1991). At Stonehenge the original alignments of the Heel Stone appear to be concerned with the lunar rather than the solar cycle. Unfortunately the more ephemeral Essex examples allow even less certainty of function.

The Bronze Age environment

Towards the end of the Neolithic period, woodland covered many parts of Essex with trees running right down to the seashore. From the Bronze Age there is evidence of decreasing tree cover which continued into the Iron Age. Woodland as a whole, though there are regional variations, was replaced gradually by grassland and cereal. Spreads of charcoal radiocarbon-dated to the later Neolithic in the estuaries suggest burning was a method of clearance (Wilkinson, 1995; Letch, 2005). Sea levels began to rise again around 1700 BC, flooding previously exploited land. However despite marshy conditions, coastal occupation continued through the late Neolithic and Early Bronze Age. Probable 'cooking holes' containing charcoal and low burnt-flint mounds have been recovered from the north-east coast (Brown, 1997, 2001)).

Beakers, widely distributed pottery vessels, approximately coinciding with the transition from Neolithic to Bronze Age around 2500-1500 BC, are well represented in Essex and Suffolk (**colour plate 3;** see Glossary). A Beaker cemetery with cockleshells was found at Southchurch. A Beaker pit at Clacton Jaywick has been carbon-dated to 2460-2144 BC. At Orsett an oval ditch about 6.5x5m diameter probably around a barrow contained within its circumference three cremation burials and Deverel-Rimbury pottery of Early or mid-Bronze Age date (Murphy, 1999; Milton, 1984; Clark, 1970).

Death and burial

Round barrow building, as evidenced by ring-ditches, continued. Indeed the majority of the pre-Roman round barrows date from the Early and Middle Bronze Ages. An extant example at Sturmer some 2m high and 120m across, formerly believed to be Roman, has now been assigned to the Bronze Age (**colour plate 4**) (Lawson, 1983). The Neolithic round barrow at Worlington (above) formed the core of a late Bronze Age mound (Briscoe, 1957; Clark, 1963). At Dedham, an oval crop mark 68x78ft across of a ring-ditch produced two Bronze Age cremation burials, of a young girl and a mature male, in urns (Blake, 1960).

Cemeteries of the Middle Bronze Age in north Essex and south Suffolk contain closely grouped circular or oval ditches (perhaps representing eroded barrows) with lines of cremations, some in urns, between the rings. Such 'Urnfields' have been excavated at Ardleigh, Brightlingsea and Stanstead (Couchman, 1975; Hinchcliffe, 1981; Clarke, 1991; Crummy, 1977; Cooke, 2008). At Ardleigh no mounds survived but the oval ditches measured 24-38ft (8-13m) in diameter. The urns are sometimes upended, with open ends face downwards. Couchman (1975) drew attention to the differences in styles between pottery found in barrows and pottery found in the 'flat' urnfields. She suggested two groups living together at Ardleigh having two different burial rites. Ring-ditches averaging 8m diameter at Brightlingsea did not themselves contain burials. The cremation burials were mostly between the rings, some in urns, others not (Clarke, 1991).

The Deverel-Rimbury type pottery (see Glossary) generally associated with these urnfields but also found in settlement sites was in use over a long time span, clustering between about 2000-1000 BC, but with examples outside this range. The pottery is tempered with flint or crushed pot (grog). In north-east Essex and south Suffolk the Deverel-Rimbury pottery is highly decorated (with, for example, finger-tip impression and comb points), and is known as Ardleigh style. In south Essex the pottery is mostly plain or the decoration much restrained, characteristic of a Lower Thames style (Brown, 1995).

In the Early and Middle Bronze Age in central and south Essex, as at Great Totham, ring-ditches and burials were widely spaced rather than clustered in the urnfields more common to the north (Wallis & Waughman, 1998). Grave goods of gold-plated shale beads and amber were found in a burial at Rochford. The cremation burials of a child and a woman dated to about 1600 bc were found a few hundred metres from a settlement at Shoebury (Wymer, Brown, 1995). There is an implication of a degree of autonomy of the northern group of south Suffolk and north-east Essex from a southern group of mid-Essex and the Thames valley, though because of the longevity of the style, such suggestions of separations need to be viewed cautiously (Thomas, 2008).

It is not unreasonable to postulate social groups in north Essex/south Suffolk having styles of burial and pottery different to those further south. Such observations raise queries as to the degree of contact there was between groups, when the need to travel was limited for all except those such as traders whose livelihood required it. Here perhaps is to be recognised an anticipation of what were later to be termed 'tribal groups'.

Metalworking

Whether metal technology was introduced to Britain by the people who made the characteristic Beaker pottery is the subject of much debate, though beaker vessels have been found with early copper mines in County Kerry. Couchman (1980) believes that the intermingling between the Beaker and indigenous populations was strictly limited. Whether the technology was introduced directly from the continent or via Ireland has some relevance for the eastern counties. If introduction was via Ireland the eastern counties of Britain might be expected to have been among the last in the islands to develop the technology and to use metalwork. The discovery of an oak paddle, diamond-shaped in cross-section and radiocarbon-dated to 1255-998 bc, from the Crouch is a reminder of the use of water as a means of transport and access (Wilkinson, Murphy, 1995). By the late third to second millennium copper and tin were being mined in North Wales and Cornwall, from where the Icknield Way would have been a cross-country trade route to Essex and Suffolk (Budd, 2000; Fitzpatrick, 2003).

Essex lacks natural copper or tin ores so metal would have been imported, perhaps in exchange for salt that was being extracted in the Crouch estuary. Evidence from Gestingthorpe of clay moulds demonstrates at least a local industry of bronze-working, though this is likely to have been of recycling rather than ore working (Draper, 1985). Metal working sites have been detected at Springfield Lyons and Mucking (Brown, Murphy, 2000). Trading was evidently widespread. Copper alloy axes found near Braintree have similarities to those from Schleswig-Holstein, the Elbe valley, Bohemia, Moravia and Gotland, Sweden (O'Connor, 1976).

The discovery of more bronze metalwork in dateable contexts is required (Sealey, 1991). Flat axes such as found at Tollesbury, relatively straightforward to cast, date from the Early Bronze Age. Finds of palstave axes (**19**), often by chance, are relatively common, and some found at widely separated sites seem to have been made from the same mould, such as those from Burnham-on-Crouch, Potton Island and Shoebury (Couchman, 1980) (see Glossary, Palstave). This suggests a class of itinerant metalworkers. Hoards (more than three or so bronze objects found together) become increasingly common by the end of the Middle Bronze Age and into the Late Bronze and Early Iron Ages (Butcher, 1923). Whether these were for recycling or concealed to be recovered in more peaceful times is unclear (Cuddeford, Sealey, 2000; Crowe, 2003).

A ritual of deposition of metalwork into water is suggested from the quantity of bronze-work found in rivers and estuaries (O'Connor, 1980; Eddy, 1982). This has echoes of the Neolithic siting of monuments in relation to water. Evidence of leather-working may be implied from the bronze knife which was found at Sheering, perhaps dropped by a Middle Bronze Age worker settled by or making their way along Pincey Brook towards the higher Boulder Clay towards the Harlow region (Brown, Bartlett, 1992).

Structures, landscape and fields

Evidence of building structures and settlement in the Early and Middle Bronze Ages has been discovered in the lower Blackwater valley. Here a rectangular eight-posted timber structure about 8x3m containing a loom-weight has been found (Wallis, Waughman, 1998). Wells containing Deverel-Rimbury pottery have been excavated by the Blackwater estuary and at Goldhanger (Adkins et al, 1984; Waughman, 1989). Here there was also a large enclosure of 200x100m surrounded by a ditch interpreted as an animal stockade.

Substantial postholes arranged in roughly rectangular shape at Maldon Elms Farm below an Iron Age temple may represent a Middle Bronze Age shrine (Atkinson, 2001). Perhaps of Middle Bronze Age date is the rectangular 10-post building c.4.5x2.2m at Boreham interpreted as a shrine demolished when the ritual was removed to nearby Springfield Lyons (Brown, 2001). At Stansted has been excavated a Middle Bronze Age settlement, dated c.1600 BC, 500 m south of a slightly earlier barrow containing burials of a neonate, an infant, a juvenile and an adult. Four timber post-built roundhouses were built surrounded by a rectangular shallow ditch and fence. The house diameters ranged from 5.5 to 7.6m and the larger two houses had southeast-facing porches. The entrance to the settlement, flanked by two large timber posts, was from the southeast. In the centre of

19   *Palstave axe from Easthorpe*

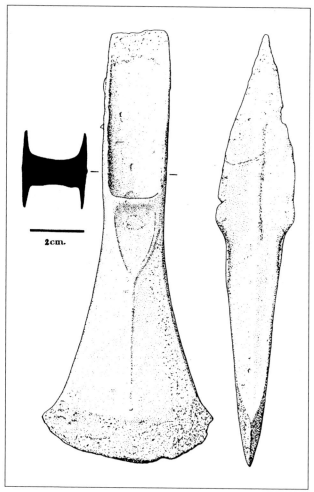

the settlement was a large red sandstone sarsen which may have been a Neolthic feature. (Since excavation, it has been moved to Takeley road junction). Some three or four generations later, three new roundhouses were built. The larger houses can be interpreted as perhaps for domestic occupation, the smaller for animals, an extended family group of maybe 15–25 persons at any one time living at the settlement pursuing a pastoral life-style (Cooke, 2008).

Before the creation of enclosed fields the landscape was divided up by natural features (notable trees, streams and rivers) or by the monuments. The earliest known ditched or embanked fields occur around 1800-1600 BC (Bradley, 1993). The need to form enclosed boundaries may have arisen because of an increasing population and concentration of occupation rather than any more fundamental change in farming practices. Certainly, the creation of such boundaries in the Middle Bronze Age was a practice which continued into the Iron Age and Roman periods (Pryor, 1998). Such field boundaries have been excavated at Great Wakering close to a settlement area (Crowe, 1984; Reidy, 1997). Mixed farming was evidently practised at North Shoebury where several field enclosures were surrounded by ditches. Storage pits, burnt remains, animal bones, querns and loom weights indicate that wheat and probably oats had been cultivated and ground, cattle and pigs kept for milk and meat, and sheep for wool. The diet included mussel from the estuary (Wymer, Brown, 1995; Manning 2003).

The value of the sea and seashore to the Bronze Age population is being appreciated through the examination of previously buried land surfaces now exposed in the estuaries. Access to the marsh was made easier by the laying down of wattle platforms or tracks. Such a platform found near Althorne on the Crouch estuary consisted of 16 vertical oak posts on which were raised horizontal planks, radiocarbon-dated to 1300 BC (Wilkinson, 1987). Brushwood tracks have been located in the Thames estuary at Rainham and Barking, the longest at least 80m (Meddens, 1995). The marsh is prime sheep-grazing and continued to be exploited for this purpose for many millennia.

4 Metal, defended sites and the invisible dead

c.1000-50 BC

Late Bronze Age (*c*.1000-800 BC): industry and economy

In the Late Bronze Age, the foreshore and estuaries continued to be used as a resource. The clay hearth, brine containers and troughs examined at South Woodham Ferrers constitute an early site of salt production carbon-dated to about 1070 BC. Excavations at Mucking in the Thames estuary have also produced Late Bronze Age salt-working sites (Barford, 1988; Murphy, Brown, 1999). The increasing incidence of salterns gives an indication of the importance of salt for meat preservation and its value for trade in the Late Bronze and Iron Age. The sea and rivers were means of communication. An Essex oak-plank Bronze Age boat similar to that found in 1992 at Dover may await discovery off the foreshore or in an estuary (Parfitt, 1993; Wilkinson, 1987; Clark, 2004).

The reduction of woodland on a larger scale is apparent from the Late Bronze Age onwards, particularly as investigated at Stansted, indicating exploitation of the heavier boulder clay regions. But even on the lower levels, as at Little Waltham, an open grass landscape was in existence by about 1400 BC (Drury, 1978). There was soil erosion and the silting of streams and channels at Asheldham and the River Chelmer (Murphy, 1996). In the Blackwater basin, Late Bronze Age environmental samples show a cover of wet grassland, weed, scrub, rushes and sedge (Adkins et al, 1984; Wiltshire, Murphy, 1998).

A new better-yielding wheat, spelt, was more intensively grown on Mid-Late Bronze and Early Iron Age sites, and gained popularity into the later Iron Age (Brown, Murphy, 2000). A storage pit at Orsett contained largely spelt wheat, though both emmer and spelt were cultivated into the Middle Iron Age at Asheldham (Murphy, 1988; Bedwin, 1991). Near Maldon Heybridge, most of the wheat was emmer, though some spelt was being grown together with naked and hulled barley (Brown, 1988). Beans, *Vicia faba,* were also cultivated in the Late Bronze at sites such as Chelmsford and Springfield Lyons (Buckley, Hedges, 1987).

The Late Bronze Age enclosure at Springfield Lyons, one of many, was constructed close to the Neolithic causewayed ditch (above, Chapter 3), overlooking the Chelmer valley and cursus, which may have still been visible. It consisted of an oval ditch about 65m in diameter, inside which was an earth rampart bank with a timber walkway. Six earth causeways crossed the ditch around the circumference (**20**). The main entrance from the east was guarded by a substantial timber gate structure. The presence of a high-level walkway just inside the bank and the strong entrance gate structure echoes the defensive forts of the Early Iron Age, but the presence of six causeways across the ditch make a defendable enclosure improbable (**colour plates 9 & 25**) (Bradley, 1996).

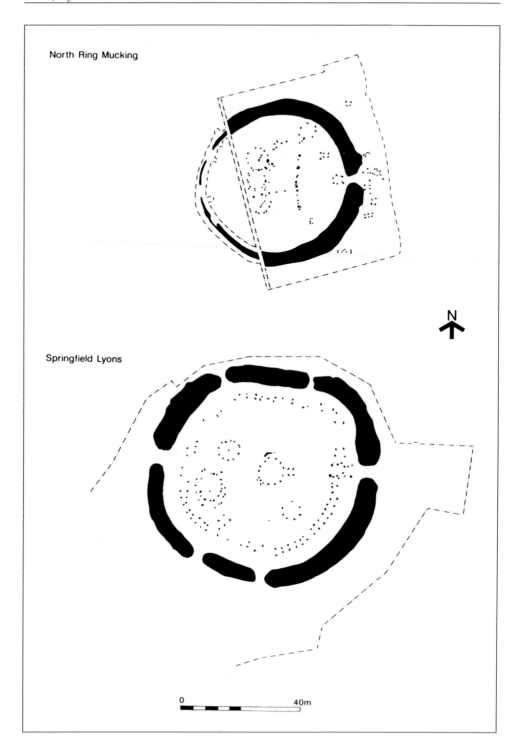

North Ring Mucking

Springfield Lyons

N

0   40m

20   *Circular Late Bronze Age Enclosures*

Springfield Lyons, Chelmsford

From 1981, to the east of Springfield Lyons House the excavation took place of a circular earthwork consisting of a bank and encircling ditch, crossed at six points by earthen causeways. The site commands views over the Chelmer valley about 200ft (70m) above sea level. Pits to the east of the enclosure contained a polished flint axe, charcoal giving a date of within 70 years of 1810 bc and pottery similar to that found at Mildenhall, Suffolk and at Orsett, Essex. Within the bank of the enclosure was evidence for a timber rampart. A large central roundhouse had its porched entrance facing east towards the main gateway. At least two other large houses, about 5m in diameter, stood within the enclosure. Clay moulds from which bronze swords had been cast were found. These moulds were bivalved, with a hole into which the molten bronze could be poured. The halves could be separated when the metal was solid. The type suggests a date of ninth to eighth century BC. Loom-weights and spindle-whorls indicated a weaving industry. Environmental samples were taken from the postholes, ditch and pits. These showed that crops of six-hulled barley, spelt and einkorn wheat were being cultivated. Hazelnuts, elder seeds and beans had been used, cooked or roasted. The site was abandoned but the finding buried in a pit of a Late Iron Age iron sword and scabbard (the sword had been bent double suggesting ritual destruction) indicated that the site was still recognisable and 'venerated'. An unexpected discovery was that in the Saxon period the area had been reused as a cemetery by which time the bank and ditch must have been unrecognisable.

From the artefacts of clay moulds, loom-weights and spindle whorls, it seems clear that bronze and textile working industries were in existence. Many of the clay moulds were for casting swords. Impressions on the outside of the moulds showed that the two valves had been bound together to keep them in place during the hardening process. A radiocarbon date within the enclosure of about 830 bc was obtained. A mould for casting bronze sickles in the enclosure at Mucking reinforces the probability that these monuments represent specialist production centres (Buckley, 1984; Buckley, Hedges, 1987; Needham, 1988).

Another enclosure, this time a rectangle of about 48x42m with surrounding double ditches, has been extensively investigated at Lofts Farm near Great Totham (**colour plate 10**). The only entrance causeway across the ditches, about 7m wide, faced east. A space between the two ditches about 2m wide would have allowed earth from them to be piled up as a bank. Inside the enclosure there was at least one roundhouse, about 11m in diameter with a south-facing porch (**21**), and a rectangular timber-post structure about 15.5m long and with 2m between the post-lines (2). If this was a building, the closeness of the post-lines suggests an aisled one, rather than the posts being an outer wall perhaps of wattle fencing. Two four-timber post structures, possibly granaries, lay south of the roundhouse (3,4). A line of (?fence) posts across the enclosure from east to west (13) divided it into a smaller northern third and a larger southern two-thirds (in which were all the four buildings). Quantities of pottery were recovered mainly from the ditches.

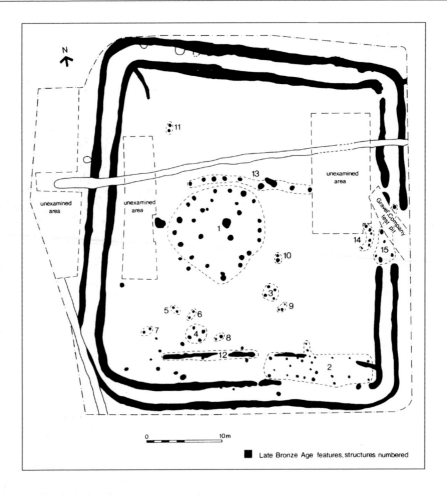

21   Double-ditched enclosure at Great Totham

Eighty-four metres south of the enclosure was a well which contained evidence of a wooden ladder and Darmsden-Linton style pottery (see Glossary) (Brown, 1988).

   The functions of the Great Totham enclosure seem to differ significantly from Springfield Lyons. A single fragment of a bronze-socketed axe was found in the outer ditch, bent and crushed in antiquity, but there was no evidence of metalworking. Evidence for a textile industry was minimal. It is possible that pottery was being made but this does not appear to have taken place inside the enclosure. The evidence of plant remains and dung from grazing animals suggests a mixed cereal and animal husbandry economy with grazing on the nearby grassland and open salt marsh. The enclosure perhaps was used for a stock corral north of the dividing fence, grain storage and, if the roundhouse was domestic, a farmer's house in the southern part (Brown, 1988). The explanation for the double ditching may lie in the need to obtain sufficient soil for a bank high enough to exclude the animals from domestic and grain storage areas on a site where the water-table was close to the surface. Digging for soil deeper, particularly in winter, may have been impracticable. Indeed digging one deep ditch and throwing earth from its bottom onto the top of the bank requires a greater effort than digging two shallower ditches. Stone (and no doubt wooden) tools, most made locally, were still much in use, though metal could be available to farmers from traders and from special metalworking sites.

An apparently similar rectangular banked enclosure occurs at Chelmsford Broomfield, single-ditched, about 35x44m, with an east-facing entrance. It contained at least one roundhouse or hut-circle. Evidence of fence-lines suggests some areas of subdivision. Stock corralling associated with a domestic dwelling is a possible function of the enclosure, though evidence is less complete than at Great Totham (Atkinson, 1995).

Evidence of crop marks suggests an increasingly dense occupation along the coastal zone, estuaries and river valleys from the Late Bronze Age (Jones, Bond, 1980; Buckley et al, 1986). There is mounting evidence of 'open' (not surrounded by ditches) settlements. Examples are known at Great Waltham and Boreham (Brown, 1988; Brown, Lavender, 1995). Just as discoveries of Neolithic occupation of wooded and low-lying sites on clay around the Blackwater have meant discarding the notion that these soils were unsuitable to be exploited in the Neolithic, settlement at Stansted makes necessary a re-evaluation of the view that the heavy boulder clay was not exploited for agriculture and occupation until the Iron Age. The expansion of settlements onto such less easily worked soil is evidence of fairly rapid increase in population by the Late Bronze Age causing land-pressure (Havis and Brooks, 2004; Cooke, 2008).

Stansted

Large-scale excavations preceding the expansion of the airport since 1985 have shown occupation since at least the Neolithic period. Animal drove roads (for cattle and sheep herding) joined large fields surrounded by ditches. On this boulder clay area, woodland is likely to have been managed by regular coppicing and the wood used for building, tools and utensils. By the first century BC there was certainly a settlement here. It consisted of several roundhouses arranged around a central square building, possibly a shrine. The settlement was surrounded by a ditch either to keep farm animals from straying among the houses or to mark the perimeter. The way of life continued largely unchanged into the Roman period, when the inhabitants started to make use of some Roman techniques and occasionally to import Samian pottery. Roman bronze brooches, some of good quality, have been found, but on the whole a basic pastoral economy seems to have continued. On the northern edge of the settlement was a six-post timber building that may have been a storage granary. The cemetery lay to one side; sometimes a horse skull buried nearby suggests an offering at the time of the burial of its owner. One cremation burial in a wooden box, long since decayed away, was accompanied by a bronze bowl, two jugs, a glass cup and two bottles, Samian plates and an iron knife. Close by, a female burial contained a bronze mirror, a container for perfume and a pair of sandals. By this time, much of the earlier woodland had been cleared leaving large areas for fields. However timber continued to be an important resource and woodland was still present on the north-east.

In the Late Bronze Age more certain evidence for buildings such as the 17-post rectangular structure 9.3x6.5m containing internal partitions, pottery, worked stone, charcoal and burnt clay has been found c.200m to the east of the Springfield Lyons enclosure (reminiscent of a medieval longhouse divided for animal and domestic habitation). An ovoid 8-timber post structure c.6.4x4.8m within which was buried a crushed pot was found at Fingringhoe, and a post-built roundhouse with a central hearth at Chelmsford Howe Green (Manning, 2003; Brooks, 2002; Dale, 2005).

Bronze

Some extensive bronze hoards dating from the Late Bronze Age have been recovered. In the five years to 1995, the number had increased by about 50 per cent from the recoveries in the previous decade, no doubt at least in part due to the popularity of metal-detectors, and to the better reporting of finds to museum curators for identification (Buckley et al, 1986). The 174 pieces found at Vange, Basildon, included spearheads, blades, swords, axes, an adze, rough pieces of casting metal and fragments. A hoard from north Basildon seems to have been originally deposited in a bag (Brown, 1996, 1998). Other Late Bronze Age hoards have been found at Little Oakley, Hacton, Fingringhoe, Little Baddow, Barling, Great Bromley, Dovercourt, High Easter and Layer Marney (Sealey, 1987, 1991, 1997; Couchman, 1977; Cuddeford, 2000; Crowe, 2003), mostly dating to the ninth and eighth centuries BC. In Essex, apart from a few sites such as Springfield Lyons and Mucking (above), bronze hoards are all too often reported unassociated with pottery or other dateable material. Examples which are discovered with other finds (in context) are required to understand the full production, use and trading implications of bronze.

Ritual and burial

Rare from the Late Bronze Age are discoveries of burial. It is apparent that burial under barrows or in 'flat' urnfields was no longer usual, and a dearth of burial evidence from the Late Bronze Age into the Early and Mid-Iron Age has produced suggestions of excarnation or burial into running water. The five unurned cremations in pits at Great Waltham are unusual and may be from earlier in the Bronze Age or indicate the lingering of an older tradition (Brown, 1988).

Rituals associated with water and pits apparently continued. In the Crouch estuary two human skulls were deposited on a wooden platform, dated about 900 bc (Wilkinson, Murphy, 1995). Similar instances of human bones deposited in pits and ditches have been noted elsewhere in southern England as in Sussex (Bedwin, 1979) and Surrey (Needham, 1992). At Mucking a cremation burial accompanied by two gold rings had been placed at the entrance to a settlement in a ditch (Bond, 1988). Shrines have been postulated for timber structures at Boreham and Great Waltham though agricultural uses are also possible (Brown, 1996). In general evidence for ritual and burial from this period is sparse.

Climate and population

The transition from Bronze to Iron Age, about 800-600 BC, accompanied a period of deteriorating weather conditions from relatively warm to moister and cooler. In Essex and Suffolk, unlike on Dartmoor where Bronze Age field-systems are still recognisable on marginal and now-unprofitable upland (Rackham, 1987; Fleming, 1988; Everson, Williamson, 1998), there is little evidence for abandonment of the higher boulder clay regions as cool wet conditions intensified. Indeed there is some suggestion that the Late Bronze/Early Iron Age economy, predominantly agricultural and pastoral, was increasingly exploiting previously underused land.

Evidence from Stansted shows a rising water-table towards the end of the Bronze Age into the Iron Age, indicating increasing rainfall. Trees continued to be removed. Heath invaded uncultivated land but increasingly new areas were coming under cultivation (Brück, 1995; Murphy, 1996; Havis, Brooks, 2004; Guttman, 2000). Reynolds (1987) points out that wetter climates release soil nitrogen and favour cereal growth. If this encouraged a population increase, the expansion of agricultural land may have been in response to such pressure.

The increasing density of settlement sites and houses throughout the Iron Age suggests the population continued to rise. Population estimates of this time are largely guesswork. Based on the medieval figure of about 120 acres of land required to support a peasant family, the acreage of non-metropolitan Essex and Suffolk being 925,000 and 950,000 acres respectively a population of about 7700 families for Essex and 7900 families for Suffolk might be guessed if the land was fully exploited. Clearly there are many opportunities for error in such an estimate.

Ironworking

Ironworking in Essex is first attested at Mucking (Clark, 1993). An iron cauldron found at Colchester Sheepen has been dated to the seventh century BC and an iron-socketed axe from Walthamstow is also probably from the Early Iron Age (Hawkes, Smith, 1957; Smith, 1925). The large numbers of hoards of bronze found (such as at Grays, Orsett Cock, Fingringhoe and Waltham Abbey) may have been abandoned (perhaps as scrap) as iron became available as a replacement, or collected for recycling.

Hot iron-work demands much more precise oxidation conditions and higher temperatures (in excess of 1000°C) than copper alloys. Molten iron for casting (needing 1535°C) was never achievable by prehistoric people (Collard, 2004). In short, iron is a more difficult metal than bronze to work and, while it is unlikely that bronzeworking was rapidly abandoned, the rewards of iron are a more durable and sharper cutting edge. Iron ores are more widely distributed than copper and tin so that local sources, available in some Essex gravels (*Orsett* may contain the Anglo-Saxon word-element (Gelling, Cole, 2000)), would have been used wherever available, although little is known of iron ore production at this time in Essex and Suffolk (Going, Plouviez, 2000). Large amounts of wood and charcoal would been burned at iron-working sites, which would therefore have been near to managed woodland. The environmental evidence from pollen studies such as from Mar

Dyke in south Essex confirms that tree cover continued to diminish from the Bronze Age into the Roman period (Murphy, 1996).

That bronze continued to be worked is attested by bronze waste found at Southchurch and a spearhead from Plaistow (Rodwell, 1977; Burgess, 1969). Bronze was being worked in the Middle/Late Iron Age near the Blackwater estuary to produce studs for shields and decorative items such as rings (Brown, 1985; Sealey, 1996). While tools for domestic and agricultural use could have been made by local smiths, the emergence by the first century BC of regional styles of construction and decoration strongly implies either itinerant specialists or regional production centres. The spectacular discovery of three gold torcs at Woodham Walter (*see* **6**) attests to specialist metalworkers whose products and styles were widely distributed from Shropshire to south and east England (Meeks, Varndell, 1994). The gold torcs of Ipswich are paralleled in Norfolk and Lincolnshire, implying an East Anglian style.

Early and Middle Iron Age iron-working sites in Essex are known at Tilbury Gun Hill (Drury, Rodwell, 1973) and Little Waltham (Tylecote, 1978), but the apparent scarcity of sites suggests many articles were imported. The bronze bridle-bit found at Fingringhoe, dated tentatively to the earliest years of the first century AD, and the Late Iron Age horse brooch from Bocking, enamelled with glass from the Mediterranean or Somerset, imply trading routes by sea and land that may have been in use for several centuries (Sealey, 1991). What products did Essex and Suffolk produce for barter exchange?

The salt and marine industries, and farming

The importance of the salt-producing industry has become increasing apparent from the investigation of the 'red hills' along the coast and estuaries of the Crouch, Blackwater and Stour. That many of these are now some distance inland reflects the higher sea levels and the then-absence of sea walls, making land marsh and mud which is now pasture and arable (Murphy, 1996). The red hills and the wooden trackways which enabled access to the marsh pasture, such as that found in the Blackwater estuary radiocarbon dated 516-390 BC, are evidence of a significant industry (Jones, 1978; Fawn, 1990; Wilkinson, 1995). Fishing was probably still an important food resource and a line of posts in the Blackwater estuary, interpreted as fish traps, has been dated to around 400 bc (Wilkinson, Murphy, 1995). Oysters and cockles were harvested at Shoebury (Murphy, Brown, 1999).

The main preoccupations of most of the population were raising sheep and cattle and agriculture, unaltered from the Bronze Age. Before the end of the Bronze Age there had been a significant change in the types of wheat and barley which were being grown. While in the Early Bronze Age the main grains were emmer wheat (*Triticum dicoccum*) and naked barley (*Hordeum tetrasticum*), by the Late Bronze Age spelt wheat (*T. spelta*) and hulled barley (*H. hexasticum*) were grown widely. The changing climate conditions favoured these varieties which, autumn-sown, would ripen earlier than varieties sown in spring. Oats, rye and Celtic bean (*Vicia faba*) are known, usually in small crops, from Iron Age excavations (Brown, 1996; Murphy, 1996).

Ploughing of fields was undertaken with the ard (see Glossary) pushed by hand or drawn by one or two shorthorn oxen. Drove roads for herding cattle and sheep probably bounded by hedges and ditches have been identified at Clacton and Stansted, dating from the very end of the Bronze or start of the Iron Age and at West Tilbury dating to the Middle Iron Age. From sheep and cattle were derived the raw materials on which the weaving and leather industries depended, evidence for has been found in the form of weaving combs, round and later triangular clay loom-weights, bone needles and spindle-whorls (**colour plate 11**). For leather tanning, Pliny the Elder mentions the trading of oak galls in the first century BC. The agricultural economy will be considered in greater detail in the next chapter (Letch, 2005; Havis, 2004; Drury, 1973).

Land management and social organisation

Evidence from East Anglia, Wessex and Devon (Pryor, 1998; Fleming, 1998) suggests that already underway was a much greater degree of land-management replacing the 'small settlement' husbandry. On Dartmoor long alignments of field boundaries enclosing up to hundreds of acres have survived as collapsed stone walls, field and parish boundaries. Long boundaries in the Roding valley district and north-west of Colchester, though difficult to date, may originate from the Iron Age. Elements of possible Iron Age field systems have been demonstrated at Little Waltham, around Braintree, Chelmsford, Kelvedon and Orsett (Rodwell, 1978; Drury, 1978; Hunter, 1999; Rippon, 1991).

These suggest a degree of organisation by a central authority and a structure of possibly tribal nature willing to co-operate or coerced into compliance. When the tribe known to Julius Caesar in 54 BC as the Trinovantes came into being in Essex and south Suffolk has been discussed by Hawkes, (1983) but without certainty. A possibility remains that this occurred at a similar time to the arrival of the Arras Culture to south Yorkshire from northern France, perhaps around the fifth century BC, but an origin of the Trinovantes in Gaul is now largely discounted. More likely it was the indigenous population which acquired by trade and contacts a north Gaulish culture. The name 'Trinovantes' which Rivett and Smith (1979) translate as 'most vigorous' scarcely throws light on the origin of the tribe. Nevertheless some cohesive organisation must have been present before the Middle Iron Age around 300 BC to produce the territorial field patterns still detectable and it is difficult to see that this could have had other than a tribal nature, even it did not then call itself Trinovantes.

Iron Age settlement

Settlements of the Early and Middle Iron Age have been excavated in several areas, including Wendens Ambo, Little Waltham, Maldon, Beacon Green and Mucking (Hodder, 1982; Drury, 1978; Bedwin, 1992; Clark, 1993). The typical house was round or oval, about 10m in diameter, supported by a ring of timber posts in the outer wall and sometimes with an additional ring halfway to the centre. The outer walls were probably of turf, daub, brushwood or timber wattles (**colour plates 12 & 13**). Hearths for baking and cooking have been demonstrated both inside and outside houses. Roofs were thatched. Less common were four-sided buildings supported by four or six timber posts, which have been interpreted as granaries standing elevated above ground-level to allow air-circulation and reduce vermin and moisture. Similar constructions lifted on staddle-stones ('mushrooms') may still be seen on some farms.

Some evolutionary features in house construction have been detected at Little Waltham and Great Dunmow. Later roundhouse diameters tended to be larger than those of the Early Iron Age, and some can be shown to have had porches, often facing southeast. Earlier houses had deeper trenches dug to accommodate the wall timbers, while for later houses shallower trenches were dug, basing the wall on minimal trenching on polygonal horizontal wall plates (Drury, 1978, 1980; Lavender, 1997).

At Wendens Ambo the settlement was unenclosed. It lay at the junction of boulder clay and lighter sands and gravels. The latter could be used for arable and the former for wood and grazing, though there is increasing evidence that the productive heavier soils were cultivated early (Hunter, 1999). There is structural evidence of storage, hearths outside the houses and butchery areas (Hodder, 1982). The settlement at Rawreth was also apparently unenclosed. Here a single small oval hut or stock corral measuring 4.75x5.8m, dated from pottery to the Early Iron Age, had areas of fire-hearth outside it (Drury, 1977).

Storage pits are frequent findings on settlement sites. Reynolds (1979) has shown that grain in a pit capped with earth to exclude air and water consumed the residual oxygen and could be preserved in a carbon dioxide atmosphere for several years. A one tonne capacity pit could hold the grain produce of three to four Iron Age fields each of about 70 yards square, ploughable in one day. Meat was also stored in such pits, requiring 20kg of salt as preservative per cubic metre of pit. Clearly the height of the water-table determined whether pits could be used for storage or whether above-ground storage structures were necessary.

From the Middle Iron Age, some settlements which had previously been 'open' were wholly or partly enclosed with defensive banks and ditches, as at Sandon Brook (Dale, 2005) and Little Waltham (Drury, 1978). A spur to fortification and defensive earthworks may have resulted from the destabilisation of the economy caused by internal feuds. At Maldon an unenclosed settlement overlooking the Blackwater valley dating to the sixth century BC was later surrounded by a timber palisade (Bedwin, 1992). At Stansted a Middle Iron Age settlement was enclosed with a ditch, palisade and a substantial gate (**22**). At one corner was a timber tower, and within the enclosure were at least two roundhouses, other smaller structures and evidence of cooking hearths outside and away from the houses to avoid inadvertent fires. It had an associated track or drove road. Faunal evidence was of cattle and sheep. Some distance away a single roundhouse was sited in an 'open' settlement. Environmental studies suggest only small-scale cultivation of crops, animal husbandry seemingly predominating (Havis, Brooks, 2004).

Defended sites?

Until the Late Bronze/Early Iron Age adequate land for husbandry and cultivation appears to have been present without recourse to widespread dispute. The appearance of defended

22   The Iron Age enclosure with corner 'tower', Stansted (by N. Netherton)

sites (hillforts), dated to the Early and Middle Iron Ages, is likely to be a reflection of this land pressure and the need to defend territory against invaders. Indeed this pressure may have been a stimulus towards collective co-operation and the grouping into tribes or clans. The defended enclosures of Ambresbury in Epping Forest, Littlebury Ring Hill and Great Hallingbury Wallbury date from around 600-300 BC, and seem to have been places of occasional refuge in times of trouble rather than settlements. Their siting raises the possibility that they were a line of boundary forts to protect against attack from the west. Warfare took on a hitherto unknown intensity. This is attested by the widespread finding of swords with burials as at Whitcombe (Dorset), leather shields of which bronze bindings have been recovered from Great Totham Lofts Farm and Harlow, and the sword injuries on skeletons at Danebury near Stockbridge in Hampshire (Cunliffe, 1993).

The double-ringed enclosure ('plateau fort') at Chipping Hill, Witham is now dated from the Late Bronze/Early Iron Age (*c*.800-500 BC) with the main occupation dating to the Middle Iron Age. It commanded the crossing of the River Brain and overlooked the plain towards its junction with the River Blackwater. The outer rampart survived to 1.4m high and 10m wide in 1969 at White Horse Lane. The ditch was 10m wide and 3.6m deep (Rodwell, 1993). The inner rampart enclosed about 3.5 hectares making it comparable in size to the ditched and banked enclosures at Asheldham which is broadly contemporary, and Brentwood South Weald which seems, on limited excavation evidence, to date from the Late Iron Age (see Gazetteer) (**23**).

The 'hillforts' of East Anglia, of which Morris and Buckley (1978) identified 15 in Essex, do not take on the size or complexity of those of Wessex such as Maiden Castle, Hambledon Hill (Dorset) and Danebury (Hants) (Cunliffe, 1993; Sharples, 1991). Indeed there is some justification for considering the Essex examples, most of which are on promontories rather than hilltops, more as deterrents or places of consolidation rather than built to withstand determined attack. Defences are usually single-ditched with a bank behind. Excavation has not positively identified the technique of timber palisade or revetment (bank timber facing) construction though presumably there

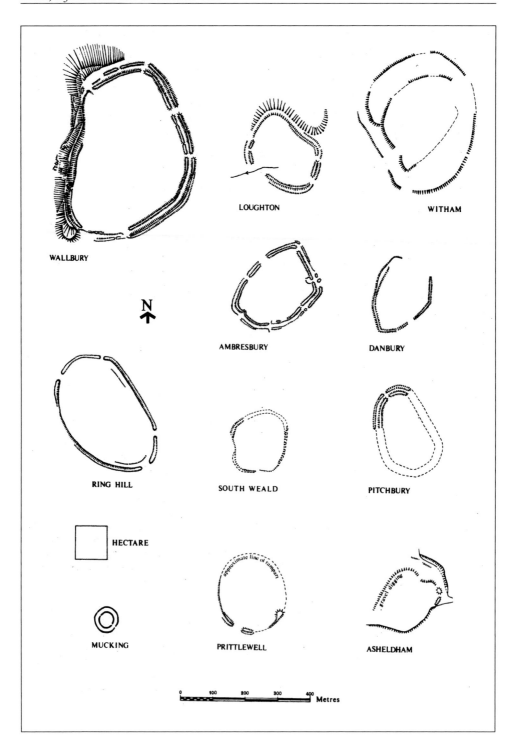

23   *Comparative plans of possible 'hillforts'*

would have been at least stake fencing along the bank top (**colour plate 14**). Entrances, where the original is known as at Ambresbury, were not the complicated earthworks which forced attackers through a series of narrow passages before reaching the gates as at Danebury, Hants.

At Ambresbury there was evidence of a solid earth causeway across the ditch and a double gate structure about 5.7m (18ft 9in wide) flanked by a stone wall in the bank leading straight into the enclosure (**24**). At Asheldham there was some evidence that the bank may have had a wooden front-revetment. Most hillforts had been at least partly abandoned by the second century BC but reoccupation appears to have occurred in the Middle and Late Iron Ages in some, as at Asheldham (Bedwin, 1991).

Danbury

The church now stands in the middle of a probable Iron Age hillfort, on the top of the ridge 360ft (115m) above sea level which commands views between the rivers Crouch and Blackwater. The surrounding bank, which is now crossed by the road to the church, still present on the east, south and west, had a ditch outside it; the ditch is still visible

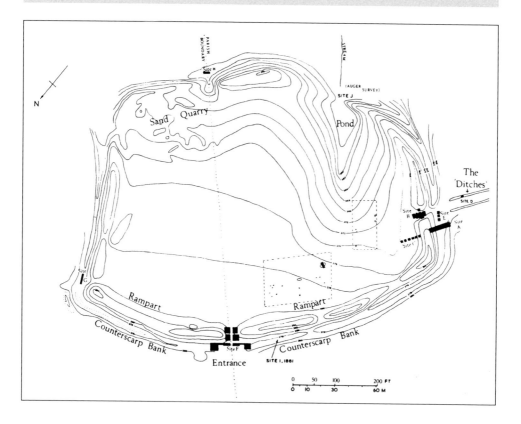

24   *Ambresbury Banks, Epping*

on the west side, in all enclosing about six acres. The bank above the bottom of the ditch created a formidable obstacle, at least 30ft (10m) high, probably with a timber palisade on the top. Seven trenches excavated in 1974 and 1977 produced Iron Age, Roman and medieval pottery. A concentration of pottery in the south-west corner of the churchyard may indicate a centre of occupation. Although certain dating evidence was not forthcoming from these excavations, it is likely that construction was begun in the Early or Middle Iron Age around 600-300 BC. Loom-weights of the fifth to seventh centuries indicate a weaving industry in the Saxon period.

There are several possible explanations for the lack of sophistication of Essex defended enclosures compared to those of Wessex. There may have been a smaller population increase in Essex and Suffolk, a greater degree of soil fertility and/or less dependence on the land due to trading links both with the interior and the mainland for essential commodities. Considerable differences in settlement patterns between the two regions exist. The Wessex hillforts such as Danebury contained large numbers of houses and storage pits within the ramparts indicating lengthy periods of habitation whereas those such as Ambresbury and Loughton in Essex did not; they seem to have been for only short-term occupation. With the emergence of an elite class it is tempting to regard this region's 'hillforts' as statements of authority to which Julius Caesar's observation that the *oppidum* of Cassivellaunus contained cattle may be pertinent.

Rituals

Evidence of burials continues to be scarce from the Early and Middle Iron Age periods (Brown, 1996), though a cremation burial in an urn was excavated at Creeting St Mary in Suffolk. The practice, widespread in the Bronze Age, of cremation burial appears to have been discontinued until it reappeared in the Late Iron Age. Evidence that broken swords were deposited as offerings in rivers suggests the continuing practice of river-burial.

Rarer still than cremation in the Middle Iron Age in Essex/Suffolk was inhumation. An infant burial was found at Shoebury (Wymer, 1995). An inhumation has been found at Mildenhall where the body was buried with a sword, gold torc, axe and two horses, presumably the property of the deceased. Finding of isolated skulls such as at Wendens Ambo, Harlow and Stifford has led to the suggestion that the head was considered to house the spirit of the departed and it alone needed to be preserved.

Ritual practices were evidently taking place. Votive offerings of food in pots have been found at Stock and Walthamstow (Hedges, 1977). Sacrifice of human beings appears also to have been practised. The bog-body, struck on the head, garrotted and strangled, preserved in the peat at Lindow Moss in Cheshire, though probably dating to the Late Iron Age or Romano-British period, is a late example of a practice probably more common in the earlier Iron Age (Stead et al, 1986). What gods were venerated can only indirectly be identified from the later Roman documentary sources; they are discussed in the next chapter. Rivers, groves, lakes and springs seem to have had special ritual significance.

A dish found in London bears the graffito *Nemet;* in Celtic *Nemet-nemeton* designated a sacred grove (Rivett, 1979). No doubt such Celtic place names which survived the Roman period were subsumed by the Anglo-Saxon writers to be lost among the hundreds of Saxon '-ton' settlement names (?Merton, possibly 'lake-settlement').

Increasing contacts with the continent

A degree of autonomy is suggested by regional and local pottery styles. In the eastern region, a characteristic Late Bronze/Early Iron Age style called Darmsden-Linton (after the sites in Suffolk and Cambridgeshire) became widespread (see Glossary). Typically these vessels are more angular (as opposed to rounded), decorated with horizontal lines, often with a pedestal base, a style associated with La Tène continental types. Crushed flint or sand and less commonly shell are the usual tempers. Some of the pottery from an Early Iron Age settlement at Linford such as an omphalos (ring)-base bowl showed affinities with Wessex styles, a jar with an angled shoulder with the Marne region of north-east France, the South Downs and Upper Thames (Barton, 1962; Sealey, 1996).

By the Middle Iron Age, pottery designed with flowing lines of the La Tène style, termed 'Mucking-Oldbury', was developed, though the majority was plain. The temper was now more usually sand or grass (**25**; **colour plate 30**). Drury (1980) drew attention to parallels in Holland. Analysis of clay from pottery found at Little Waltham shows it was obtained in the Maidstone region, traded across the Thames from Kent. Another trading route was from Glastonbury, Somerset, as shown by a bowl excavated at Maldon Heybridge. Mediterranean amphorae have been found at Middle Iron Age Stansted (Sealey, 1996) and coins of about 100 BC found at Stansted were of tin-bronze mined in central Europe (Sealey, 1996).

By the beginning of the first century BC, contacts of trade and economy were increasingly with the continent. Pottery thrown on the fast wheel (as opposed to coiled, slabbed or moulded), called 'Belgic ware' after north Gaulish types, appeared first in Britain about 50-25 BC (after Julius Caesar's expeditions) (**colour plate 15**). Grog, crushed pottery, is the typical temper. It is a new style, not an evolution from earlier native types. It often has horizontal or criss-cross decoration raised or incised into the pottery shape. A native style, found mainly in south Essex, containing shell temper was produced simultaneously and is a continuation from the Middle Iron Age. That Belgic ware was almost invariably used for cremation urns in the Late Iron Age suggests it was held in greater regard than the indigenous type. Belgic ware of Aylesford-Swarling 'culture' (named after sites in Kent) indicates the increasing links with continental Gaul available to tribes, such as the Trinovantes, friendly to Rome after Caesar's visit (Hawkes, 1980; Cunliffe, 1995).

By the middle of the first century BC, the region could be regarded as extensively occupied by farmsteads, some enclosed by a bank and ditch, others open. Some form of hedging or ditching would have separated sheep and cattle from the crop fields. At Stansted eight or nine round houses, stock pens and granaries were enclosed inside a square ditch and bank, 80x80m (**colour plate 32**). The enclosure had a small rectangular

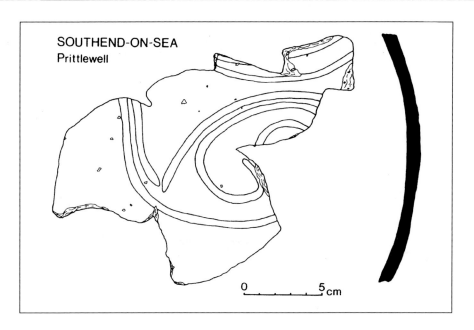

SOUTHEND-ON-SEA
Prittlewell

0 _____ 5 cm

25   Middle Iron Age decorated pottery

building 10x7.5m at the centre; this was interpreted as a shrine from the votive offerings, which included an onyx ringstone and brooches found by it. A construction date for the enclosure of about 60 BC was suggested from the pottery, but it was abandoned by 25 BC. Although the rampart bank had been reduced, its presence is shown by an area devoid of occupation between the ditch and the houses. The ditch and bank would have been a reasonable defence, in all some 3.5m from ditch bottom to bank summit, and higher with a surmounting palisade (Brooks & Bedwin, 1989; Havis & Brooks, 2004; Cooke, 2008).

Documentary evidence is of a Celtic society bound together by oaths of allegiance. Social organisation was hierarchical. Sources such as Julius Caesar (*De Bello Gallico,* VI, 13) and Strabo (IV, 4, 4-5) refer to an elite of druids, bards, Vates and knights. The druids officiated at rituals and dispensed justice. They studied the natural phenomena and moral philosophy, and influenced the supernatural powers through magic to gain a favourable result. The bards kept alive the history of the people through storytelling and inspired them with their songs and poetry. The Vates interpreted the meaning of sacrifices and divined the future. Warrior knights had at their disposal vassals on whom they called in time of war. The nobility acted under a tribal chieftain, the *Ri*, who was elected on merit, with an underclass of craftsmen. Below them were free landowners and ultimately the landless slaves. Strabo wrote that the last were traded, along with hunting dogs. Possibly the main wealth was salt and food produce, both of which were traded for imports of iron. Trade was partly by barter but by now coinage was being increasingly used.

Though Britain retained an identity of its own, the nobility and traders, especially in the south-east, were already well aware of Roman culture.

5 From Trinovantian to Roman

From the middle of the first century BC, documentary references about the Essex/Suffolk region become available to supplement the archaeological evidence. But these texts were mostly written by authors who were not native to Britain. Most had not visited the country and their accounts are therefore at best second-hand. Julius Caesar, who visited in 55 and 54 BC, had a political purpose in writing *De Bello Gallico*.

Julius Caesar's expeditions

Cassivellaunus, possibly the leader of the Catuvellauni tribe (approximately Hertfordshire/ Bedfordshire/ Buckinghamshire), had killed the king of the Trinovantes (of Essex/south Suffolk), and extended his influence into Essex. The king was identified by Caesar as Imanventius (Webster, 1993). His son Mandubracius, *Du brabwr,* 'the Black Traitor', (from Celtic sources *Avawry* whom Caswallon treated as his own son) fled to Gaul seeking the protection of Julius Caesar who ordered protection of him in Trinovantian territory at the end of 54 BC (Ellis, 1991, 1994).

Julius Caesar's account in *De Bello Gallico* is presumably contemporary. Landing probably at Walmer, Kent, he crossed the Thames 'in order to enter the territory of Cassivellaunus. The river is fordable at one point *only* and even there with difficulty'. Caesar then received envoys of the Trinovantes who sent hostages and grain.

'The Trinobantes having been defended and protected from any violence of the soldiers, the Cenimagni (?Iceni), Segontiaci, Ancalites, Bibroci and Cassi, having sent embassies, surrendered themselves to Caesar. From them he learnt that the oppidum of Cassivellaunus is not far from that place, defended by woods and marshes, and that a considerable number of men and herds have assembled there. The Britanni call it an oppidum when they have fortified dense woods with a rampart and ditch where they are accustomed to assemble to avoid the assault of enemies.' *De Bello Gallico*, v, 21, 1-3.

Evidence for the defensive *oppida* of the Britons can be traced at Wallbury (Great Hallingbury), Littlebury Ring Hill and Loughton and Ambresbury (Epping) (**colour plate 17**). In position and size, Ambresbury must be a candidate for the *oppidum* of Cassivellaunus to which Caesar refers and which he attacked. Though Cassivellaunus' probable main base at Wheathampstead near St Albans cannot be ruled out as that to which Caesar refers, if Caesar's encampment was deep in Catuvellaunian territory it is unlikely that Trinovantian envoys would venture there to surrender while Cassivellaunus remained undefeated. Excavation at Ambresbury has confirmed its occupation to the middle of the first millennium from pre-Belgic pottery (Alexander, 1978), and its situation just 15 miles, a day's march, from Chelmsford was probably on the edge of Trinovantian/Catuvellaunian territory (Black, 1990).

Iron Age settlement in the first century BC

Caesar described a thickly populated Britain, with timber as in Gaul 'with the exception of beech and pine'. He wrote that the British did not grow corn but lived on milk and meat, and that groups of 10-12 men shared wives.

Fieldwalking and excavations of first century BC/AD sites in Essex and south Suffolk suggest a largely rural economy with self-dependent farmsteads. Settlements, while averaging about 1.3 per square km, were not of uniform density across the region. They were scarcest in the north-west on the chalk soil on the sides of major 'dry' valleys, though more concentrated at their edges where water was available or could be harnessed in clay ponds (Williamson, 1984).

Bone survival is poor in much of the region, so studies of domesticated and farmed animals in the Late Iron Age are limited. At Nazeingbury and Birchanger, Late Iron Age bone assemblages showed, in order of frequency, sheep, cattle, pig and horse (bones of sheep are difficult to differentiate from goat, so for 'sheep' perhaps 'sheep or goat' should be understood).

Age-at-death studies have been informative. If mainly older cattle were being slaughtered, it might be inferred that cows were being kept for milk and draught purposes rather than being killed for beef. But at Rayne young cattle were being slaughtered, while some mature ones were being driven to market (?to Braintree) (Smoothy, 1989). At Braintree, at the junction of communicating roads (?drove ways), there was a pattern of regular yearly culls and clear evidence of butchery marks on the cattle bones (Havis, 1993). Pigs were being kept at all ages, presumably for meat, while horses could have been used for meat at the end of their life as draught or pack animals, though no butchery marks have been observed on horse bone at Braintree, Rayne or Birchanger (Medlycott, 1994). There was an increase in the size of the horse in the Romano-British period compared with those in Iron Age contexts at Nazeingbury, suggesting selective breeding or the import of continental stock. The Iron Age horse might better be described as a pony.

Indirect evidence for sheep-farming comes from the concentration of weaving industries in the Thames, Crouch and Blackwater estuaries and Dengie peninsula (from the findings of weaving-related objects such as spindle whorls and loom-weights) (**colour plate 18**) (Sealey, 1996). On many Iron Age sites sheep numbers seem to exceed cattle, with a tendency towards a decline in sheep relative to cattle into the Roman period.

The cattle known to Iron Age farmers were Celtic shorthorn (*Bos longifrons*), similar to Highland, a smaller relative to modern breeds now nearest represented by the Dexter. The Dexter can be expected to produce about 500 gallons of milk a year, perhaps a third or a quarter of modern dairy cattle, some of whose ancestors were introduced by the Romans. The *longifrons* breed was identified at Romano-British Nazeingbury (Huggins, 1978). Sheep, something akin to the present-day Soay, and, by this period, Manx Loghtan and Shetland varieties, likewise were small. Sheep were both shorn and plucked for their wool and shears have been recovered from Iron Age sites. The availability and richness of grazing land around settlement sites may have influenced the preference for sheep or cattle farming. Cattle require about four times as much hay per day as sheep, and where grazing was limited this would clearly have favoured keeping sheep and goat which can be milked and used for meat, skins and wool.

Caesar's observation that 'most do not grow corn' needs careful evaluation as it implies that the fields around the farmsteads were mainly animal pasture, and the field ditches were to restrain the stock from roaming widely, not mainly to keep them off cereal growing fields. It is unlikely that Iron Age farmers, after three millennia or more of farming experience, were unaware of the advantage of mixed agricultural and herd farming. They would have manured their fields between years of crop growing by folding their animals onto them, as well as manually spreading middens onto fields within easy carrying distance of them.

Spelt, bread (specially suited to clayey and silty soils) and emmer wheats have been isolated from Late Iron Age sites at Peldon and the Blackwater estuary, along with barley and oats (de Brisay, 1978). Indeed on most of the sites which have been analysed for cereals when preservation conditions are favourable, they have been present. At Asheldham, particularly proliferate in addition to wheat, barley and oats, was *Chenopodiaceae* (fat-hen) which was used as a vegetable. At Wendens Ambo and Maldon Heybridge (though in small amounts) wheat, barley and oats were all present (Jones, 1982; Langton, 1997), and at Billericay wheat and barley (Rudling, 1990).

Evidence from a farmstead at Boreham shows that food was being imported from the Mediterranean during the first centuries AD, and it is likely that contacts with the continent afforded a degree of affluence to this region which was restricted in areas more distant (Lavendar, 1993). On many settlement sites oyster shells have been recovered (North Shoebury (Wymer, 1995), and in Roman contexts at Braintree (Milton, 1986) but so small is the calorific value of oysters relative to meat that it is probable they were a delicacy rather than a staple.

Thus the interpretation of a pattern of settlement in small self-reliant farmsteads seems established. Though many enclosures were roughly circular, others were rectangular, such as that at Writtle, a small farmstead with a ditched and banked enclosure containing probably at least one house with evidence of domestic weaving and fires (Gobbold, 1996). The Iron Age British were not predominantly inhabitants of large nucleated settlements even though there is evidence for some small towns of the pre-Conquest era as at Great Dunmow, Harlow, Billericay and Maldon (Rodwell, 1975a). This last may have been a small port at the estuary of the River Blackwater.

Maldon, Elms Farm Heybridge

At the upper reaches of the Blackwater estuary lay an Iron Age settlement, excavated from the 1980s. The site had been occupied since at least the Mesolithic from which period was found a microlith, and a later Neolithic arrowhead. Middle Iron Age buildings were suggested by postholes and pottery. In the first century BC the settlement seems to have grown; it was primarily agricultural in nature, with scattered houses, plots and trackways. At the centre was a pagan shrine. By the early Roman period, gravel surfaces had been given to the main lanes, and the plots were more regularly spaced, separated by ditches. One area seems to have been given over to a marketplace, another to an industrial area where bronze and iron were being worked to produce hammers, axes, awls and blades. Of the wooden buildings, some had wall-plaster. Timber from the large well, 4.6m wide and at least 1.7m deep, showed well-developed carpentry techniques employing dovetail joints, chamfers and peg-holes. To the south-west was the cemetery which contained both inhumations and cremations. Remains of animal bone showed that cattle, sheep and pigs had been kept and slaughtered for food, hide, leather, wool, milk and sinew. An enlarged temple precinct contained an altar, the base plinth of which survives. A bronze stag and a stone figurine suggest the worship of Mercury and Venus.

Significant alterations in the Roman landscape and field patterns from the Iron Age are difficult to identify with certainty. A pattern of crop marks south of Colchester suggests a regular parcelling, perhaps relating to the territorium given to Roman military veterans in the late first century AD (Going, 1996; Crummy, 1978). A similar territorium may have been present around Great Chesterford (Bassett, 1989). Ditched field systems from the Roman period have been identified at Mucking. Here enclosures were replaced by larger fields by the third century which, in turn, appear, at least in part, to have been abandoned a century later (Jones, 1978; Evans, forthcoming).

Where evidence of field boundary landscapes of this period still (or at least until the period of eighteenth- and nineteenth-century maps) exist, such as Chelmsford and Little Waltham, fields appear small and rectangular, usually less than an acre in size. There is some evidence for organisation of larger tracts of land in the form of long field boundaries across several miles. Such have been traced in the areas of Rivenhall, Dengie and Roding (Drury, 1980; Hunter, 1993; Rodwell, 1975a). In this region, more environmental studies of soils from field boundaries are needed, but the banks and ditches around settlements have been sampled. These banks may have been to keep the animals away from the settlement and houses, (as did the ha-ha to the eighteenth-century country house) as much as to deter marauders. Some credence can be given to the suggestion that unenclosed settlements were chiefly agricultural or industrial (not needing a barrier to straying animals) while the enclosed were more dependent on animal husbandry. Some such unenclosed sites may have been obtaining their resources from industry (pottery, metal) to buy meat, hides and milk.

Oppida and economy

Most of the island is flat and thickly-wooded though many districts are hilly. It produces grain and cattle, gold, silver and iron. They are exported along with hides and slaves and dogs especially bred for hunting . . . They are ruled by chieftains. In war they mostly use chariots like some of the Celts. The forests are their cities for they fortify a large circular enclosure with felled trees and there make themselves huts and pen their cattle though not for a long stay. Strabo IV, 5, 2.

Strabo's observation of defendable enclosures surrounded with felled trees admits the possibility of brushwood and horizontal timber stockades rather than timbers sunk vertically into the top of a bank. Horizontally-laid timbers would leave little or no archaeological trace. Huts might then be interpreted as being unenclosed by a palisade fence unless a pattern of close-grouping into clusters could be shown, unlikely on sites where the area of excavation is limited. Strabo's comment that the large defensive enclosures were occupied for no long periods of time is born out by the lack of buildings inside the defendable sites such as Ambresbury, though some longer occupation seems to have gone on at Asheldham (Alexander, 1978; Bedwin, 1991). In the late second and first centuries BC first internal disputes and then the events of Julius Caesar's campaigns in Gaul and Britain encouraged refortification.

A large settlement developed on a spur of land between the River Roding and Loxford Water at Uphall, Ilford around 200-100 BC (**26**). A bank and ditch enclosed 24 hectares, doubled on the west (Wilkinson, 1978). Roundhouses served various functions from domestic to storage. Iron-working was being carried out. This largest Iron Age settlement may have grown as a result of its trade as a port (up the navigable river from the Thames) and as a river crossing point (Greenwood, 1988, 1989, 2001; Merriman, 1990).

The huge territories protected by linear dykes, such as Camulodunum (Colchester) with its multiple dyke system, are clearly of a different order to those at Ambresbury and Wallbury. The dykes with the Colne River to the north and east, and the Roman River to the south enclose an area of some 10 square miles (Davies, 1992; Crummy, 1997). Such a territory is to be regarded as defendable against attack mainly from the west, in which a significant population could permanently live and cultivate. Similar large territory *oppida* are known at Loose (Kent), Dorchester (Oxon) and Winchester which appear to date from the first century BC, some two or more centuries later than most of the hillfort *oppida*. (Pitts, Perring, 2006).

Currency and tribal leadership

As money they (*the Britons*) use either bronze or gold coins or iron bars with a fixed standard weight.
De Bello Gallico, v, 11,8-14,4.

The evidence for Gallo-Belgic and British coins from the pre-Conquest period includes hoards from Corringham (Thurrock), Brentwood, Epping Forest, Clacton, Chippenham and Freckenham. The 2300 potin coins from Corringham are some of the earliest issued in Britain, dated to the end of the second century BC. The Stansted hoard of 51 coins is dated to about 50 BC (Haselgrove, 1989a; Sealey, 1996). Cast potins, better known as high-tin

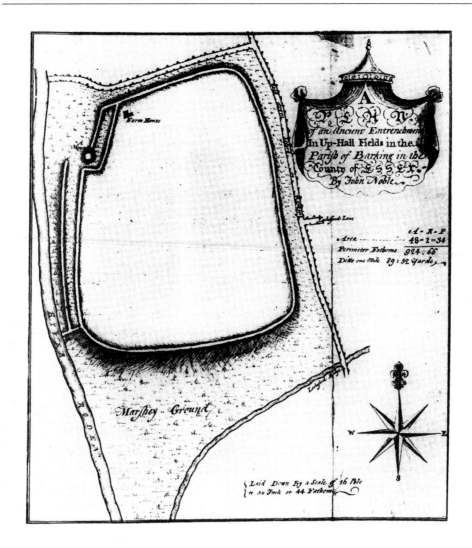

26   *Uphall Camp, Ilford, drawn c.1735*

bronzes, were made several at a time by pouring molten metal into clay moulds, the process leaving lateral flanges (sprues) of metal attached to the coins (**27**). Most coins were struck by placing a blank pellet of carefully controlled weight on a concave obverse metal die, holding on top of the pellet a reverse image die (the trussel), and striking the trussel with a hammer so that the pellet was inscribed on both sides. The issue of potins ceased towards the end of the first century BC but they continued to circulate for several decades.

By about 75 BC coins were being issued in gold and silver in Hampshire/Sussex/ Berkshire areas by the Atrebates and Regni tribes. These were of high value and used for payment of military services, dowries, tributes and bullion rather than for small trade for which barter remained the norm (it is pertinent that the Latin word for cattle, *pecus,* has the same root as *pecunia*, meaning wealth or property, and that 'cattle', 'chattels' and 'capital' all derive from the same root related to *caput,* head (Davies, 1996)). From the latter part of the first century BC the economy became increasingly coin-based, and there is some evidence of hoarding at about the time of Julius Caesar's expeditions in 55/54 BC (Haselgrove, 1979; Sealey, forthcoming).

Gold staters inscribed with a personal name were being produced north of the Thames by about 40 BC by Addedomaros, leader of the Trinovantes (Van Arsdell, 1989). On these early coins the image of a horse is a recurrent theme; sometimes there is a wolf, eagle or lion (Haselgrove, 1989b; Chadburn, 1999; Rudd, 2009).

Based on documentary evidence, mint marks on coins and the distribution of coin find-spots, the spheres of influence of the tribal leaders and their approximate succession have been estimated (Allen, 1944; Mack, 1975; Rodwell, 1976). Van Arsdell (1989) believes that coin-evidence provides no indication of a separation of the Catuvellauni and Trinovantian tribes, and considers these two tribes were united under one leadership. However, Julius Caesar recounted that while he was receiving tribute from the Trinovantes and other tribes near the Thames, Cassivellaunus' oppidum was nearby. If this is credited, the implication is that the Trinovantes at least in 54 BC were acting independently of the Catuvellauni, their nearest western neighbour, or that Cassivellaunus' forces were acting from Catuvellaunian territory. Certainly before the invasion of AD 43 the two tribes had been united under Cunobelin.

The coins of Addedomaros are found mainly to the east and north of Essex, south and east Suffolk and Hertfordshire. Addedomaros may have pushed the Trinovantian frontier westwards towards Verulamium during his reign. He lost Camulodunum to or was succeeded by Dubnovellaunus whose name appears on coins in Essex and Kent. Tasciovanus, (*c.*25-15 BC) who titled himself *Ricomus*, king, minted coins at Verulamium and soon after also at Camulodunum (Kretz, 2000; Curteis, 2006; Brooks, 2008).

Following issues of coins inscribed Sego, Andoco, Dias and Rues about AD 5 Cunobelin issued coins from Camulodunum (Webster, 1993). If the Dubnovellaunus who inscribed coins in Kent is the same person as that in Essex, Cunobelin confined him to Kent. Cunobelin inscribed some of his coins 'FIL[ius] TASC[iovani]', son of Tasciovanus, and reintroduced tin-bronzes until his death about AD 40. Some of Cunobelin's coins have an ear of corn, a galloping horseman, a boar on its haunches or a bull; a silver coin has entwined bull-headed snakes. These have been found in hoards and on temple sites (Crummy, 1994; de Jersey, 1996, 2001). The coins of Cunobelin appear widely distributed in Essex, Hertfordshire, north Kent and through mid-Suffolk, mostly south of the line from the River Deben estuary to Bury St Edmunds and the River Lark, but overlap with those of the Iceni, suggesting an approximate and fluctuating boundary between these two tribes. The coin distribution suggests either that Cunobelin was an expansionist, widening his influence from Verulamium and Trinovantian territory to parts of Kent, the south-east Midlands and the Severn valley as far as the Dorset/Hampshire border, or that his currency was widely traded (Allen, 1975; Van Arsdell, 1989).

Dio Cassius says Cunobelin divided his kingdom between his two sons Togodumnus, whom Plautius killed in AD 43, and Caratacus (Caradoc). No dateable coins of Togodumnus have been found and the few of Caratacus are not in eastern England. Caratacus escaped from Claudius after the invasion in AD 43. He continued to harass the Romans from Wales with

0   30mm

27 Potins

the Silures tribe and eventually took refuge in the north but was betrayed and handed over to the Roman authorities by Queen Cartimunda of the Brigantes (Salway, 1981).

After AD 43 Britain adopted the imperial coins of the Roman empire, probably initially through payment to the military. Claudius produced an *aureus* and a *denarius* commemorating his triumph, inscribed DE BRITANN showing a triumphal arch, and unofficial copies of his bronze were produced in Britain. In the disturbed times of the AD 270s there were copies of coins of Claudius II (268-70). The usurper Carausius (287-93) established a mint at London and possibly at Camulodunum at the end of the third century and London became an official mint after the end of the rebellion in 296, until 325. In the late fourth century appeared copies of the Constantius II bronzes.

Iron ingots or bars, about 75cm in length, of which over 1,000 are known, appeared in Britain from the second century BC and continued in use until the mid first century BC. They are of fairly standard weight, between 400 and 500 grams. Only the sword-shaped type is found in hoards, but the plough-type along the Thames valley, the spit-shaped type in Gloucestershire and Somerset, and the bay-leaf type in Cambridgeshire are found individually. Caesar's reference to their use as currency probably therefore applies only to the sword-type (Van Arsdell, 1989; Hingley, 1990). Essex has few authenticated examples of hoarded currency bars, and the reference seems to apply in the main to south and central Britain (Sealey, 1996).

The Claudian invasion of AD 43

The Roman army of Claudius under Aulus Plautius comprised probably four legions, II Augusta from Strasbourg, XIV Gemina from Mainz, XX from the Cologne region and IX Hispana from Pannonia (the Danube); including auxiliaries it totalled perhaps 40,000 men (Salway, 1981). Where Plautius landed in Briton in AD 43 has long been a subject of discussion, to which Richborough seems the most probable answer, possibly with a second arm through Sussex (Webster, 1993; Frere, Fulford, 2001).

> ... From there the Britons withdrew to the Thames at a point where it flows into the sea and at high tide forms a lake. This they crossed with ease since they knew exactly where the ground was firm. The Romans however in pursuing them got into difficulties here. Once again Celts (*of the Roman army*) swam across while the others crossed by a bridge a little way upstream, and engaged the enemy from several sides at once cutting many down. On account of this and the fact that the death of Togodumnus (*son of Cunobelinus, king of the Trinobantes who was now dead*), far from causing the Britons to give in, had united them all the more to avenge him, Plautius became afraid and advanced no further. Instead he hung on to what was already in his possession and sent for Claudius... He joined the army which was waiting for him at the Thames. Taking over command he crossed the river and engaging the natives, defeated them, and took Camulodunum, the capital of Cunobelinus...Claudius came back to Rome after an absence of six months, of which he had spent only sixteen days in Britain, and celebrated his triumph.
> Dio Cassius, LX, 19-23.

> From there *(Boulogne)* Claudius crossed to Britain. In the space of a very few days he received the surrender of part of the island without a single battle or any bloodshed, returned to Rome within six months of setting out, and celebrated his triumph.
> Suetonius, second century AD, Claudius 17.

Having secured and then broken out from his beachhead at Richborough without resistance, Plautius encountered British skirmishes again at a river taken to be the Medway. He then pressed on to make a crossing of the Thames. The crossing place, upstream of a tidal lake, had marshes on the north shore. Known crossing places of the Thames in prehistoric times recovered by archaeology include Vauxhall and possibly Lambeth and Southwark (Sloane, 1995; Orton, 1998; Denison, 1999). Though the topography is now much altered, the marshes of the River Lea (now East India Dock) are a candidate, which could be described as 'on the way' to *Camulodunum*. A crossing at East Tilbury marshes would have had the advantage of a greatly shortened supply line into Essex (Chapman, 1973; Thornhill, 1976). The British army had made its stand at the river; being defeated here many may have defected, but clearly Plautius still considered there to be a threat.

There is evidently a difference of opinion between Dio Cassius and Suetonius as to what extent Claudius himself had to fight his way to Camulodunum and to what extent the British had already retired before he arrived. Dio says that the British were engaged again by the legions now nominally under Claudius' direct command. Where this engagement occurred Dio does not state, though judging by the Britons' previous form of defending river crossings, the Lea or the Chelmer/Can rivers at Chelmsford are possibilities; both strategic crossing places, at the latter there was a prehistoric earthwork (Drury, 1972). A case has been made for a temporary encampment (traces of which have been excavated) having been made by Julius Caesar almost a century earlier at Chelmsford of which at least the earthworks would still have been standing inviting refortification by Plautius (Black, 1990; Wickenden, 1990; Kemble, 2000). A victory by Claudius here might justify the Roman name *Caesaromagus*, 'Caesar's market'. As Claudius was in Britain only 16 days, any resistance cannot have been long or sustained. Indeed some sectors of Trinovantian society may have welcomed an easy Roman advance which did not lay waste the land (Rodwell, K, 1979). Caesar having departed, the legionaries constructed a large (50 acre) fort some two miles east of the native centre (Gosbecks) of *Camulodunum*, the base for *Legio XX*, now the western part of Colchester town east of the Balkerne Gate.

The revolt of AD 60 against Roman occupation

Probably under Roman patronage, Prasutagus came to the Icenian throne sometime after AD 43 and was dead before the Boudican revolt of AD 60. Coins inscribed SUBESVPRASTO ESICO FECIT, formerly believed to be issued under Prasutagus, are now thought to be issues of Esuprastus (Chadburn, 2006; Williams, 2007). Although uninscribed, Van Arsdell (1989) identifies coins of Prasutagus' widow Boudica which occur mainly in hoards confined to Norfolk and north Suffolk, almost unworn suggesting their use was short-lived.

Two sources record the events of the Boudican Revolt, Tacitus and Dio Cassius, to which archaeology has added much detail. The recently-deceased Prasutagus had left his wealth to his two daughters and to Caesar in the hope that at least part of his kingdom would remain within his family. The Procurator, Decianus Catus, and his officials treated Boudica's and the daughters' expectations not only with contempt but with abuse, to the extent of flogging then of raping them. The elite families' possessions were seized. Unsurprisingly the Iceni took up arms (Dennis, 2008).

The historical accounts make it clear that the Roman administration and military centred on Colchester were acting in a provocative manner likely to inflame the native British. In AD 49 a *colonia* was established within and beyond the fort at Colchester to which retired Roman soldiers were billeted with their families, and it was Roman practice to provide them with land carved out of the surrounding natives' property. The veterans were behaving towards the local Trinovantes contemptuously. The Icenian rising soon attracted large numbers of supporters from disaffected Trinovantes (Webster, 1993).

> Boudica, a woman of the British royal family, having collected an army of 120,000, mounted a tribunal made in the Roman fashion out of earth. In stature she was very tall and grim in appearance, with a piercing gaze and a harsh voice. She had a mass of very fair hair which she wore to her hips, and wore a great gold torc and a multicoloured tunic folded round her, over which was a thick cloak fastened with a brooch. Taking a spear in her hand so as to present an impressive appearance she spoke as follows . . . She then engaged

in a type of divination by releasing a hare from the fold of her tunic, and since it ran on what was for them the lucky side, the whole mass of people shouted for joy . . .
Epitome of Dio Cassius, LXII, 1-6.

Evidence for the burning of the *colonia* at Colchester is clearly apparent in many of the excavations there from the red soil layer up to a metre thick, the burnt timbers and furniture. These signs of burning do not appear at Gosbecks, which was the native area. The completion (or rebuilding) of the Claudian temple in which the Romans and their families sought final sanctuary is dated to after the revolt. The defences of the earlier legionary fortress had been levelled to the timbers at the base of the rampart after *Legio XX* was deployed to south Wales and the veterans' town developed. Booty probably taken back to Suffolk from Colchester has been found: a large bronze head of Claudius hacked off a monumental statue in the River Alde and a fragment of a bronze equine statue at Ashill, Norfolk (Lawson, 1986; Sealey, 1997; Crummy, 1997).

As it left the *colonia*, the Boudican force smashed Roman tombstones in the cemetery along the roadside, and continued to London. Other tribes were probably involved but they are not specified; apparently not included were the Catuvellauni, some of whose native settlements were burned by the Boudican army on its way to Verulamium (Salway, 1981).

Tacitus refers to the forts and garrisons which the Boudican force avoided on its way to London. Where were these bases? On the grounds of topography they might be expected between Colchester and London at Kelvedon, Witham, Chelmsford, Romford, Braintree, Coggeshall and Chigwell. An early fort has been excavated just south of the River Chelmer at Chelmsford. Although there is evidence of fire at about this time in Chelmsford it is unclear whether this is associated with the rebellion (Drury, 1972). The presence of a fort at Kelvedon, postulated by Rodwell (W & K, 1975), has been queried by Eddy (1982). The Iron Age *oppidum* at Witham was apparently not refortified by the Roman army (Rodwell, 1993). No fort has been positively identified at Romford or at Chigwell, the proposed site of *Durolitum*. A first century ditched enclosure has been found at Coggeshall, but a military use not established (Clarke, 1988). In short, the forts to which Tacitus refers are unidentified. Eventually, the revolt was put down by the Governor Suetonius Paullinus.

Caesar increased troop numbers with 2,000 legionary soldiers sent from Germany with 8 auxiliary cohorts and 1,000 cavalry. The IX legion was brought up to strength in terms of legionary troops. The cohorts and cavalry squadrons were stationed in new winter quarters and any tribe that had wavered in its loyalty or had been hostile was ravaged with fire and sword.
Tacitus, *Annals XIV*, 38-9.

Wary of such an appalling opposition to their authority, the Romans replaced Paullinus with Petronius Turpilianus, a retired consul, who would both pursue less provocative policies and strengthen the army's hold. New garrisons were stationed at Coddenham, Pakenham, and Great Chesterford (Wickenden, 1996). Two forts have been excavated at Chelmsford at

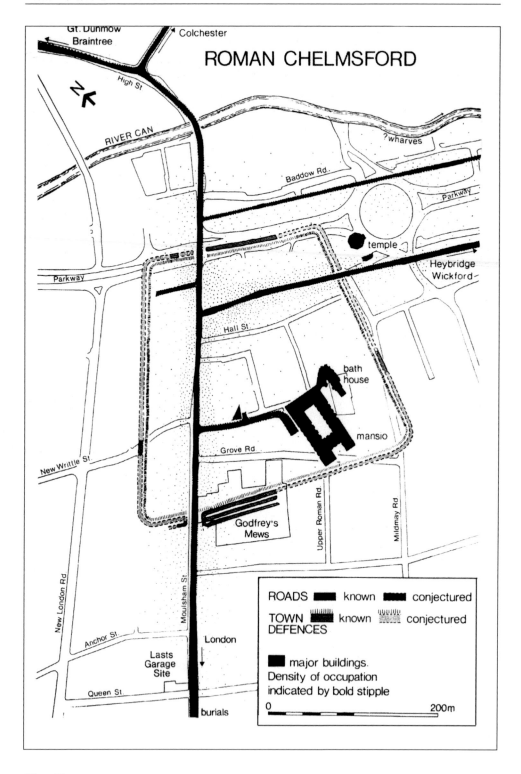

28   *Caesaromagus*

the strategic crossing over the river at a small Iron Age farmstead, and defences were updated towards the end of the second century (**28**) (Drury, 1988; Allen, 1988; Wickenden, 1991, 1996). The River Chelmer crossing of Stane Street was a suitable site for a fort at Great Dunmow which grew to occupy about 10 hectares (Wickenden, 1988).

A fort was established at Colchester Gosbecks (not yet excavated) to overlook the native centre, where some autonomy was allowed in the building of a Romano-British temple and theatre. Excavation of the theatre has shown it capable of seating 5,000 people in tiers looking towards the stage southwards. Above the foundations built of septaria (a hard black stone probably from the Harwich area), the entrance corridor was cobble set in a pink mortar. The stage was of timber and was replaced at least once (Dunnett, 1971). The temple immediately adjacent was surrounded by a ditch (into which it subsequently collapsed together with its mock-marble pillars and red-tiled roof) and outside that was a four-sided roofed portico 400 yards long (Crummy, 1997). The temple ditch in 1995 produced an exquisite finger-ring gemstone engraved with the figure of Mars, especially appropriate for a place called Camulodunum, 'the fortress of the Celtic war god Camulos'.

The *colonia* in Camulodunum, protected on the north by the River Colne, became the site of the capital of the new province but the town was eclipsed by the port entry at Londinium.

For many away from the turbulence of politics, the Iron Age way of life continued. Probable native Romano-British farmsteads have been excavated at Orsett and Boreham (see Gazetteer). Both were enclosed with ditches and internal features include timber houses, stock pens, granaries and kilns. The farmstead at Mucking, including a granary and a well enclosed by a double ditch, burned down around the end of the second century.

Orsett Cock

This late Iron Age and Romano-British enclosure was rhomboidal in shape, each side about 85m long, some 0.7 hectares (1.7 acres). The south and west sides were enclosed by three ditches (with banks) and the north side by two; the east side is under the roadway. The two inner ditches and banks were dug in the earlier first century AD, probably as part of a defendable area like those at West Tilbury and Mucking (see Gazetteer), though there is no evidence of military occupation. In these ditches were found six iron spears, all of a similar pattern suggesting they were part of a set. Later in the same century the third ditch was dug outside and parallel to the other two, its bank partly filling the older (middle) ditch. Across the middle of the enclosure was dug an east-west ditch, dividing it into two halves. The enclosure seems to have been a native farmstead, making pottery for local use. Later, a Saxon village developed close by.

Ritual, burial and religion

> You would find in Britain the rites and religious beliefs of the Gauls.
> Tacitus, first to second century AD, *Agricola*.

[*The Gallic nation*] worship Mercury most of all and have very many images of him regarding him as an inventor in all crafts, their guide on all journeys, and they consider him to be especially important for the acquisition of money in trade. After him, they worship Apollo, Mars, Jupiter and Minerva about whom they hold much the same ideas as do other races; that Apollo repels disease, that Minerva teaches the principles of arts and crafts, that Jupiter reigns in heaven, that Mars is Lord of warfare, and it is to him, when they have decided to fight a battle, that they generally promise the booty they look forward to taking. When they are victorious they sacrifice the captured animals and assemble the other booty in one spot. The Gauls claim they are descended from the Father Dis, and they claim this is a tradition of the Druids.
De Bello Gallico VI, 13-18.

Roman administration at Colchester did not impose a religion on the British. Emperor-worship was not at this time firmly entrenched, indeed it is likely to have been largely an attitude adopted by those in close contact with imperial Rome. The deification of Claudius and the building of the temple dedicated to him at Colchester may have been a factor in arousing the natives' opprobrium.

The Roman administrators and soldiers brought the Roman cults with them (examples of temples to Isis and Mithras are known in London). British gods were integrated with Roman gods into native beliefs. The Celtic practice of worship in 'natural' settings such as woods and rivers is illustrated by a dedication to the wood-god Silvanus Callirius on a copper plaque found with a bronze stag figurine at Colchester. The affix Callirius recalls Callirrhoe, daughter of the river Achelous, and may associate the river Colne with the forest protecting Camulodunum on the north (Breeze, 2004).

Animals were venerated. In the Lexden tumulus, possibly the burial of Addedomaros (*c.*15 BC), were bull and boar figurines. The horse appears on his coinage, that of Dubnovellaunus and of Cunobelin. Indeed the horse, sometimes mounted, is a frequent depiction on Cunobelin's coins, though the boar, bull, ram, snakes and wolf also appear. A horse burial was excavated at Witham. A horse and rider figurine was found at Braintree (**29**); many appear in ritual contexts. The godess Epona, patroness of cavalry officers, is sometimes shown mounted on a horse and is associated with fertility, a theme which the ear of corn also found on his coins may represent. The horse-burial at Chelmsford suggests this cult. The horse was a sky-god and was apparently worshipped at Kelvedon where a pot stamped with a mounted horse was found at the shrine.

An alternative to Epona was the Celtic warrior-mounted god Mars Corotiacus whose statuette has been found at Martlesham in Suffolk within Trinovantian territory. A dedication to Mars Medocius was found in Abbey Field at Colchester and a finger ring gemstone of Mars has recently been excavated at Gosbecks. Mucking has produced a clay statuette of Mars draped with a cloak over one shoulder and it is clear that there was a fusion of the Roman Mars with the Celtic war-god Camulos as a dedication to Mars Camulos has been recovered on the Antonine Wall (Green, 1992).

To the god Mars Medocius of the Campeses and to the victory of our emperor

29   *Romano-British copper alloy figurine, Braintree*

Alexander Pius Felix, Lossio Veda, grandson (*or nephew*) of the caledonian
Vepogenus, set this up as a gift from his own resources.
Bronze inscribed plate found in 1891 on south side of Colchester, RIB 191.
Now in British Museum.

After adoption or assimilation of the Roman gods into Celtic practice, names can
more often be given to the deities found. Mars, Jupiter, Mercury and Venus appear on
the fine eight-sided stone monument from Great Chesterford (to be seen in the British
Museum), possibly at the base of a tall Jupiter column. The column substituted the Celtic
oak tree reaching to the sky-god. The huge posthole for what may have been a similar
column has been excavated at Ivy Chimneys, Witham (Turner, 1982, 1999). This sky-god
was worshiped in a Celtic form before the Roman invasion as a wheel, sometimes with
an eagle (Jupiter's emblem), the wheel representing the sun. The wheel-tomb at Mersea
may have celestial significance.

A Hercules statuette has been recovered at Epping Forest (in the British Museum, ?
a modern cast), Venuses (Southend and Thurrock Museums and from Heybridge) and
a Bacchus (Chelmsford Museum). An interesting example of an eastern deity figure
wearing a Phrygian (pointed) cap, possibly associated with Cybele worship, was found in

the villa at Whitton, Ipswich (Clarke, 1963). The prohibition of this Anatolian cult of the mother-goddess Cybele and her shepherd-consort Atys, which involved self-flagellation, castration of initiates and *hilaria*, ecstatic ceremonies, was lifted during Claudius' reign and became popular in Norfolk and Suffolk.

More mythical in depiction is the three-horned bull clay figurine found in a child's grave at Colchester which resembles the bronze macehead bull at Maiden Castle (Green, 1983). The figure three is recurrent in Celtic ritual, and appears in the three-fold *genii cucullati,* the hooded dwarves, which were found on a pot at Chadwell St Mary. They are associated with prosperity and fertility (Rodwell, 1975b).

> To the Mother goddesses the Suleviae, Similis, son of Attus, a tribesman of the
> Cantiacii, willingly fulfilled his vow.
> Stone inscription from Colchester, RIB 192.

> To the divine power of the Emperors and Mercury Andescocivovcus, Imilico,
> the freedman of Aesurilinus, gave this marble altar from his own resources'.
> Inscription from Colchester, RIB193.

Also found at Balkerne Lane, Colchester was a dedication to the *Suleviae*, the goddesses of healing, often prominent near springs. The bronze Mercury at Gosbecks was a Roman import but has been found frequently in Gaul. He seems to have represented trade, and, with an animal, a herald. Associated with him was the cockerel, as found at Chelmsford. A plaque to Mercury Andescosis appears at Colchester. The chalk-carved human figure with bare arms wearing a tunic found at the temple at Witham is interpreted as a votive offering (**30**). The clay phallus at the temple and those at Maldon Heybridge may be fertility symbols (Frere, 1970, 1973).

There is some evidence that Celtic leaders may have aspired to godlike status. The names of many of the tribal leaders are unknown to us but the dedication to the god Ocelus Vellaunus is recorded at Caerwent, and Vellaunus is a Celtic god known from Gaul associated with the god of success and the arts, Mercury. The Trinovantian leader Dubnovellaunus and Cassivellaunus, leader of the British against Julius Caesar, may have added the suffix to their names to reflect the god's attributes. The suffix appears on a gold stater of the Corotini of the Midlands in Volisios Dumnovellaunus and a silver stater of Volisios Cartivel. Cunobelin's name incorporates the cult name Belenus known in Gaul, Italy and the Alps, and is associated with the sun and, as a sky-god, with horses, venerated at the festival of Beltane on 1 May as a prelude to summer.

> [*The Gauls*] wear not only golden ornaments, torcs round their necks and
> bracelets round their arms and wrists, but those in high positions wear clothes
> that have been dyed and shot through with gold. [*There is also*] the barbaric
> practice of fastening on enemy heads to their horses when they leave battle,
> and once they have taken them home nailing the spectacle to their doorposts.
> However the Romans put an end to the practice of these customs.
> Strabo, first century BC-first century AD, IV,4,4-5.

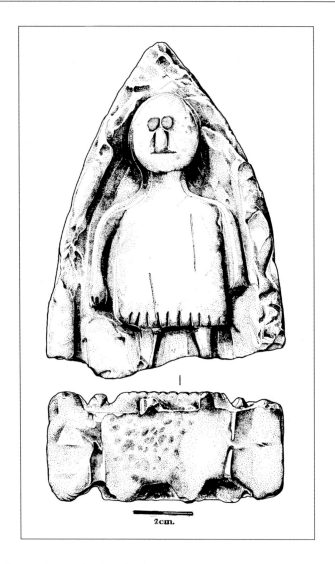

2cm.

30   Romano-British chalk votive from Witham

The Severed Head Cult appears in burials and may be represented on a bronze coin of Cunobelin. The heads of enemies were displayed by Celtic victors, attached to their horses after battle, and at *oppida* stuck on poles. Known from burials are skeletons in which the amputated head was placed (usually) between or beside the legs. Over 70 severed head burial sites are known in England, mostly dating from the Romano-British and Anglo-Saxon periods (**31**). Examples in Essex and Suffolk include Icklingham, five at Chignall St James and six at Ipswich Dales Road. At Harlow the head of a young man was found in a pit with an iron spear and a bronze ring, dated to about 50 BC. Prone (face-down) burial suggests judicial execution or disposal of an outcast, especially when it is at the edge of a cemetery, but ritual burial, not necessarily dishonourable, has been suggested

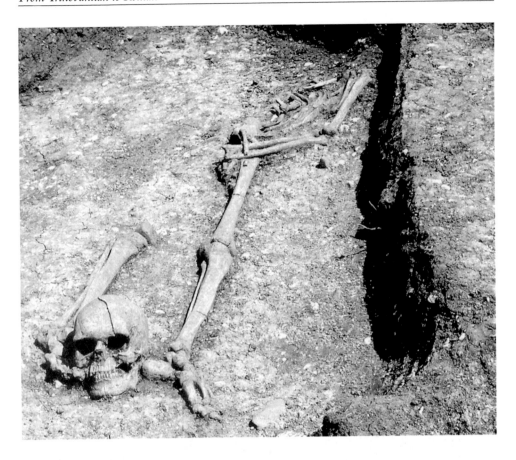

31   Decapitation burial, Cressing

(Philpott, 1991) (**32**). The archaeological evidence clearly conflicts with Stabo's comment that such practices had been ended by the Roman authorities; it is more likely that though suppressed it had not been entirely erased.

> A belief the Druids particularly wish to inculcate is that the soul does not perish but after death passes from one person to another.
> *De Bello Gallico.*

Clearly this belief continued into the Roman period amongst the native British. Cremation on a pyre was the usual rite, in the Middle Iron Age with slaves and dependants, but into Caesar's time with their possessions. The excavation of the late Iron Age and Roman cemetery at Stansted (Havis, 2004) provides evidence of burial practices to the latter part of the second century. Two of the late Iron Age burials may have had mounds over them. Some had evidence of wooden boxes, one with a lock, to hold the cremation (**colour plate 19**). In two of the graves with the richest grave goods were glass vessels, but neither contained cremated bone. Only one burial contained metal vessels, a jug, patera, saucer,

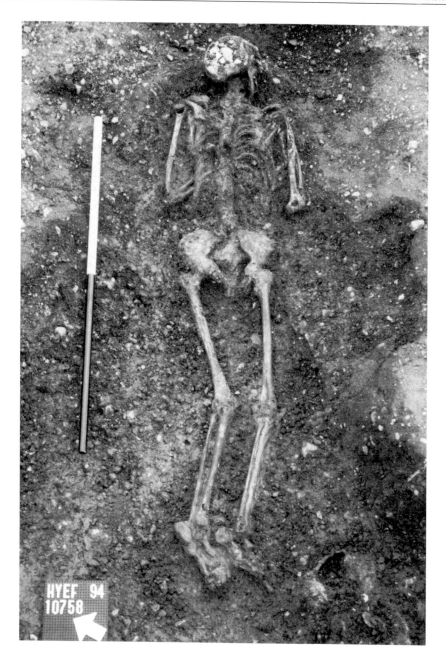

32   Face-down burial of young woman in a Roman pit, Maldon

amphora, a bowl and another vessel, dating to the first century. Animal bones, especially chicken and pig, suggest provision for the afterlife. Overall the evidence is that this was a cemetery of a moderately high-status land-owning family who may have farmed the same area for 200 years (Cooke, 2008).

A similar high-status family is suggested from burials at Bartlow (**colour plate 20**). These contained a glass phial with ashes, an enamelled casket and food on a samian dish, probably of the second century. Unfortunately many of the recoveries from these impressive mounds have been lost, but records suggest there were similarities with Stansted (VCH Essex, 1963, 44). At a higher social level are the first century aristocratic graves at Colchester Stanway. Here grave goods are richer and more abundant. They include a warrior's grave with goods needed for the afterlife, amphora, a spear and shield, pottery and glass vessels, a doctor's grave with his set of surgical instruments and a scribe's with writing equipment and inkwell (Crummy, 1997). Other high-status burials of the Roman period are at Mersea, White Notley and East Ham, with cemeteries at Mucking, Colchester and Kelvedon.

Graves of soldiers who served with the Roman army and died far from their native homelands, such as Longinus and Marcus Facilis (see Gazetteer for Colchester), were marked with elaborate gravestones along the Lexden Road outside the *Colonia*. Gradually, into the second and third centuries, inhumation replaced cremation as the commoner form of burial. Burials such as those of two young women and an eight year old child at Great Chesterford lying north-west to south-east, probably of the second century, may have been in graves unmarked or marked only by a wooden stake (Hooper, 1967).

A third century altar dedicated to Isis, found in Upper Thames Street, London, reused in the riverside wall, announces: 'In honour of the Divine House, M(arcus) Martianius Pulcher, of senatorial rank, governor of the emperors, ordered the temple of Isis...which had collapsed through old age to be restored' (Britannia (1976) 7, 378).

A graffito on a jug from London states: *'In London at the shrine of Isis'* (Merrifield, 1983).

The usual form of the Romano-Celtic temple was a square *cella* (although sometimes it was round or polygonal as at fourth century Chelmsford), with an encompassing ambulatory, as at Harlow (France, Goble, 1985). The ditch around the temple at Colchester Gosbecks may belong to an earlier (?pre-Conquest) ritual site. Here the temple was built off-centre of the ditched enclosure suggesting perhaps a more venerated earlier structure in the middle. The huge surrounding portico was a Roman-inspired embellishment, an extension of the Celtic ambulatory. Recent excavations at Maldon Heybridge have revealed the foundations of Iron Age shrines, which were replaced by a circular temple. A particularly large temple complex was excavated at Witham Allectus Way (**colour plate 21**). This began as an Iron Age settlement and, about AD 70, became a Celtic pagan centre with a timber shrine near a ritual spring. This spring was later converted into a pond into which ritual deposits such as 'thunderbolts' (palaeolithic flint handaxes) were thrown. In the third century a large timber temple was erected with a sacred *temenos* and sometime after it was converted into a Christian church (Turner, 1982, 1999).

A personal 'rite' was the Curse-tablet *(defixio)* often written on lead sheets of which several have been found at shrines. Their 'magical' nature may have been enhanced by writing them backwards. 'I curse Tretia Maria and her life and mind and memory and liver and lungs mixed together, and her words, thoughts and memory. May she be unable to speak what is secret nor be able...' (Inscription from London, RIB 7). From Harlow another inscription runs: 'To Mercury I entrust to you my affair with Eterna and herself, and may Timotneus [*sic*] feel no jealousy of me at the risk of his life'. From Kelvedon one reads 'Whoever has stolen the property of Valenus, whether woman or man, in his own blood and from the money he has consumed let him pay gifts to Mercury and sacred offerings to Virtue' (Wright, 1958; Rodwell, 1975b).

Recreation

The discovery and excavation from 2004 of the horse-racing circus 400 metres south of the Roman town of Colchester, to date unique to Britain, shows the extent to which Roman culture had permeated urban life in the capital. With a capacity for perhaps 15,000 people, the circus was around 447m long and around 72m wide with a semicircular east end and 8 starting gates at the west end. From the central barrier or spina was recovered part of a brick cone covered with opus signinum painted pink; such cones were sited at the ends of the barrier. The circus was probably built in the 2nd century but apparently did not survive as a functioning structure into the fourth (Crummy, 2005, 2008).

The stone-built theatre in the Roman town immediately northwest of the Temple of Claudius had its seats arranged in a semicircle facing north towards the River Colne. This no doubt served the Roman veterans, the administrators and their families. The native British probably patronised the theatre 2½ miles southwest of the colonia at Gosbecks, the tribal capital. Above the foundations of septaria, the upper courses were of ragstone brought from Kent. The entrance corridor to the theatre through the auditorium led to the orchestra. Two large stairways led up to the rear seats of the auditorium which in all may have seated 5,000 people. The second century building replaced an earlier timber theatre, and it seems that the building ceased to be in use after about AD 250 (Dunnett, 1971).

A bath suite with hypocaust has been excavated at Chigwell, a possible site for Durolitum, and a bath house has been postulated adjacent to Chignall St James villa. The owners added a bath suite to their villa at Little Oakley, possibly in the late second century, and a bath house formed part of the Rivenhall villa complex (Clarke, 1998; Barford, 2002; Rodwell, 1985). For more public use, a probable bath building pre-dating the Boudican destruction was excavated just southwest of the theatre in Colchester town, and a bath complex was found next to the Chelmsford mansion (Allen, 1988; Wickenden, 1990).

6 High Britannia, success and disruption

Following the Boudican Revolt, early documentary references specifically to Essex and Suffolk are meagre. Interpretation depends on archaeology and literature of a wider British context (Frere, 1973; Salway, 1981).

Towns such as Kelvedon, Coggeshall and Great Chesterford were enlarged and some were used as administrative and military centres. Roman Colchester developed on and around the earlier fort some two miles east of the Iron Age nucleus of Gosbecks. Some such as Billericay, Long Melford, Wickford and Braintree have evidence of previous Iron Age hamlets or farms (Wickenden, 1996). Chelmsford on the main road between Colchester and London developed a way-station *(mansio)* near the river crossing (**colour plate 22**). If the excavated site at Chigwell Little London at the crossing over the River Roding is Durolitum, it may be another example of a Roman riverside settlement on a main road whose name is known (Clarke, 1998). Hacheston and Gestingthorpe developed near roads (Rodwell, 1975a). Maldon Heybridge and Fingringhoe near Colchester, the former an Iron Age settlement, were used as ports by the second half of the first century AD. Harlow may have enlarged in response to the presence of the temple.

Chelmsford, Moulsham

The junction of Grove and Roman Roads marks the south-west corner of the Roman *mansio*, or inn, the official guest-house for travellers. The platform on which it was constructed still produces a slight rise in the road level in Roman Road and the northern end was about 75m north of the Grove Road-Roman Road junction. First built in wood about AD 125 and later in stone, a central courtyard was surrounded by guestrooms. Tesserae and painted plaster from the floor and walls have been recovered. To the north was a temple complex. On the north-east corner was a bathhouse constructed in the mid-second century. It consisted of a *caldarium* (hot room), *tepidarium*, a cold plunge room and a furnace room. The *hypocaust* and iron bands of the water pipes survived. A sauna, *laconium*, circular in shape, lay between the *mansio* and the baths. The *mansio* fell into disuse in the fourth century (Drury, 1988; Allen, 1988; Wickenden, 1991, 1996).

An urban economy increased as trade and communications improved. Freer links with the Roman Empire implied the easier trade of goods made in Gaul and elsewhere. The plate brooch of a hare probably made in central Gaul found at Great Dunmow is no doubt representative of such imports (**33**).

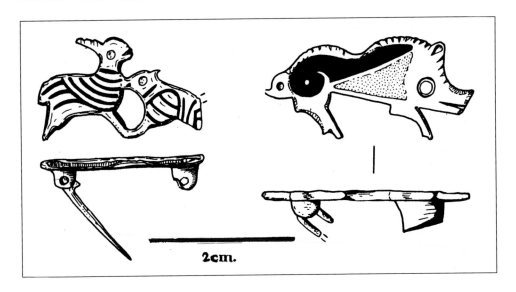

33   Hare and boar brooches, first-/second-century AD, Great Dunmow

As wealth amongst the Romano-British increased, some were able to establish large villa estates employing workers who lived on the land in timber houses similar to those of their forefathers. Building of higher-status villas and villa estates increased from the latter part of the first century into the second. A cluster occurs around Colchester. Examples which have been excavated include Wendens Ambo, Gestingthorpe, Pakenham and Ipswich (see Gazetteers and Glossary 'Romano-British villas'). At least one, at Rivenhall, may have employed water-power in a mill, and other mills have been identified at Ardleigh and Great Chesterford (Going, 1996).

The more prosperous villas such as Rivenhall, Mersea, Wanstead and Whitton were often well-appointed with decorated plastered walls, corridors, hypocaust heating and bathhouses. The sites of over 35 villas in Essex and over 15 in south Suffolk are now known. The extent of the associated land-holding is difficult to ascertain, though there is the possibility that some holdings are represented in the medieval royal vills and ecclesiastical boundaries (Dark, 1994; Morris, 1980; Williamson, 1986; Yorke, 1999).

Romano-British industries

Fulling troughs at Great Chesterford, and maltings at Stebbing and Mildenhall (Bates, 2004) suggest local industry. Small farms producing enough to sustain the owners or tenants with hopefully a surplus to send to the *vicus* for sale and distribution are difficult to identify outside the villa estates so long as the extents of these estates are unknown, but surely must have existed in considerable numbers (Brooks, 2006). At Mucking extensive excavations have revealed the ditches and field boundaries of what may be such a farm showing continuity with the Iron Age predecessor (Jones, 1978). Tools such as cropping shears found at Great Chesterford and pottery kilns, particularly around Colchester but also at Hacheston, Ardleigh, Rettenden and along the Thames at Tilbury, Mucking and Shoebury attest to other industries providing produce for local use and trade.

The extensive industry of salt-production which had begun in the prehistoric period continued. By AD 200 the Roman coastline, as plotted from salt-production sites, was in places several hundreds of metres inland of the present coast. Largely unprotected by sea dykes, there were extensive tracts of mudflats, creeks and marsh. Dumping of spoil such as shells, refuse and soil to raise the ground level has been detected at Canvey and Bradwell Othona (Murphy, 1996). 'Red Hills' 2-3ft high but now often reduced to a flattened earthen patch are widely distributed along the coast and estuaries. Salt water was evaporated in large clay pans, leaving the debris of the pottery pedestals which supported the pans over the furnaces and the burnt earth as archaeological evidence.

Sites of brick and tile industry have been found at Mount Bures, Colchester and Great Braxted. The occasional impressed stamps of the potter's or his owner's initials found on them at widely separated sites indicate a larger than local distribution (Rodwell, 1975b).

The considerable amount of building involved a large timber industry, both in growing and managing woodland, and in carpentry. The enclosure at Hatfield Broad Oak formerly in Hatfield Forest, Portingbury Rings, may represent a small forest-workers' community settlement (**34**). Coppicing and pollarding were well known to the efficient and experienced Romano-British and from much earlier centuries. Ancient coppice stools are found in Stour Wood and Holbrook Park near Ipswich (Rackham, 1986). The Romans introduced the sweet chestnut and walnut. Surviving waterlogged timbers such as those found lining wells at Boreham, Great Totham and Wickford speak eloquently of the capabilities of the Romano-British carpenter.

Metal industrial sites include Colchester Sheepen, Harlow, Hacheston and Gestingthorpe. These industries required large amounts of wood and charcoal for the furnaces in addition to the bronze and iron ores or scrap. They depended for their supplies and distribution on river and marine ports, and on cross-country road networks begun probably in the Neolithic period and expanded in the Roman. Trackways such as the Icknield Way from Wessex to north Essex and Norfolk, Stane Street (Braughing — Great Dunmow — Colchester) predating the Roman period, and Cavendish — Long Melford — Coddenham — Hacheston provided the main east-west routes. The Stratford — Romford — Marks Tey road and the Chigwell — Chelmsford — Braintree — Long Melford roads developed as north-south routes, the former possibly first for military purposes, later for commerce. Many in existence in the Iron Age are still in use as bridleways, tracks and roads, now being recognised by field-work (Going, 1996).

Towards the end of the second century there appears to have been some destruction by fires at Chelmsford, Billericay, Wickford, Gestingthorpe, Kelvedon, Mucking and Braintree, though not on the scale of London and Verulamium (Going, 1996; Wickenden, 1996). There is also evidence of coin hoarding. The documentary record for Essex and Suffolk as to the causes is silent and the fires may not have been simultaneous. Theories of military mutiny, civil war and barbarian invasion remain speculation (Rodwell, 1975a; Salway, 1981; Gardner, 2007)

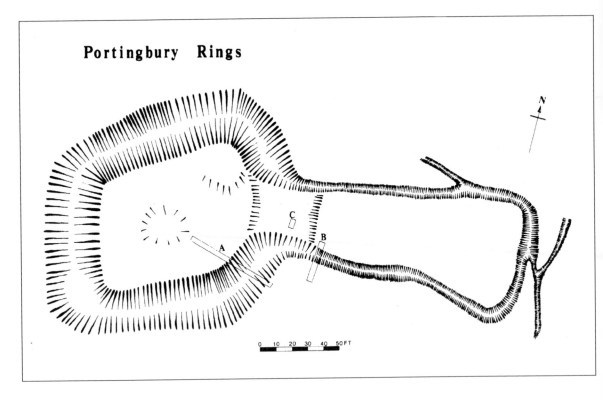

34   *Hatfield Broad Oak, enclosure*

Christianity

> Eborius bishop of the city of York, in the province of Britain, Restitutus bishop
> of the city of London in the above-mentioned province, Adelphius bishop of
> the civitate colonia Londiniensi [?Lindinensium, Lincoln or Legionensium,
> Caerlon], also Sacerdus, presbyter and Arminius, deacon.
> British representatives at the Council of Arles, Gaul, AD 314.

A year after the Edict of Milan which, for the first time, gave freedom of worship
to the Christian church, the representatives of the church in Britain called to Gaul
probably represented the four provinces, of which Colchester was, by 312-4, in *Maxima
Caesariensis*. Its bishop Restitutus was from London, not Colchester. The small church
and cemetery at Butt Road on the south side of Colchester is dated to about this time.
Buildings, probably of the fourth century, interpreted as churches have been excavated
also at Witham. The piece of pottery scratched with a chi-rho symbol found near the
Colchester Temple of Claudius cannot be interpreted as proof of its conversion to a
church (Crummy, 1997).

The transition from pagan to Christian was accommodated within Celtic tradition by
invoking the multiplicity of saints in place of the panoply of gods. Christian burials usually

lack grave-goods, but may be recognised by the body's orientation east-west, head to the west. According to Tertullian (7,4) Christianity had been practised in Britain at least since the beginning of the third century, possibly earlier.

The martyrdom of St Alban at Verulamium for concealing a Christian priest from the Roman authorities has been dated to the first half or middle of the third century. A lead tank with Christian symbols found at Icklingham (see Gazetteer), at Brentwood a gold finger-ring bearing a chi-rho, at Wickford a tile with an alpha-omega motif, from Hoxne Christian crosses and from Mildenhall 'baptismal' spoons all indicate observance of the religion. To these may be added a fish (?representing *ichthys*) on a glass bowl at Colchester, a late Roman bronze buckle plate from Harlow temple with a peacock representing a Christian soul eating from the Tree of Life (Bartlett, 1987), and a strap-end with a peacock and griffin design from Rivenhall (Tonnochy, Hawkes, 1931) (**35**). Though few are closely dated the majority appear to be of the fourth century (Rodwell, 1975b; West, 1976; Turner, 1999). At Long Melford is a probable fourth century Christian burial. The estate-workers' inhumation cemetery at Chignall St James dating to the third and fourth centuries may at least in part be Christian, grave-goods being few (Clarke, 1988) (see Gazetteer).

The extent to which Christianity permeated Romano-British society in the region is difficult to estimate (Major, Eddy, 1986; Wickenden, 1986). It seems to have failed in being embraced wholeheartedly by the subsequent leaders of the population, the spur for the British cleric Gildas about AD 530 to denounce their lapses. Pagan practices continued until Christianity was brought again by Cedd from Lindesfarne about AD 653 when he set up his church at Bradwell Othona at the request of King Sigebert Sanctus (Yorke, 1985).

Witham, Ivy Chimneys, Allectus Way

In the third century AD at the Romano-Celtic temple, coins and jewellery were deposited as votive offerings to the gods. The temple had a double entrance on the east. Also to the east was a pond and east of that a large timber column beside a tiled platform. To the north of the temple was a pottery kiln archaeo-magnetically dated to within 25 years of AD 325. Pottery wasters of dishes and jars were found. This pottery may have been for ritual use. Close by was a potter's shed packed with tiles. There is evidence of a small rectangular semi-masonry building, possibly a chapel, from the late fourth to early fifth century. A font 2m wide was built where the earlier temple pool had been, perhaps to acknowledge previous religious practices. Three construction phases were recovered. The earliest font was octagonal with tile walls supplied by water from a small ditch, the second an octagonal wooden box and the last a square with wooden walls and a cobble surface surround. Forty metres east of the font was a small square building with walls of septaria stone and a tiled floor. The walls were covered with painted plaster and the windows may have been glazed. Later, probably in the fifth century, the stones were robbed for other uses and the pond silted up (**colour plate 21**).

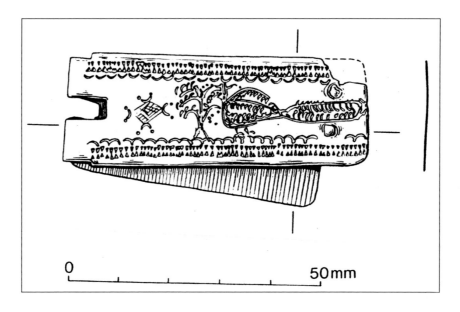

35   *Late Roman bronze buckle with peacock design from Harlow*

Disruption and incursion

> Comes [*Count*] of the Saxon Shore in Britain:
> Under the control of the Vir Spectabilis are:
> Praepositus [*commander*] of the Unit of Fortenses at Othona [*Bradwell*] . . .
> Praepositus of the Stablesian cavalry of Gariannonenses at Gariannonum
> [*Burgh Castle*].
> Praepositus of the unit of scouts at Portus Adurni [*?Felixstowe Walton Castle or
> Porchester, Hants*].
> From *Notitia Dignitatum*, 28.

The impetus of the first and second centuries to building, commerce and wealth appears to have been on the wane by the latter part of the fourth. Perhaps the evidence of the need from the middle of the third century to provide a defensive system of forts along the south-eastern coastline of Britain against piratical raids (of which the forts at Bradwell Othona, Felixstowe Walton and Burgh Castle are the regional examples) provides a clue to one of the causes of decline, but this is unlikely to be the only one.

The fort at Bradwell Othona is still traceable on its west and parts of its north and south sides, the rest having been inundated by salt-marsh. The walls are of tile and septaria, 4.2m wide at the base, and bastions protected the corners. The west gate may underlie the Saxon chapel attributed to St Cedd whose walls contain stone from Lincoln and Kent, reused probably from the fort. The identification of Portus Adurni as Walton Castle, Felixstowe is more controversial. Only seventeenth- and eighteenth-century records of a fort here exist; it is now wholly lost to the sea. In 1722 its walls stood 1.5m high and 3.6m wide, made of tile and stone, and, like at Othona and Burgh, having corner bastions. The occurrence of Romano-Saxon pottery at the forts at Burgh, Bradwell Othona and Richborough raises the possibility that they were manned at some time by Germanic militia under Romano-British supervision. Their use may have changed between the third and fourth centuries from shore-based points from which naval sorties could be launched to deter sea-borne marauders to policing stations for the coastal-based Saxons.

There is some evidence that the forts on the east shore were constructed later than those of Kent. Romano-Saxon pottery is scarcer in Kent than Essex and Suffolk, and this has been explained as a success of the defences in the English Channel against incursions while the eastern shore was, for a while, unprotected (Roberts, 1982; Rodwell, 1970). Certainly it is likely that the Roman navy *Classis Britannica* would have had its traditional ports and shore installations at places such as Richborough, Lympne and Dover, which subsequently became Saxon Shore forts. The size of the extant Roman walled town at Richborough suggests it remained a major port.

Close dating is difficult but Myers (1986) claims a possible construction date for the forts at Reculver in Kent and Brancaster in north Norfolk around AD 230. The intermediate forts at Felixstowe Walton and Bradwell Othona may not have been built until the earlier second half of the century. About AD 285, Carausius (subsequently usurper emperor, *c.*287-93) was put in command of a fleet to repel Germanic intruders. Himself from coastal Belgium, he proved unreliable, helping himself to booty from the pirates (Aurelius Victor, fourth century). Frere (1973) credits him with the development of the fort system, though Burgh, Othona and, by association, Walton, were probably already built by the time he received his command (Johnson, 1979; Fairclough, 2000). The beacon signal-towers postulated at Hadleigh, Dunwich and Corton, Suffolk, may be part of these defences (Johnson, 1975; Moore, 1948; Pearson, 2002; Douglas, 2004).

Germanic presence

After the murder of Emperor Constans in AD 350, Magnentius became effective Augustus of most of the West for some three-and-a-half years. That his family derived from Germanic *laeti* (mercenaries) may have a bearing on the progressive installation of Saxons in Britain to deter the raids from the north and east (Salway, 1981). Constantius' (337-61) purge of Britain to hunt out adversaries caused much alarm, soon to be compounded by further concerted attacks from the north. His cousin Julian, Caesar of Britain and Gaul, a confirmed pagan, set about reintroducing the pagan cults which had been in decline for more than a century, and removed privileges from Christians. These upheavals amongst the aristocracy and the army left Britain ill prepared to combat incursions. Having been simmering for a generation, around AD 367 these insurrections of simultaneous but perhaps uncoordinated attacks by Picts, Attacotti, Franks and Saxons reached a crescendo along the coasts of Britain and Gaul, reaching as far as London (Ammianus Marcellinus, xxvii, 8). Bartholomew (1984) claims these were compounded by revolt of the Roman army driven by hunger from food-shortage due, at least in part, to corruption within the administration.

Evidence of the extent of the disruption in Essex/Suffolk is difficult to estimate. Direct attack may have been minimal. The evidence of bronze military metalwork, indicative of mercenaries, may be early fifth century rather than evidence of the troops, the Batavi (from the region of the Netherlands), Heruli and Jovii (from northern Italy and Croatia) and Victores, brought in by Count Theodosius, father of Theodosius the Great, to rescue the province in the fourth century (Dunnett, 1975). Such metalwork has been found at Bradwell, Mucking, Colchester and Gestingthorpe in Essex, Ixworth and Icklingham in Suffolk. Great Chesterford was reinforced with a wall and ditch. A series of imperial usurpers, bad internal administration and breakdown of co-operation between the native Romano-British and the Roman command may have played a major part in the disruption (Jones, 1996).

The probable estate-workers' cemetery excavated at Chignall villa gives an interesting insight into the health and burial practices of the native British in the third and fourth centuries (Clarke, 1998), but villas and farmsteads seem to have been in decline by the fourth century. Building of new large villas appears to have ceased by about AD 350. Use of some continued into the early Anglo-Saxon period at Rivenhall and Colchester Lion Walk, when some larger rooms were modified with timber partitions or stone building material was re-used. Many showed an unspectacular, gradual decline into the post-Roman period, as might be expected if Dark (1994, 1997) is correct that Essex/Suffolk remained a Romano-British enclave until the sixth century. A worsening climate, loss of arable to marshland, decline in trade with the mainland as Gaul became subject to Germanic invasions, incursions by the Picts and internal dissent may be factors contributing to decreasing individual prosperity.

In the fourth century a population increase in Britain was accompanied by destruction of woodland (Taylor, 1983). Wood was in great demand not only for building but also for kilns, hearths and furnaces. The evidence for clearance in Essex is equivocal. Much land was already under cultivation and had been at least since the Iron Age (Williamson, 1984) but the increasing population, reinforced from the continent, would have exacerbated difficulties of supply. Local people's requirements could no longer be satisfied from a weakening central authority and rural economies, such as the specialist pottery works making Romano-Saxon ware just over the border into Hertfordshire at Much Hadham, were set up. The attractions which had drawn the immigrants from their continental homelands to Britain could no longer be guaranteed. Gildas makes it clear that this failure was a major reason in the fifth century for the mercenaries breaking out of their shore-lined bases to seek land in compensation, but the process may have begun in a lesser way half a century or so before.

Other evidence attests to Germanic presence, or at least a Germanic influence on the Romano-British population, in Essex by the late fourth or early fifth century. From Chelmsford near the temple was recovered Romano-Saxon pottery (**36**). At Billericay a wheel-turned pot in Roman ware has Saxon decoration of cruciform pattern, line and dots and a swastika. It contained a human cremation and had a fourth century Roman jar as a lid (Weller et al, 1974).

At Mucking, early Saxon occupation is shown by characteristic Germanic pedestal pots dated around AD 400 which may have been brought by *laeti* mercenaries, commissioned

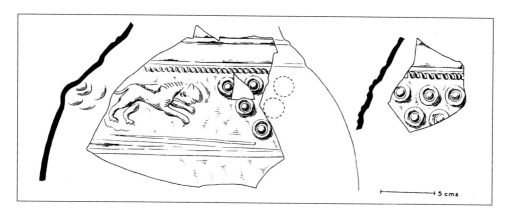

36   Romano-Saxon pottery from Chelmsford temple area

by the Romano-British authorities to defend the country against marauders. Miltary style buckles and belt-fastenings are found in association with Germanic pottery, as at Bradwell and Mucking, emphasising an official Roman connection. A silver equal-arm brooch of early to mid fifth century Germanic form has been found at Mucking, equivalents to which have been found in the Rhine-Weser region (Jones, 1980; Myers, 1986). The recognition of Roman units of measurement in the buildings of the Saxon halls here supports the view that the immigrants were using Roman practices, perhaps Romano-British builders (Tyler, 1996).

Early fifth-century Saxon houses, *grubenhäuser*, in a late Roman small town have been excavated at Maldon Heybridge suggesting continuity of or simultaneous Romano-British and Saxon settlement (Drury, Wickenden, 1982). Early Saxon settlement is suggested by pottery and *grubenhäuser* at Feering, Rivenhall, Shoebury, Wickford and Tilbury. Even though late shell-tempered pottery is deemed not to have been made much after AD 410, precise dating is difficult and some may be late fifth-century (Going, 1996). The mercenaries brought in or tolerated by an increasingly beleaguered Romano-British administration to combat incursions may have been followed by increasing numbers of their families, traders and merchants. The letter in AD 410 which the emperor Honorius wrote to the cities in Britain bidding them to take precautions on their own behalf' (Zosimus, VI, 10.2), marks the traditional end of the Roman period. After Honorius (393-425), coins of Arcadius (395-408), Constantine III the usurper of the West (407-11) and Valentinian (425-55) are among the last to appear in Britain for about two centuries.

However in Essex, while buildings were not maintained to the same quality, building certainly continued, often using available local materials. A turf-and-rubble early Saxon building reused Roman material at Wickford (Drury, Rodwell, 1980). The dearth of fifth- century Saxon remains in Essex relative to regions further north, west and south (with the exception of the margins as at Mucking and along some river valleys) supports the view that Saxon influence here was limited (Jones, 1980; Dark, 1994). Early Saxon pottery found at Little Oakley and an early Saxon glass recovered at the Roman villa at Rivenhall show that the villa sites continued to be used (Farrands, 1958; Rodwell

& Rodwell, 1985; Tyler, 1996). This does not necessarily of course imply occupation by Saxons; the Romano-British owners may merely have been acquiring more modern merchandise.

The Saxon cemetery at Great Chesterford dates to the early Saxon period. Here the pagan cremations were just outside the gates of the Romano-British town, again showing continuity of settlement (Evison, 1994).

The historical account of the cleric Gildas that

> All the members of the [*British*] council, together with the proud tyrant [*Vortigern*], devised for our land, that those fierce Saxons, like wolves into the fold . . . should be let into this island, to repel the people of the north. Then a pack of cubs broke forth from their lair . . . [*and*] fixed their terrible claws in the eastern part of the island. The barbarians asked to be given supplies . . . which for a long time shut the dog's mouth. Then they again complained their allowance was insufficient…swore they would break their agreement and plunder the whole of the island. They put their threats into immediate effect.

may be represented by the cemetery at Shoebury, dated to the fifth century, which contains Roman military equipment. These may be the graves of the mercenaries brought by Vortigern to protect against the incursions of pirates and the Picts. The Saxon site at Mucking, never occupied by many more than about 100 people at any one time, but which lasted until the eighth century, may have had a similar origin, later becoming a settlement for a developing Saxon population (Jones, 1980; Hamerow, 1993).

Bede, as often quoted, wrote that

> the newcomers were Saxons, Angles and Jutes. From the Jutes are descended the people of Kent and the Isle of Wight. From the Saxons, the land of the Old Saxons [*Rhine and Weser coast*], came the east, south and west Saxons and from the Angles, that is the country of Angulus [*southern Denmark and Schleswig*] are descended the east and middle Angles, the Mercians, all the Northumbrian stock and the other English people.

In spite of the fourth-/fifth-century Roman name '*Litus Saxonicum,* the Saxon Shore', most of Roman Britain did not become 'New Saxony', rather 'England'. Only Essex, Middlesex, Sussex, Surrey ('south region') and Wessex retained the Saxon memory in the names of the later kingdoms.

Artefacts found in Kent affirm links and influence with northern Denmark ('Jutland'), and from Norfolk and Suffolk with Frisia (northern Netherlands), whose lands were invaded by Germanic tribes from further east in Schleswig. Close reading of Bede's wording suggests the explanation for the name 'England' surviving. While the Saxons were the earliest invaders or immigrants, the Angles from the south Jutland peninsula (Morris, 1995) came in significant numbers later in the fifth century, to be the largest group by the eighth century. Some additional support for such a proposal comes in the Anglo-Saxon Chronicle for AD 443 when the British called on 'the chiefs of the Angles', the earliest documentation of the name for the immigrants. Indeed the legendary Hengist who led the mercenaries called by the king of the British Vortigern about AD 449, or perhaps a little earlier, may have been from Angeln stock (Myers, 1986; Williams, 2007).

Post-Roman London continued for a while to be a trading and civil centre. It was the refuge behind whose walls the native Britons retreated after the defeat by the Saxons at Crecganford, probably Crayford in Kent, in 457. A military presence is suggested by the finding of late Roman buckles in the Walbrook and at Smithfield, and fifth century Mediterranean pottery from the waterfront point to continuing but greatly reduced trade with southern Europe. Pagan cemeteries around the south of London suggest an increasing Saxon presence in the fifth and sixth centuries, though London and its immediate surroundings may have remained a beleaguered and declining British enclave. It became the capital of the future kingdom of the East Saxons, and the place where the first bishop to the East Saxons, Mellitus, had his church dedicated to St. Paul built by king Æthelbert of Kent in 604, the first documentary evidence of a Christian presence since the mention of a bishop of London at Arles in 314. The extent of the early East Saxon kingdom may be preserved in the diocese of London which included Middlesex, Surrey and southeast Hertfordshire. Early land-holdings may be preserved in place-names such as Roding, Tendring and Ginge. Although there was some intensification of settlement in south Suffolk in the fifth and sixth centuries, and in the sixth century at Wicken Bonhunt there was new settlement on a Roman site, there is little firm evidence of continuity from the Roman (Bassett, 1989; 1997).

It is from this period onwards that the study of Anglo-Saxon place-names has much to contribute with other disciplines to an understanding of the development of settlements (Baker, 2006; Kemble, 2007). While very few villa names are known to us (*Villa Faustini*, ?Scole or Stoke Ash), none has given its name to villages, hamlets or estates into the Saxon period. Their demise seems complete. But evidence from field-walking (Williamson, 1984) is that settlement continued even in the heavier boulder clay uplands in the west into the Saxon and later periods.

From the Iron Age of the Trinovantes, the people had become Romanised in administration and outlook, but many retained and adapted their tribal customs. In the Essex/Hertfordshire region at least (the area of the former Trinovantes/ Catuvellauni tribes) they coexisted with a Germanic presence, remaining the major influence until the beginning of the sixth century, perhaps half a century longer than much of the rest of the country (Dark, 1994). Only in the later part of that century did the region emerge as the independent kingdoms of the East Saxons under Sledd and Sabert, and of the East Angles under Weahha and Wuffa (Yorke, 1990; Bailey, 1988; Boulter, 2003; Plunkett, 2005). Not until the seventh century was coinage again minted here, such as an early gold *thrymsa* inscribed with the mint mark LONDVNIV, and a silver *sceat* (penny) of East Anglian type about 750 (Mitchell, 1997).

Gazetteer of Prehistoric and Roman sites

Abbreviations used are:

EAA — East Anglian Archaeology Journal

EAH — Essex Archaeology & History. Published annually by the Essex Society for Archaeology & History.

PSIAH — Proceedings of the Suffolk Institute of Archaeology & History

OS — Ordnance Survey 1:50000 (Landranger) series, followed by National Grid Reference.

Trans EAS — Transactions of Essex Archaeological Society (predecessor of EAH)

VCH — Victoria County History of Essex or Suffolk

★ — site has visible remains.

The Gazetteer contains a selection of the sites subjected to archaeological investigation. Many sites have Scheduled Protection making it an offence to disturb the soil or remove any object. When sites are on private land, permission to visit should be sought from the owner; in our experience it is rarely withheld without good reason.

ESSEX

1. Abbotstone. *OS* map 168. TL 9423. Bellhouse Farm, Warren Lane, Stanway.

Middle Iron Age pottery and a roundhouse of a settlement within the influence of *Camulodunum*. An unusual cremation burial was interred beneath a timber post. Flue tiles and window glass indicate a nearby Roman villa.

Colchester Archaeologist (2000), 13, 4.

2. Alphamstone★. *OS* map 155. TL 878354. 3.2km (two miles) north-west of Bures, via Lamarsh.

Four large stones in the churchyard, deposited by glacial action, may have been a prehistoric pagan monument (see Ingatestone and Newport). Bronze Age cremation urns have been found near the church. A first century AD Romano-British villa lies partly under the churchyard.

VCH Essex (1963), iii, 35. Essex Sites & Monuments Record nos 9319 and 9320.

3. Alresford. *OS* map 168. TM 0620, TM 0720. Broomfield Plantation quarry, 500m (0.3 miles) north of Alresford Creek.

Half a mile east of the Alresford Creek Roman villa was a Late Iron Age (50 BC-AD 50) oval enclosure and two Romano-British four-sided enclosures surrounded by ditch and bank, perhaps related to the villa estate. The villa explored in 1884 contained tesserae pavements and

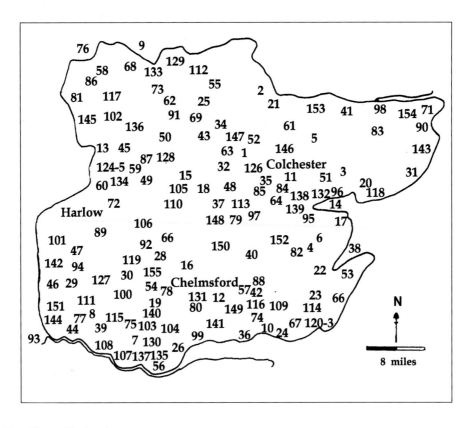

37   Essex, Site location map

corridors 162ft long on the south side and 97ft long on the north side.

Laver, H, Trans EAS (1889) ns iii, 136. Priddy, D, EAH (1985) 16, 123. VCH Essex (1963) iii, 37.

Bedwin, O, EAH (1986) 17, 69.

4. Althorne, Crouch estuary. *OS* map 168. TQ 9297. East of Bridgemarsh Island. On the foreshore are five posts, 8-14cm in diameter, a pole 1.25m long, stakes and brushwood, in all 1.5x1.3m. Preserved in the mud and water, this has been interpreted as a wattle 'hurdle' (fence), radiocarbon dated to 1000-900 BC.

Wilkinson, TJ, East Anglian Archaeology (1995) 71, 135.

5. Ardleigh. *OS* map 168. Centred around TM 0528. 800m (half a mile) south-east of Ardleigh church, either side of the road to Burnt Heath and Great Bromley, B1029. Detected by aerial photography, dating from the Bronze Age about 1200 BC, was a cemetery from which 92 clay pottery burial urns were excavated. The urns were buried in clusters within rings of ditches and may have been covered by earth mounds. Urns had finger-mark decoration and horse shoe bands (**38**). Some contained ashes, others were upturned over the cremation remains. To the north, east of Elm Park TM 0629, was an Iron Age house surrounded by a bank and ditch.

38   *Ardleigh style pottery (by Sue*
      Holden)

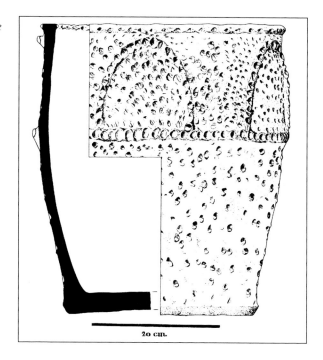

20 cm.

Erith, FH, et al, Proceedings of the Prehistoric
Society (1960) 26,178. Couchman, CR, EAH
(1975) 7, 14. Couchman, C, et al, EAH
(1983) 15,1. Brown, N, EAA (1999) 90.
Brooks, H. EAH (2001) 32, 75.

6. Asheldham★. Iron age fort. OS map
168. TM972012. 2km (1.2 miles) north-
east of Southminster, immediately south
of Asheldham village.

A banked and ditched oval fort, about
3.5ha (8.75 acres), sited on a plateau. The
defences are traceable on the west, south
and east, in spite of past quarrying. The
road may follow the line of the northern
bank, with the ditch on the road's northern
side. There is an earthen mound within
the enclosure to the east. Excavation in
1985 showed that before the fort was
constructed the area had been cultivated
with cereal and used for pasture. There
was evidence of roasting (cooking or
drying) of cereals. Three types of cereal
were recovered, emmer and spelt wheat,
and six-row hulled barley. Most of the
activity dates from about 400-150 BC after
which the fort was abandoned.
Laver, PG, Trans EAS (1898) ns vi, 350.
Laver, PG, Trans EAS (1930) xix, 180. Erith,
MR, EAH (1980) 12, 58. Bedwin, O, EAH
(1991) 22, 13.

7. Aveley. OS map 177. TQ 5581. Sandy
Lane and Purfleet Road, A13.

Woolly mammoth and straight-tusked
elephant (now in the Natural History
Museum) have been found since an amateur
archaeologist, John Hesketh, noticed
fossil bones sticking out of a cliff in 1964.
Excavations (at TQ5580) have found jungle
cat, lion, giant deer, brown bear, rhino and
bison. These animals were living during the
late Wolstonian Stage, 200,000 years ago, or
perhaps a warm phase, provisionally named
the Aveley interstadial.
Foreman, S, EAH (1997) 28, 215. Wymer,
J., Prehistoric Sites in East Anglia (1985) Geo
Books, p305.

7. Aveley, Mitchells Wood. Dene holes. OS map 177. TQ 5879. 220m south of Mar Dyke, by the M25 motorway.

Cut into chalk under up to 80m of sand and gravel, three chambers at the end of a tunnel 10m long. The chambers were about 1.5m wide and the arched roof 2.6m high, just high enough to be within reach of a man wielding a pick. The roof showed pick or hammer marks. This had been a flint quarry. In Hangman's Wood, Grays, 72 holes in 4 acres were recorded with vertical shafts 50-100ft going through the sand into the underlying chalk. Shafts of 3-4ft diameter ended in branching chambers 20ft long. Bands of flint were noted in the chamber walls with metal pick marks. Dene holes in the Grays area have yielded finds dating from the Roman period to thirteenth century, though chalk was mined at the Stifford, Ardale School site (qv) in the Middle Iron Age (about 200 BC).

VCH Essex, (1903) i, 309. Wilkinson, T.J., East Anglian Archaeology (1988) 42, 59.

8. Barking. OS map 177. TQ439837. Unit 7 Retail Park (Tesco site), west side of Abbey road opposite the site of Barking Abbey.

A pit contained Neolithic pottery and flint implements. Two brushwood trackways date to the Bronze Age. On the line of the old course of the River Roding a Roman timber jetty was excavated, dating to first/second century AD.

Meddens, F (1995) Current Archaeology, 143, 415. Hull, G, London Archaeologist, (1999) vol 9, suppl 1, 1.

9. Bartlow, Cambs★, [near Ashdon]. Roman burial mounds. OS map 154. TL 586449. 250m south of Bartlow crossroads (**colour plate 20**).

Only four of the original eight mounds survive, one being destroyed after 1586 and the western three having been removed in 1832. One lies north of the railway. Morant (1768) (who wrongly dated the barrows to the Viking period) recorded that two bodies in a stone coffin and another two stone coffins with bones and chain of iron like horse bits were found. The remaining four barrows were investigated in 1840. The largest measures 12m (40ft) high, 45m (147ft) in diameter. It contained cremated bones in a glass vessel, long-necked vessels, two bronze strigils (body scrapers), and an enamelled casket. The second highest (nearest to the road) contained a wooden box with cremated bones in an urn, a bronze jug and a samian dish containing chicken bones. This high-status family or community, dated to the second century AD, may have lived at the villas in Bartlow Park and/or Ashdon. Many of the finds were destroyed in a house fire in 1847; the remainder are in Saffron Walden Museum.

Morant, P, History of Essex (1768) ii, 539. VCH Essex (1903) i, 304 and (1963) iii, 44. Goddard, AR, Trans EAS (1900) ns vii, 349. Gage, J, Archaeologia (1833) 25, 1 and 26, 300 and (1850) 28, 1. Taylor, A, Archaeology of Cambridgeshire (1998) 2, 18, Cambridgeshire County Council. Rodwell, W. in Todd, M (1978) Studies in the Romano-British Villa, Leicester University, p31.

141. Basildon. OS map 178. TQ7291. At Great Wasketts.

Socketed bronze axes dating to the Late Bronze/Early Iron Age. [Cater Museum, High Street, Billericay].

Brown, N, EAH (1986) 17, 141.

10. Benfleet, South. OS map 178. TQ 7987. South of A13, at Badger Hall.

From a garden were found over several

years flint axes, adzes, scrapers and cutting blades which date from the Mesolithic period (7000-4000 BC). There are plentiful outcrops of good flint in the area, and it is likely that seasonal camps were set up for flint tool-making.

Crowe, K, EAH (1992) 23, 1.

11. Berechurch. OS map 168. TL 9920. At Park Farm on the south bank of Roman River.

Roof tiles and painted plaster suggest a Romano-British villa.

Dunnett, R, The Trinovantes, Duckworth, 1975, p97.

12. Billericay★. OS map 167. TQ 6794. (**colour plate 15**).

Norsey Wood (TQ 6899) has an extensive bank and ditch circuit containing first century BC pottery indicative of Iron Age settlement. Within the wood in two tumuli opened from 1865, wheel-turned cremation burial urns and Roman tiles have been excavated. Chance finds and small excavations have produced Neolithic flint tools and Bronze Age burials and Deverel-Rimbury pottery (2500-1000 BC). The Late Iron Age settlement and Roman town (after about 25 BC) seem to be confined mainly to the area south of Sun Street/London Road. Roman buildings have been found at Sun Corner. Excavations at School Road, Roman Way and Billericay Secondary School (TQ 675938) in 1987-8 revealed cremation burials, wells and ditches of the first to fourth century AD. The size of the cemetery areas and burial grave goods suggest a relatively large but poor population. A pottery kiln, archaeo-magnetically dated AD 43-100, was discovered to the south of the school in Buckenhams field, just north

of the junction of Laindon and Noak Hill roads.

Cutts, JEK, Trans EAS (1873) old series v, 208. Branfill, BR, Trans EAS (1895) ns, v, 226. Britannia (1977) 8, 405. VCH Essex (1963) iii, 49. Rudling, DR, EAH (1990) 21,19.

13. Birchanger, Uttlesford. OS map 167 TL506219. Woodside Industrial Park, south of A120.

A human skull and the base of a round house dating from about 200 BC were excavated here in 1992. After 200 BC, the site was largely abandoned but used for a cremation burial of an adult about AD 50. With the burial was pottery imported from Gaul, bronze brooches, the cleavered skull and leg of a pig (for the afterlife?).

Medlycott, M, EAH (1994) 25,28.

54. Blackmore. OS map 167. TL6001. A shafthole adze. *EAH (1990) 21, 140.*

14, 38. Blackwater, Crouch and Thames estuaries. Submerged forests, land surfaces and foreshore.

In the late Neolithic period (about 2000 BC), sea levels rose engulfing low-lying forests. The water preserved the tree stumps (usually oak) in a layer of peat and mud, now to be seen at low tides, especially in the Crouch, Thames and Blackwater estuaries (**colour plate 2; 39**). Survey reveals mesolithic to medieval activity. At Fen Creek, River Crouch, there may have been a mesolithic occupation site where 'tool kits' were discarded.

Warren, SH, Piggott, S et al, Proceedings of the Prehistoric Society (1936) 9, 178. Jacobi, RM, Council for British Archaeology Research Report (1980) 34, 24. Wilkinson, TJ, East Anglian Archaeology (1995) 71, 90. Strachan, D, EAH (1999) 30, 198. Wallis, SP, Waughman, M, East Anglian Archaeology (1998) 82.

39   Prehistoric wood hurdle, Blackwater estuary

15. Bocking End. OS map 167. TL 763244.

Bradford Street lies on the Roman road from Braintree (qv) to Long Melford. Just north of Bradford Bridge on the east bank of the River Blackwater a horse brooch 5x3cm made of bronze was found and reported to the Museum by a metal-detectorist. It has a hatched curved decoration and two crescent rings inset with red enamel which was produced in the Mediterranean or in Somerset. Such brooches were attached to horse tackle in the Late Iron Age and Roman periods. *Sealey, PR, EAH (1991) 22, 1.*

16. Boreham. OS map 167. TL 7409. South of the A12-B1137 (Colchester Road) road junction, north of Sheepcotes.

An enclosure surrounded by a ditch produced Late Bronze Age flints (about 1000 BC), with cremation burials. Evidence of one building suggests a shrine. *Lavender, NJ, EAH (1999) 30, 1.*

16. Boreham, Great Holts Farm. OS map 167. TL 7512. South of Boreham-Little Waltham road.

A Roman farmstead dating from the first to the fourth century AD contained at least four buildings including a farmhouse, bathhouse, a store and wells (**colour plate 23**). The farmer was reasonably affluent and could afford to eat food imported from the Mediterranean. *Germany, M, EAH (1995) 26, 247. EAA (2003) 105.*

16. Boreham. OS map 167. TL 7511. North-east of Bulls Lodge Farm dairy.

A Roman building was detected by field-walking in 1990 (**2**). Excavations subsequently revealed that in the third century AD a large building with a rounded west end, 22m square with aisles and arcades, had been constructed to the west of a hypocaust (underfloor heating) room. Both were of mortared flint with tiles. The third century round-ended building had an apse-shaped north room 6x4m. This was interpreted as an estate governor's audience-chamber (*principia*), as an early Christian church, or as a pagan temple. A Roman villa close to the church (TL7609) is suggested by first century pottery finds.

Lavender, NJ, EAH(1993) 24,1. Wallace, C, EAH (1995) 26, 264. VCH Essex (1963, iii, 51.

17. Bradwell-on-Sea★. Roman fort. *OS* map 168. TM 032082. At the sea edge along a lane 2.5km (one-and-a-half miles) north-east of Bradwell village church.

In the later third century AD, the fort was built on a natural promontory as part of the Saxon Shore fortifications. The fort was probably nearly square (the western, 160m long, and part of the northern and southern defences remain) (**40**). The mortared rubble walls (which can be seen in the south side) were 13ft thick with a horseshoe bastion at the north-west and south-west corners. The walls were surrounded by a ditch at least 8ft deep and 25ft wide. The entrance gate was probably where the Saxon chapel now stands on the west wall, with a quay gate on the east, now eroded by the sea. Excavations in 1864 and 1947 produced brooches, a cameo ring and a Frankish throwing-axe. Geophysical survey in 1999 has located barrack blocks. An extramural third/fourth century Roman settlement lay to the north. When Cedd, a monk from Lindisfarne (Northumberland), came to Essex at the request of the king Sigebert Sanctus in AD 653, he built his monastery at Othona on the foundations of the Roman wall using the stone from the fort. A seventh-century chapel survives because it subsequently found a use as a sea beacon and a barn.

Johnson, JS, Roman Forts of the Saxon Shore, 1979. Carter, HM, The Fort of Othona,

Chelmsford, 1966. VCH Essex (1973) iii, 52. Rodwell, W, EAH (1976) 8, 234. Maxfield, V, (ed), The Saxon Shore (1989), Exeter. Pearson, A, Roman Shore Forts, 2002. Gilman, P, EAH (1993) 24, 203. Lavender, NJ, et al, Othona Bradwell on Sea, Essex County Council Report, 2000.

18. Braintree. OS map 167. TL 755233. At the junction of Roman roads Colchester-Great Dunmow (Stane Street, A120), and Little Waltham-Gosfield, A131.

A socketed bronze axe made in Gotland (Sweden) about 700 BC, found near Braintree, indicates trade with Scandinavia at this time. There is evidence for a banked and ditched settlement dating to the Late Iron Age (50 BC-AD 50) to the south-east of the A131-A120 junction, around George Yard. Settlement here continued into the Roman period. It appears to have enlarged in the late second century along the Rayne road westwards. Excavation west of the south end of High Street produced evidence of iron-working; the presence of numerous horseshoes attests to a horse-involved economy. The quality of 'finds' indicates a reasonable degree of prosperity in the town, but there is little evidence of masonry in building materials. In Sandpit Road was found a copper alloy horse and rider figurine 8cm high; the rider's right arm is raised, possibly to hold a spear (**29**). The Roman cemetery was in the Grenville Road area. After the mid-fourth century the town declined, to be abandoned at the end of the century. The present line of London Road lies approximately on the Roman road but the present High Street deviates eastwards of the line. The main east-west road, Stane Street, probably lay north of Coggeshall Road, but excavations have so far not positively identified its precise

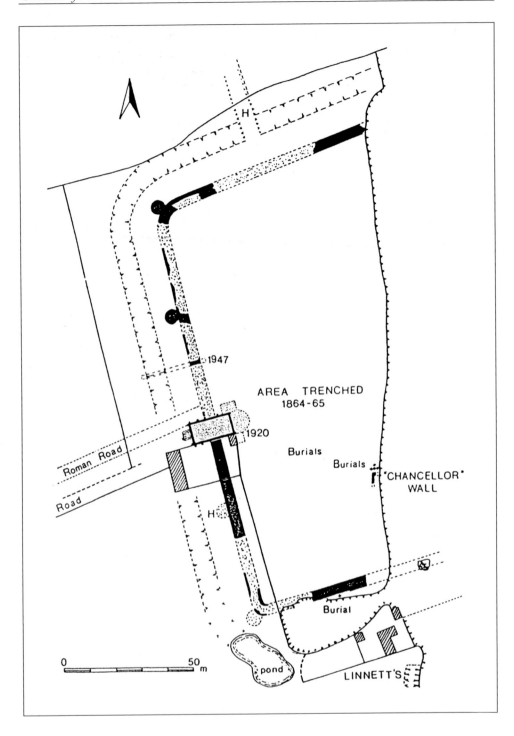

40   *Bradwell Othona Roman fort*

line. The junction may have been in the vicinity of White Hart Hotel.

Kenworthy, JW, Essex Naturalist (1898) 10, 405. O'Connor, B, EAH (1976) 8,279. Drury, PJ, EAH (1976) 8,1. Essex Journal (1977) 12(iv) 89. Eddy, MR, EAH (1983) 15,36. Milton, BH, EAH (1986) 17,82. Havis, R, EAH (1993) 24, 22. Garwood, A, EAH (2000) 31, 94. EAH (2002) 33, 98.

19. Brentwood. Roman road. OS map 167. TQ 574928.

Excavations at Brook Street and Spital Lane have shown that the Roman road from *Londinium* to Colchester *(Camulodunum)* is on the approximate line of the present Brook Street, A1023. Found at Wealdcote, Hillside Walk (TQ 5893), was a Roman gold ring. Three-quarters of an inch in diameter, it had a chi-rho (Christian) motif and a dotted border.

Gobbold, S, EAH (1990) 21, 153. Journal of Roman Studies (1949) 39, 115.

19. Brentwood, Weald Park★. Iron Age encampment. OS map 177. TQ 5895. From Brentwood Wilsons Corner, take the Ongar Road, A128, to Pilgrims Hatch. After crossing over the A12 dual carriageway take first turning left into Sandpit Lane, almost opposite a petrol station. After 1km (0.6 mile), Sandpit Lane runs through the centre of the enclosure at the cricket pitch (on the left), and Weald Park (fenced) on the right, at a right-hand bend. [The western rampart within Weald Park can be inspected by a walk of about 15 minutes north-east from Weald Road carpark] (**Colour plate 24**).

A fort surrounded by a single bank and ditch occupying 7 acres (2.8 hectares) can be traced within the boundary fence of Weald Park and, on the east of Sandpit Lane (less easily), at the southern side of the cricket pitch. The steepest escarpment is in Weald Park on the west. There is evidence of a rampart within the bank. An entrance from the south is now pierced by Sandpit Lane which takes a turn north-west as soon as it enters the enclosure. The original track continued straight on towards the centre of the fortification. Excavations in 1990 produced Late Iron Age pottery (first century BC-first century AD).

Isserlin, RMJ, EAH (1995) 26, 40. Medlycott, M et al, EAH (1995) 26, 53.

20. Brightlingsea. OS map 168. TM 0718. South of Moverons, 1km (0.6 mile) west of Samsons Corner, B1029.

A D-shaped ditched (and banked) enclosure about 23m in diameter was excavated in 1994-5 revealing Early Neolithic (*c*.3000 BC) pottery. It had an entrance across the ditch on the east by an earth causeway. In the centre was a smaller circular ditch (perhaps with a central mound) with a cremation burial. A large Middle Bronze Age cemetery (1500-1000 BC) excavated in 1989 (TM0718) contained 31 ring-shaped ditches about 8m in diameter and cremation burials in urns between the ditch circles. Several large (Deverel-Rimbury type) urns were lifted intact. A probable Roman villa was found during the First World War at Moverons Farm (TM0619) from which second century pottery, including flagons, amphorae and samian ware, was recovered in the 1970s. Two other villas (at TM0817, and under the Hall church TM0819) have been found.

VCH Essex (1963) iii, 57. Clarke, P, Current Archaeology (1991) 126, 272. Lavender, N, EAH (1996) 27, 266. Martin, TS, EAH (1996) 27, 311. EAA (2009) 126.

21. Bures. OS map 168. TL 9132.
Near the railway, a grave of a Romano-British nobleman accompanied by two brass knobs attached to iron bars. Aerial survey in 1996 at Mount Bures showed a possible long barrow and ring ditches, and 450m of the Wormingford 'cursus' (See also Chelmsford, Springfield).
VCH Essex (1963) iii, 60. McMaster, I, Colchester Archaeology Group Annual Bulletin (1967) 10, 46 & (1982) 25,6.
Strachan, D, Essex from the Air (1998), Essex Co Council, p 11. Buckley, DG, Hedges, JD, Brown, N, Proceedings of the Prehistoric Society (2001), 67, The Springfield Cursus.

22. Burnham-on-Crouch. OS map 168. TQ 9396. Cliff Reach.
From the north shore of the River Crouch and adjacent fields flint implements such as blades, scrapers, arrowheads and a knife, dating from Palaeolithic, Mesolithic (7000-4000 BC) and Neolithic (4000-2000 BC) periods.
Martingell, HE, EAH (1980) 12, 51. Murphy, P, in Barringer, C (ed), (1984) Aspects of East Anglian Pre-History, Norwich, Geo Books, p2.

23. Canewdon. OS map 168. TQ 9296. South Crouch estuary.
In 1983 was found an oak paddle in the foreshore, 2.08m long with a leaf-shaped blade 63cm long, 14cm wide at its widest, with a diamond-shaped cross-section. The shaft was 5cm diameter and had an expanded end. There was no wear to suggest its use in a rowlock or as a steerage oar. It was radiocarbon dated to about 1100 BC.
Wilkinson, TJ, East Anglian Archaeology (1995) 71, 152.

24. Canvey Island★. OS map 178. TQ 779842. South-east of Russellhead, Canvey Road, Dutch Village.
The Red Hill (see Glossary), the last known surviving on Canvey, was first established in the Roman period and reused in the medieval period.
Linder, E, Essex Naturalist (1937-40) 26, 136. Essex Journal (1980) 15(i), 10. Topping, P, EAH (1995) 26, 255.

25. Castle Hedingham. OS map 155. TL 786347. 0.5km east of Sible Hedingham.
At Sheepcote Road immediately north of Maiden Ley Farm (Anglian Water Co), excavations in 1992 found second-fourth century AD settlement of ploughed fields and paddocks. Hearths may have been used for corn-drying. It is probable that the main building was close by. On the west bank of the River Colne was a small Roman settlement or farm.
Lavender, NJ, EAH (1996) 27, 22. Medlycott, M, Historic Towns Survey (1998), Essex County Council.

26. Chadwell St Mary. OS map177. TQ 6578. 150m south-east of the church.
A farmstead or villa dating to the Late Iron Age (50 BC-AD 50) was surrounded by an enclosure ditch. Outside the ditch was a coffin burial lying east-west. Urns in oak chests with metal fittings and mortaria have been found at TQ6578. Early Neolithic pottery has been found east of St Francis Way.
Manning, WH, Trans EAS (1962), 1(ii), 127. VCH Essex (1968) iii, 62. Ennis, T, Brown, N, EAH (1999) 30, 258.

27. Chelmsford★, Caesaromagus. Roman town. OS map 167. TL 7107.
Moulsham Street (continuation of the High Street pedestrian precinct south

of the Stone Bridge and Parkway dual carriageway) represents the Roman road alignment of the road to *Londinium*. The Roman road continued northwards to Colchester probably along the line of Springfield Road (**28**).

At the start of the first century AD there was a farmstead south of the River Can east of Moulsham Street between Parkway and Hall Street. After the Roman invasion in AD 43, the military built a fort south of the river crossing in Moulsham over the farmstead. It was replaced by a more substantial fort defended by a bank and steep ditch (centred on Godfreys Mews) of 1.5 acres. About AD 120 a hostel for travellers (*mansio*) was built with a central rectangular courtyard, painted wall plaster and mosaic floors with a bathhouse, east of the junction of Grove and Roman Roads (**colour plate 22**). Its position is still marked by a slight rise in Roman Road. A pottery industry (kilns) was in operation near Goldlay Road. At the end of the second century the native settlement which had grown up was surrounded by banks and ditches 2m (6ft) deep which encompassed Moulsham street extending northwards to Parkway, eastwards to Mildmay Road and southwards to Godfreys Mews. About AD 325, on the south-west side of the Baddow Road roundabout was an eight-sided masonary temple, probably dedicated to Mercury. A stone coffin containing a burial with a jet rod (?symbol of office) and another (partly burned) body beside the coffin were found at the Godfreys Mews site. *Caesaromagus* (the Roman name for Chelmsford) traded with north Italy, Gaul, Germany, Yugoslavia, Syria and Egypt. After AD 400 the town seems to have decayed and the bridge over the Can collapsed, not to be rebuilt until around 1100.

Drury, PJ, EAH (1972) 4, 3. Going, CJ, Council for British Archaeology Research Report (1987) No 62. Drury, PJ, Council for British Archaeology Research Report (1988), 66. Allen, P, Essex Journal (1988), 23(ii), 27. Wickenden, NP, Council for British Archaeology Research Report (1992), 75. Wickenden, NP, Essex Journal (1990) 25(iii) 58.

27. Chelmsford, Broomfield. OS map 169. TL 7011. North End of Broomfield, 500m south-east of Broomfield Hospital at Court Road and The Windmills.

Previously identified by aerial photography, a four-sided enclosure was surrounded by a ditch and bank about 35x44m with an entrance to the east. The ditch was 0.95m deep and 2m wide. Within its circumference was a circular hut 8m in diameter, a possible (?corn) drying rack and several storage pits. Flint scrapers, cutting blades and awls were found. The farmstead was dated to about 900-800 BC. 1km (0.6 mile) south-west of Broomfield Hospital (TL6911), a Romano-British villa.

Kettle, BM, Trans EAS (1965), third series, 1, 264. Atkinson, M, EAH (1995) 26, 1.

27. Chelmsford, Springfield. Neolithic Cursus. OS map 167. TL 732069. North of Barnes Farm, 800m north-east of the junction at the Army & Navy roundabout, 200m north of the River Chelmer. The north-eastern end is under the Asda store car park, the south-western end at B&Q superstore (Dukes Lane roundabout).

Running from north-east to south-west were two ditches parallel to each other for 690m, about 40m apart, squared to join at the ends (**colour plate 28**). There were gaps across the ditches at intervals. The earth from the ditches may have been piled into the middle to produce a long mound, though long since ploughed down (about 300m north-east of the northern end the ditches 'pointed' to a possible long barrow) (**17**). In 1979 the eastern end of the enclosure was excavated before housing and shopping complexes were built over it. Fourteen substantial postholes formed part of a circle 26m in diameter (the remainder have been disturbed by a recent sewer trench). This could represent a large roofed building or an unroofed wooden monument. A pit contained cremated animal (cattle, sheep, pig) bones and a saddle-quern, another a large amount of pottery. Dated to the Neolithic (about 2000 BC).

Hedges, J, Buckley, DG, Essex County Council, Occasional paper No 1, 1981. Buckley, DG, Hedges, JD, Brown, N, Proceedings of the Prehistoric Society (2001) 67.

27. Chelmsford, Springfield Lyons★.

OS map 167. TL 736082. East of the B1137 Boreham Road, south of the junction with the A12 Chelmsford bypass. From Chelmsford Parkway A138 junction with the A414 (Army & Navy roundabout), take Chelmer Road A138 northwards across River Chelmer. At the next two roundabouts keep left. 800m (half a mile) north of the second roundabout take the slip road left, signposted Springfield. At the top of the slip road at Aloi store roundabout turn right (north). Bear right under the bridge, and immediately take the first exit from the roundabout, singposted Boreham. In 300m at 'Hedgerows' roundabout turn right (third exit), signposted Springfield Lyons. Take the second right and in 100m park north of the Territorial Army HQ. Walk south-eastwards for 100m along a metalled track

then veer south along a grass track towards a spinney of three tall oak trees. The site ditches are 30m south of the trees.

A circular enclosure with ditch, bank and timber internal rampart excavated in 1981-3 (**20; colour plates 9, 25**). The ditch was about 1.2m deep and 5m wide. The enclosure was entered by a causeway from the east guarded by a timber gate. In the centre was a large timber round house, 7m in diameter, with a porch facing east, surrounded by several smaller houses. Clay moulds for casting bronze swords were recovered . Loom weights and spindle whorls indicated a weaving and spinning industry. Crops had been barley, emmer and spelt wheat and beans, and charcoal suggested the burning of oak, ash and hazel wood. The enclosure was in use in the Late Bronze Age (about 900 BC) and was then abandoned but nearby there had been Iron Age occupation from which a broken sword and iron scabbard (of La Tène type, about 100 BC) had been deposited in a pit (?as an offering). Close by had been dug a ditch from which Neolithic pottery was excavated. The site had later been used as a Saxon cemetery from which 100 cremation and 103 inhumation burials were identified dating from the mid-fifth century AD. *Buckley, D, Essex Co. Council, occ paper 5, 1987. Essex Jnl (1986) 21 (iii), 57. Brown, N, EAH (2001) 32, 92*

28. Chignall St James. Roman villa, estate and cemetery. *OS* map 167. TL 6611. North of Chignall Hall.

The outline of a Roman villa photographed from the air in 1974 shows three ranges, each about 60m long, on three sides of a square, each range fronting onto the central courtyard with a portico (**41; colour plate 26**). Round the outside

41   *Plan of Roman
     villa, Chignall
     St James*

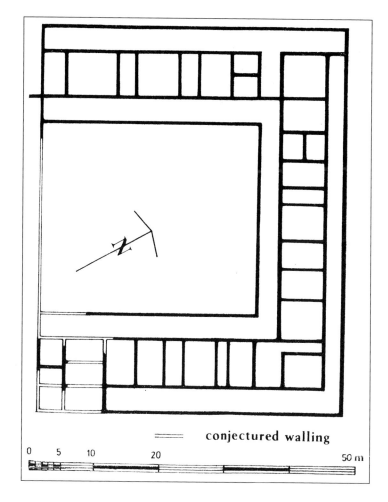

conjectured walling

0   5   10   20   50 m

of each range is a gallery. To the west is ?the bathhouse. One hundred and fifty metres south of the villa, excavations have found a round (timber) house and a cemetery dating to the third/fourth century AD. The 28 burials do not suggest much prosperity, though, if Christian, grave-goods would not be expected. It may have been the cemetery of the *coloni* (villa estate workers). Life expectancy was about 30 years. One person had had a congenitally dislocated hip but had lived into adulthood. Another was buried with hobnail boots. Four of the burials were of children, one an infant and one with a small shale bracelet. Five skeletons had been decapitated after death, with the heads placed by the legs. Such burials are well known in Roman cemeteries but whether this means they were regarded as malefactors or victims of affray is unclear. The most affluent structure was a cenotaph in which no body had been interred (or had been subsequently removed) into the coffin, which contained a fine glass cup.

Britannia (1975) 6, 263, and (1977) 8, 406. McMaster,I, Colchester Archaeology Group Annual Bulletin (1975) 18, 7. Going, C, Essex Archaeology News (Winter 1976) p12. Buckley, D, Going, C, Aerial Archaeology (1977) 1, 10. Essex Journal (1980) 15(i), 3. Clarke, CP, East Anglian Archaeology (1998), 83.

29. Chigwell, Little London. OS map 177. TQ4596. On A113 south-east of Epping, west of the Chigwell-Abridge road, south-west of The Chase.

The Antonine Itinerary is a third-fourth-century collection of routes through the Roman Empire which gives mileages between stopping places. Route IX names a place *Durolitum* as 16 (Roman) miles from *Caesaromagus* (Chelmsford) and 15 miles from *Lundinium*. *Litum* indicates a ford and *Duro* a military post(?) for which (at present) evidence here is lacking. Though Romford has been suggested, *Durolitum* may be near Chigwell which is on a known Roman road that crosses the River Roding to Colliers Hatch, Moreton (TL535070) and Great Dunmow. At Claybury Hospital, the line of the Roman road, which lies north-west of the present road (A113) as it bends eastwards, has been confirmed by excavation. Excavations at Little London have revealed a bathhouse and a well which was timber-planked with upright squared posts secured by nails. Of 46 burials, one of a child, 40 were cremations in an urn, and five marked with a post at the base of which had been placed a coin (?to pay for the ferryman to cross the River Styx). A villa at Hill Farm is 1km to the west. Also have been found a tessellated pavement and urns at TQ4596 east of Woolston Hall. *Clarke, F, et al, Romano-British Settlement at Little London Chigwell, West Essex Archaeological Group (1998). Rivett, ALF, Smith,C, Place-Names of Roman Britain, Batsford (1979), p 170. Rodwell, WJ, Britannia (1975) 6,76. VCH Essex (1963) iii, 88. Fulcher, EA, Essex Journal (1983) 18(i), 12.*

30. Chipping Ongar★. OS map 167. TL 553030.

The church of St Martin of Tours of Norman flint rubble contains Roman brick in its walls. 3km (1.9 miles) to the west of the town is the main Roman road from Chigwell, qv, (possibly *Durolitum*) to Great Dunmow, qv.
VCH (1956) ii. Aspects of the History of Ongar, Ongar Millennium Group, 1999.

31. Clacton-on-Sea. OS map 169. TM 1613, east of Golf Green Road, Jaywick. TM 1714, Marine Parade.

Since 1840 butchered remains have been discovered of straight-tusked elephant, deer, giant beaver, lion and bison, together with flint and quartzite choppers, axe-edges, scrapers, piercers and flakes (used to fashion wood or bone). They have been dated to a warm phase at the end of the Anglian Iceage (or soon after), about 425,000 years ago (Oxygen Isotope stages 11-12). This is approximately contemporary with the human skull found at Swanscombe, Kent, just on the opposite side of the Thames, which has been regarded as of a young girl of an archaic form of *Homo sapiens*. Stone which originated in north Kent suggests that Clacton was a channel of the Thames-Medway river (see Glossary, Anglian Iceage). A unique wooden spear, one of the earliest wooden implements to be found in Europe, was found near the Palace Hotel in 1911, dated to about 350,000 years old. It was made from yew, measured 15.25in long, broken at the shaft end. It had been sharpened with a flint tool to a long point while the wood was freshly cut, and its shape suggested it was a thrusting spear which would easily have penetrated animal hide.
Warren, SH, Essex Naturalist (1932-35) 24, 1. Oakley, KP, Proceedings Prehistoric Society (1937). Singer, R, et al, Proceedings Prehistoric Society (1973) 39,6. Wymer, JJ, Palaeolithic

Sites of E Anglia (1985) Geo Books Norwich, p264. Oakley, KP et al, Proceedings Prehistoric Society (1977) 43,13. Bridgland, DR, Quaternary of the Thames, Chapman &Hall (1994). Wymer, J, Palaeolithic Occupation of Britain (1999), Wessex Archaeology/English Heritage.

32. Coggeshall. OS map 168. TL 8522.

The Roman road, Stane Street, runs east-west through the town, probably on or close to the present alignment of East Street. Timbers, probably Roman, of the ford or bridge over the River Brain, were found by the present bridge in 1855, indicating a road to *Canonium* (Kelvedon, qv). A settlement (?farm) was begun about 700 BC with timber-post buildings at St Peter's School (TL855229). The Roman enclosure in the first century AD extended from immediately north of the main road (East Street) to south of the church of St Peter ad Vincula and was surrounded by a double ditch and bank. The pronounced kink in East Street 250m east of the 'town square' may represent the south-west corner of the enclosure bank as it turns northwards. About AD 120 the town was, at least partly, abandoned for reasons not yet clear, but seemingly revitalised in the third century for the next 100 years when there is evidence of renewed activity with buildings at Woolpack Inn and East Street. The villa building or a *mansio* (travellers hostel) may have been south of and near to the church. In the seventeenth century a Roman brick-arched vault was found containing an urn, ashes and samian ware inscribed with the potter's mark COCCILIM.
Cutts, EL, Trans EAS (1858) old series i, 99. Clarke, CP, EAH (1988) 19,47. Isserlin, R, EAH (1995) 26, 82. VCH Essex (1963) iii, 90.

33. Colchester Town★, *Colonia* Victricensis. OS map 168. TL 9925.

The Roman town, now within the walls, was a new foundation after the arrival of the Roman army in AD 43, starting with a fort in the North Hill area. The principal visible sites within the town are the town walls, best seen in the Priory Street carpark by St Botolphs Priory, in St Marys churchyard and in Castle Park; the Norman Colchester Castle which has the foundations of the Roman Temple dedicated to Claudius (guided visits from the Castle Museum); remnants of the Roman street layout; extensive amounts of Roman brick and tile in the tower of Holy Trinity Church, and the site of the Roman theatre in Maidenburgh Street (west of Castle Park). The Balkerne Gate (west of the jumbo water tower), was excavated in 1920; it has two carriageways 17ft (5.5m) wide flanked by 2 footways 6ft (2m) wide) *Wheeler, M, Trans EAS (1921) ns, 15, 179*. At Lyon Walk, a Roman courtyard house, built about AD 150 and excavated in 1971-4, contained large mosaic floors, one with a depiction of a grey, olive and brown lion with a red tongue and black mane, another 3.6m diameter with a billowing robe of a woman (view in Colchester Castle Museum).Circus 400m south of town.
Trans EAS especially Vol III (third series) (1971). VCH Essex, especially Vols III (1963) and IX (1994). Rainey, A (1973) Mosaics in Roman Britain, David & Charles, p53. Crummy, P, Britannia (1977) 8,65; (1999) 30,57; (2008) 39, 15. Drury, P, Britannia (1984) 15, 7. Colchester Archaeological Reports, especially Vols 3(1984), 6(1992), 9(1993) and 11(1995). Crummy, P, CBA Res Rep (1994) 93. Colchester Archaeologist (2001) 14, pp5, 9; (2002) 15,19. Current Archaeology (2003) 185, 205.

33. Colchester Castle Museum★. Some Roman Tombstones, Dedication Stones, Statues and Statuettes.

'M(arcus) Favon(ius) Facilis, son of Marcus, of the Pollian tribe, Centurion of the XX legion, lies here. Verecundus and Novicius his freedmen set this up'. A tombstone 3ft 7in high and the relief of a centurion holding a vinestick was found in 1868 west of Colchester near a lead container with cremated bone. (Beverley Road, Colchester). RIB 200. *c*.AD 45. *Lodge, B, Trans EAS (1873) old series v, 87. Phillips, EJ, Britannia (1975) VI, 102.*

'Longinus, Sdepeze son of Matyeus, duplicarius *[soldier on double pay, i.e. second in command]* of the first cavalry squadron of Thracians from the district of Sardica *[Sofia]* aged 40 with 15 years service lies here. His heirs had this put up under his will'. A tombstone and the relief of a mounted cavalryman were found in 1928 west of Colchester (off Beverley Road, Lexden, TL980248). RIB 201. *c*.AD 45. *Maxfield, VA, 1995, Inscriptions of Roman Britain, London Assocn of Classical Teachers 4. Colchester Arch (1996) 10, 10. Fawn, J, EAH (1997) 28, 217. Cleary, ASC, Britannia (1997) 28, 432. Minerva (2001) 12(3),43.*

Found in 1907 in the River Alde at Rendham was a bronze head 13in high, broken off at the neck, probably of Emperor Claudius. The attitude suggests it may have been from an equestrian statue a leg of which was found at Ashill, Norfolk. A likely source is Colchester at the time of the Boudican revolt in AD 60/61, taken back to Suffolk as booty. *MacDonald, G, Journal of Roman Studies (1926) 16, 3.*

Found east of Colchester North railway station in 1845 was a 5in high bronze bust of ?Emperor Gaius (Caligula, AD 37-41) mounted on a globe of the world. If the identification is correct it was presumably brought to Colchester by a Romanophile Gaul before the Roman invasion of AD 43. *Strong, A, Journal of Roman Studies (1916) 6, 27.*

Ploughed in the 1940s from a field at Gosbecks, a bronze figure of Mercury, 12in high. *Hull, MR. Trans EAS (1951) 24, 43.*

Found at Lexden, an ivory figure of a gladiator 2.8in high with a crested helmet. *Toynbee, JMC, Trans EAS (1955) ns 25(i), 9*

'…Macri..us a Roman knight (*eques*) lived 20 years. Val(eria) Fron(t)ina his wife and Flor(ius) Cogitatus and Flor(ius) Fidelis set this up'. Tombstone found in grounds of Colchester Grammar School 1910. RIB 202. Undated. *Maxfield, VA, Dodson, B, 1995, Inscriptions of Roman Britain, London Assocn of Classical Teachers 4.*

'To the god Silvanus Callirius, Cintusmus the coppersmith willingly and deservedly fulfilled as a gift his vow'.
Bronze plate found in 1946 in temple precinct in grounds of Colchester Grammar School, close by another dedication to Silvanus by Hermes (RIB 195). RIB 194. Undated. *Hull, MR, 1958, Roman Colchester, Report to Soc Antiquaries. Maxfield, VA, Dodson, B, 1995, Inscriptions of Roman Britain, London Assocn Class Teachers 4.*

'To the mother goddesses Suleviae, Similis son of Attius a citizen of the Cantiaci *[in Kent]* willingly fulfilled his vow'. Dedication stone found in 1881 west of the west town walls. RIB 192. Undated. *Maxfield, VA, Dodson, B, 1995, Inscriptions of Roman Britain, London Association of Classical Teachers 4.*

33. Colchester, Butt Road (B1026)★. *OS* map 168. TL 993248. Continuation of Head Street south of Southway dual carriageway, by the Police Station. Beaumont Seymour premises.

One of several Roman cemeteries here that has been recorded since 1840. In 1976-88 the cemetery of 739 burials was excavated and shown to contain pagan burials from the first and second centuries AD, followed by Christian burials from the third and fourth. Burials were mostly in oak coffins with the body in a shroud. A few were accompanied by jewellery, belts, purses and coins. One burial was decapitated with several cutmarks on the back of the skull and neck and the head placed between the legs. The adjacent masonry building was a small church 25x7.4m with stone and tiled walls and roof. It had an eastern apse and a wooden screen near the east end. Coins indicate its building about AD 320, remaining in use until after AD 400. Since Christianity was legalised in the Roman empire only in AD 313, the Butt Road church is one of the earliest known in Britain.

Essex Journal (1977) 12(iv), 90. Crummy, P, Current Archaeology (1990) 120, 406. Colchester Arch Reps (1993) 9. Crummy, P, Secrets of the Grave, Colchester Archaeology Trust. Crummy, P, Colchester Archaeologist (1987) 1, 1; (2000) 13, 19; (2007) 20, 10.

33. Colchester Dykes★. *OS* map 168. TL9624. Most lie to the west of the walled town, around Lexden Road.

An intricate system of defensive banks and ditches, probably begun at the end of the first century BC (Heath Dyke), delimited the Iron Age *oppidum* (territory) of *Camulodunum* on the west, with the River Colne and forest on the north and Roman River on the south. Several additions, possibly by the Roman military, were made in the following century. The deepest ditches were 13ft deep with a bank (usually on the east, behind). The best sections publicly visible are on the east side of Straight Road north of Heath Road (Triple Dyke), in Lexden Park, Prettygate Road, Beacon End park (Lexden Road, New Farm Road), Heath Road, Dugard Avenue (Gryme's Dyke) and east of Stanway Hall.

Laver, H, Trans EAS (1889) ns iii, 133; (1900) ns vi, 17 and 87; (1903) ns viii, 108; (1911) ns xi,19. Round, H, Trans EAS (1928) ns xviii, 1. Hawkes, CFC, Hull, MR, Camulodunum (1947) Oxford. Hawkes, CFC, Crummy, P, Camulodunum Two, Colchester Arch Reps (1995) 11, 24. Fishwick, D, Britannia (1997) 23, 31. Colchester Arch (1987) 1,4; (2007) 20,30.

33.   Colchester,   Gosbecks★, Camulodunum. *OS* map 168. TL 967224. Gosbecks Park, Olivers Lane, 2km (1.2 miles) east of Colchester Stanway zoo. From Colchester town Southway roundabout take the B1022 Stanway, Tiptree and Maldon road south-west for 2.5km (1.5 miles). At the double mini-roundabout turn left into Gosbecks Road, then at the next roundabout turn right and immediately left into Olivers Lane.

The Romano-British temple and theatre capable of seating 5,000 spectators are marked out on the grass. The square temple was surrounded by a large columned portico built of mortared septaria with a tile roof. A brick pillar covered with a white simulated marble coating and black and white flooring tesserae (small square stones) were excavated from the ditch which may have predated the temple, which dates to about AD 60-80. A statuette of Mercury 30cm high was found in the 1940s. A gemstone with a carving of Mars found within the temple site had been used to make an impression on wax seals. The Roman military built a small fort (to the north-east at TL9623), of 2.2ha, to overlook the native settlement up against the Iron Age dyke (north of Stanway Road).

Dunnett, R, EAH (1971) 3(i), 95 and Britannia (1971) ii, 27. Wilson, DR, Britannia (1977) 8,185. Colchester Arch Gp Ann Bull (1983) 26, 19. Colchester Archaeologist (1994-5) 8, 8, (1995-6) 9, 1; (1999) 12, 20; (2003) 16,7. Crummy, P, City of Victory (1997) p105. Fishwick, D, Britannia (1997) 28, 31. Crummy, P, EAH (1998), 29, 206. Current Arch (2007) 208,16. Benfield, S, EAH (1999) 30, 216.

33. Colchester, Lexden Tumulus★. Iron Age burial. *OS* map 168. TL 975247. From Colchester town Southway roundabout take Lexden Road A1124 (A604). Take second turning left after Norman Way into St Clare Road. Tumulus is in private gardens of Nos 30-36 Fitzwalter Road at the junction with St Clare Road.

The large round earthen mound, 70ft diameter, now about 5ft high, was excavated in 1924. Under it in a pit, probably originally in a wooden chamber, were cremated human bones, a copper-alloy cupid and griffin, a bronze foot, bronze bull and bear, chain-mail with silver studs, a copper axehead which was 1,000 years older than the grave, a leather jerkin and the remains of a chair or stool, a metal bowl with vineleaf fittings and an inlaid glass casket. A medallion made from a copy of a coin of Augustus (suggesting the dead person admired the emperor) dates the burial to after 16 BC. It may be relevant that Julius Caesar, who had invaded Britain in 54 BC, records that 'the Trinovantes

had been protected against Cassivellaunus (leader of the British tribes) and spared any injury on the part of the Roman troops'. The grave may be the burial of the British king Addedomaros who died around 15/10 BC.

Laver, H, Archaeologia (1927), 76, 241. Hawkes,CFC, Crummy, P, Camulodunum Two, Colchester Archaeological Reports (1995) No 11, p85. Foster, JAA, British Archaeological Reports (1986) 156. Crummy, P, City of Victory, Colchester Archaeological Trust, 1997. Colchester Archaeologist (1999) 10.

33. Colchester, Lexden Mount★. OS map 168. TL 969249. The Mount, Wordsworth Road, in a garden. From Colchester town Southway roundabout take Lexden Road, A1124 (A604). Take the first turning left after St Clares Road into Church Lane, then right into Shakespeare Road, and right again into Thompson Avenue at end of which is
Wordsworth Road.

A trench 16ft deep at its centre was dug through this barrow in 1910. The ashes of a burial were identified with Roman tile, samian pottery and glass. A Georgian halfpenny indicated it had been dug into before.

Laver, H, Reader, FW, Trans EAS (1913) ns xii, 186. Hawkes, CFC, Crummy, P, Camulodunum Two, Colchester Archaeological Reports (1995) No 11.

33. Colchester, Sheepen. OS map 168. TL9825. Area around Sussex and Sheepen Roads and the Technical College.

Large quantities of metalworking tools, smithing, bronze-casting and scrap metal, dating to the first century BC and first century AD were excavated in the 1930s and in 1970. The mint of Cunobelin,

26　*Villa at Chignall St James (by Frank Gardiner)*

27 *Enamelled bronze* pyxis *from Elsenham, second century AD*

28 *Chelmsford Springfield cursus (by Frank Gardiner)*

29   Reproduction bow ard

30   Middle Iron Age
pottery vessel, Little
Waltham

31   Experimental clay pottery kiln

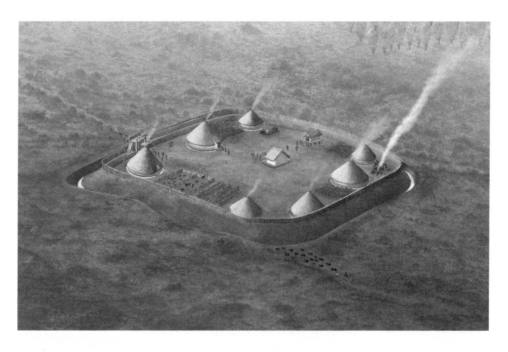

32   Enclosure with round houses, Stansted (by Frank Gardiner)

leader of the Trinovantes (died about AD 40) was here and was destroyed by the Roman military in AD 43. There was also a leather factory. The area was burnt in the revolt under Queen Boudica in AD 60/61, but it seems to have resumed as a commercial market, no doubt due to its proximity to the River Colne, and the presence of four Romano-British temples indicates it to have been a native sanctuary.

Hull, MR, Trans EAS, ns xx, 270, ns xxi, 29,300 and ns xxii (i), 1. Hawkes, CFC, et al, Camulodunum (1947). Niblett, R (1985) Council for British Archaeol Res Rep 57. Crummy, P, City of Victory, Colchester Arch Trust,1997. Colchester Arch (2003) 16,16; (2008) 21,11.

33. Colchester, Stanway. OS map 168. TL9523. North of B1022, 500m north-east of Colchester Stanway zoo.

High-status graves probably of native Britons, dating to the first century AD, were excavated from 1990. The cremation burials were within square or rectangular banked and ditched enclosures in timber-lined chambers. They contained grave-goods such as brooches, necklaces, gaming boards, glass and bronze vessels. In a grave thought to be that of a doctor were found surgical instruments (viewable in the British Museum). In a warrior's grave were a shield, a spear, a copper-alloy armlet and a wine amphora from Pompeii. A military fort was built overseeing the native settlement.

Webster, The Roman Invasion of Britain (1980) p129. Colchester Archaeologist (1991-2) 5, 1 & (1992-3) 6, 1; (2008) 21,14. Crummy, P, EAH (1993) 24, 206. Current Archaeology (1993) 132, 492 & (1997) 153, 337. Crummy, P, Minerva (1997), 8(ii), 5. Jackson, RPJ, The Lancet (1997) 350, 1471.

Britannia (2007) monograph 24. Brit Arch (2008) 99,29.

34. Colne Engaine. OS map 168. TL 8731.

In Abbey Field has been found the probable site of a Roman villa.

VCH Essex (1963) iii, 122.

35. Copford. OS map 168. TL 9323. 1km (0.6 miles) north-east of Copford Green. The presence of a Roman villa is suggested by surface finds.

VCH Essex (1963) iii, 123.

36. Corringham. OS map 178. TQ 7183. Over 2,300 coins made of tin-bronze (potins), some of the earliest in England dating to about 100 BC, were found in Corringham. They are now in Thurrock Museum.

Van Arsdell, RD (1989) Celtic Coinage of Britain, London.

37. Cressing. OS map 167. TL 800186. In Dovehouse field south-east of Cressing barns, excavations in 1998-2000 have shown Iron Age and Roman ditches and indicate occupation enclosures. Loom-weights and animal jawbones indicate local industry. At the church (TL7920) have been excavated first-century BC pottery and brooches, a bronze mirror and bronze depilator. *EAH (2004) 34, 36. Atkinson, M, EAH (1999) 30, 218. Hope, JH, Essex Journal (1983) 18(iii), 72. Hope, JH (1984) Excavations at All Saints Church, Essex County Council, occasional paper 4, p28.*

38. Dagenham. OS map 177. TQ4984. Hays warehouse.

In the peat was an artificial causeway across muddy land made of pebbles, flints, sand

and silt up to 30cm thick, 4m wide and at least 23m long, probably a cattle droveway dating to the Bronze Age.
Meddens, F, Current Archaeology (1995), 143, 414.

39. Dagenham. The Dagenham Idol. *OS* map 177. TQ4882. A few yards south of London-Tilbury road where it crosses Gores Brook.
9ft (3m) below the surface, a wooden figure 19 $\frac{1}{2}$ in (48cm) high, 3 $\frac{1}{2}$ in (9cm) wide at the shoulders was found in a marsh deposit in the Thames bank at Dagenham in 1922, next to a deer skeleton ?sacrifice. The wood was Scots Pine. The figurine is without arms; it has eye sockets and 6in (15cm) long legs and a notch for an erect phallus. The survival is remarkable, carbon dating to 2351-2139 BC and is believed to be a religious object of a fertility cult.
Wright AG, Trans EAS (1923) ns 16, 288. Drury, P, in Buckley, D, (1980) Archaeology in Essex, CBA Research Reports 34, p53. Coles, B, Proceedings of the Prehistoric Society (1990) 56, 315.

40. Danbury.★. Iron Age/Saxon hillfort. *OS* map 167. TL 779052. At Danbury church.
The fort occupies the western end of the promontory between the Rivers Blackwater and Crouch at 111m (365ft) above sea level. The bank and ditch enclose an oval area of 2.4ha (6 acres), and are best seen on the south-east, south-west and west sides (south of the church which is within the enclosure). The original entrance is unknown. Excavations in 1974 and 1977 produced Iron Age, Roman and Saxon pottery, a Saxon bone comb and a loom-weight (from a weaving loom). Though named

in the Domesday Book *Danengeberiam* (stronghold of the Saxon Daenningas tribe), the fort may originally either be of Iron Age (perhaps about 200 BC) or Saxon construction. Examples of Saxon refortification of old Iron Age defences are known, such as at Asheldham and Witham, qv.
Spurrell, FC, Essex Naturalist (1890) iv, 138. Hull, MR, Essex Naturalist (1935-37) 25, 109. Morris, S, and Buckley, D, EAH (1978) 10,1.

41. Dedham. *OS* map 168. TM 0732. 1.2 km ($\frac{3}{4}$ mile) south-east of Dedham on the lower road to Manningtree.
In 1958-9 a cremation burial of a young girl was excavated. Nearby was the burial of an adult male whose ashes had been put into a leather or cloth bag. The remains of both were in earthenware urns. A ditch 3ft 6in deep and 11ft wide had been dug round the burials, and a mound raised over them. The burials were dated to the Iron Age.
Blake, BP, Trans EAS (1960) 25(iii), 344.

42. Downham. *OS* map 167. TQ 735957. The Grange.
500m south-east of the village on the top of the south-pointing spur, a substantial Iron Age settlement/hillfort was sectioned in 1965-6. In a trench dug east of a sunken lane on the east of the spur was found Early Iron Age flint-tempered pottery. From within the enclosure has been recovered Iron Age, Roman and Saxon pottery.
Rodwell, W, Trans EAS (1966) third series, 2(i), 95. Drury, P, EAH (1977) 9, 43. Drury, P, (1980), CBA Research Reports 34, 47. Wickford Archaeology Group unpublished papers in Essex Record Office, ref T/P206.

43. Earls Colne. *OS* map 168. TL 8629. Excavations at The Priory suggest the presence of a Roman villa which may have been quarried for later buildings.
Fairweather, FH, Archaeologia (1937) 87, 275. Medlycott, M, Historic Towns Survey (1998) Essex County Council.

44. East Ham. *OS* map 177. TQ 4283. A quarter of a mile (400m) west of East Ham church on the line of the great London sewer outlet.
In 1863 a stone sepulchral and lead coffin dating to the Roman period was found. It contained two skeletons of adults in middle age. It is now in the British Museum.
Boyle, EF, Trans EAS (1865) old series iii, 104.

45. Elsenham. *OS* map 167. TL 5425.
A Roman *pyxis* (box) 4.6cm high is an extremely rare find, only part of one before having been found in Britain (**colour plate 27**). Each of its six sides has a bronze panel with *millefiori* enamel decoration, probably made in Gaul and buried here after AD 145. Careful note of its location by the metal detectorists allowed subsequent excavation and the recovery of a grave, three Samian bowls, animal bone, game counters and an iron lamp. The *pyxis* was acquired by the British Museum.
Havis, R, & Medlycott, M, EAH (1992) 23, 112. Johns, CM, Antiquaries Journal (1994) 73, 161.

46. Enfield Lock. *OS* map 177. TQ 3799, TQ 3798. Moxeys Nursery, Rammey Marsh, and Royal Ordnance Factory.
The ice of the Devensian Glacial Stage about 25,000 years ago (see Glossary) has preserved arctic mosses, birch and willow in peat. Also found were woolly mammoth including a tusk, rhinoceros and bison. Probably of approximately the same date, a Levallois flint flake tool (see Glossary) was recovered from the base of a well. Pollen analysis from a nearby site in a meander of the River Lea suggested a formation date about 6500 BC for an oak/alder woodland.
Wymer, J, Palaeolithic Sites in East Anglia (1985) Geo Books, p301. Bedwin,O, EAH (1991) 22, 161.

47. Epping Forest, Ambresbury Banks★.
Iron Age fort. *OS* map 167. TL 438004. Beside and east of B1393 (old A11) 3.2km (two miles) south-west of Epping, nearly opposite the road to Copthall Green and Upshire.
On one of the highest parts of Epping Forest, an area covering about 11.7 acres (4.6 hectares) is surrounded by a bank still about 2m high which would have been surmounted by a wooden palisade, and an external ditch which was 3m deep and 6.7m wide (**24; colour plate 17**). The 'fort' was probably constructed between 400-100 BC, maybe by the Trinovantes tribe against attack from the neighbouring Catuvellauni. The original entrance was on the west. A causeway crossed the bank which here was made up of unmortared puddingstone blocks forming a parallel-sided passage through the bank. There is evidence of inner and outer double wooden gates at the entrance to the passage and as it passed through the bank. A spring rises within the enclosed area, providing a water supply. The name has been associated with the military leader of the British, Ambrosius Aurelianus, against the Saxon invaders in the fifth century AD.
Pitt-Rivers, A, Trans Essex Field Club (1882), 2, 55. VCH Essex (1903) i, 279. Cotton, MA, Essex Naturalist (1957) 30, 43. Alexander JA et al, EAH (1978) 10, 189.

47. Epping, Hill Wood, High Beach. OS map 167. TQ4197. 1km (0.6 mile) south of Epping Forest Conservation Centre. Conserved in the British Museum is a collection of a flint scrapers (for animal hides), cores from which tools have been fashioned, a hammerstone, burins and awls ('arrowheads' and borers) and punches which date from the Mesolithic period (7000-4000 BC). They were found in a series of excavations from about 1913 in a pit at High Beach.
Warren, SH, Essex Naturalist (1913) 17, 292. Clarke, JDG, The Mesolithic Age in Britain (1932) p62. Jacobi, RM, Martingell, HE, Huggins, PJ, EAH (1978) 10, 206.

48. Feering. OS map 168. TL8720.
A long mortuary enclosure 65m long has been found from aerial survey (**17**). It has twin parallel ditches, curved but not joining, at the south end, which faces the river Brain. To the east was a 25m diameter round barrow.
Strachan, D, Essex from the Air (1998), Essex County Council, p 12.

49. Felsted. OS map 167. TL 6621.
1 km (0.6 mile) east of Little Dunmow by the disused railway track a small excavation produced evidence of a Roman villa.
VCH Essex (1963) iii, 126.

50. Finchingfield. OS map 167. TL 6734 and TL 6932.
1.5km (0.9 mile) east of Little Sampford church and 500m south-east of Finchingfield church small excavations suggest the presence of Roman villas.
VCH Essex (1963) iii, 129,130.

51. Fingringhoe. OS map 168. TM 0320. Plane Hall Farm.
A hoard of bronze axes, gouges, a sickle (**42**), chisels and rings dated to about 700 BC at the end of the Bronze Age was found in plough-soil in 1985 and reported to Colchester Museum for recording. It may have been abandoned as scrap at a time when bronze was being superseded by iron. In the Nature Reserve east of South Green (TM 0519) are (?villa) stone buildings on the site of early first century AD and Roman military buildings. Beside

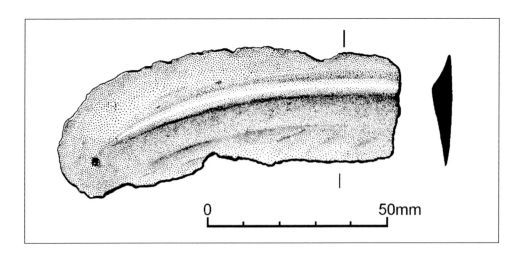

0   50mm

42   Late Bronze Age copper alloy sickle from Fingringhoe

the River Crouch is the site of a Roman fort (TM 0519).
VCH Essex (1963) iii, 131. Britannia, (1970) i, 181. Sealey, P, EAH (1987) 18,7; (1991) 22, 3. Brooks, H, EAH (2002) 33,54

52. Fordham. *OS* map 168. TL9228. Fordham Hall Farm.
A villa and burials, one a female in a lead coffin 140x40cm wide 31cm deep having a bead and roll moulding decorative border on the lid, inside a nailed wooden coffin, laid north-east south-west. A second burial was of a child.
Davies, GMR, Colchester Archaeology Group Annual Bulletin (1984) 27, 44.

53. Foulness, Little Shelford. *OS* map 178. TQ9891. 200m south-west of Little Shelford House, 100m west of the site of a Romano-British tumulus.
Five burial urns dating to second century AD containing cremations were excavated in 1972.
James, DJ & HR, EAH (1978) 10, 227.

54. Fryerning*. *OS* map 167. TL 6201. Mapletree Lane. From the centre of Ingatestone High Street, take Fryerning Lane, turning right and left into Beggar Hill at the Woolpack Inn. At the end of this lane Mapletree Lane (track) crosses north and south. From 300m north-west of Woodbarns Farm off the Furze Hall-Blackmore road, 1.5km (0.9 mile) of straight track leads north-east. It has lateral ditches silted to about 0.5m below the top of the external banks along its length. The alignment towards Writtle (north-east) is towards another straight stretch at Bumsteads Farm (TL6705) and south-west to Doddinghurst. Church (TQ 5999). This may be a Roman road but is unexcavated.

200m west of the church (TL6300) is a ploughed out mound 25m wide showing as a slightly raised mound and lighter soil. A further 50m west is an earth mound 7m across, 1m high with brick and ironwork debris; both of these are in Millhill (field) but, close to the twelfth century church and a spring, may be of prehistoric origin with later reuse (**colour plate 1**).
Margery, ID, Roman Roads in Britain, 1973. Kemble, J, Essex Journal (1993) 28(i), 16.

55. Gestingthorpe. *OS* map 155. TL 8339. Hill Farm, east of Wiggery Wood.
An Early Bronze Age flanged axe survived in a field subsequently occupied by a Roman building. The site was occupied from the Late Iron Age to the fourth century AD. From 1949 the landowner excavated a villa near the main Roman Braintree to Long Melford road. A bronze industry producing statuettes, buckles and jewellery was indicated by clay moulds. The finding of moulds for casting a bronze male figure was the first excavated evidence for bronze casting in this region. The villa measured 36mx18.4m; the foundations were of mortared flints. Along the south-west side had been a timber aisle (?veranda). An apsidal room had a hypocaust. The walls were covered with red-painted plaster. On the west was a bath block with red, blue, grey and yellow plaster. The villa was destroyed by fire about AD 185, rebuilt and probably in use until the late fourth/early fifth century (dated from recovery of Romano-Saxon pottery).
Brown, N, EAH (1987) 18, 88. Frere, SS, Britannia (1970) i, 266. VCH Essex (1963) iii, 133. Rodwell, W, in Todd, M (ed) (1978) Studies in the Romano-British Villa. Leicester University. Draper, J, East Anglian Archaeology (1985) 25.

56. Grays. Stifford Clay Road. *OS* map 177. TQ620809. William Edwards school, to the south-east of the A13 flyover/Stifford Clays road junction.

The site of Mesolithic (7000-4000 BC) flint-knapping which continued into the Neolithic period (3500-1500 BC). Flint projectile points, blades and an arrowhead were found. The settlement may have been further east near Bloomfields Farm. There was a farmstead here in the Roman period from the first to fourth century from which coins were recovered. Primrose Island pond probably existed in Roman times, since a pristine storage jar was found in the silts. *Lavender, NJ, EAH (1998) 29,19.*

56. Grays. Chadwell Road. *OS* map 177. TQ 635787. Palmers Grammar School (Sixth Form College)

In 1970 here was found a clay Roman pottery kiln, 1.3m in diameter. There was an appreciable quantity of pottery, urns, beakers, dishes and flasks from the final firing still in situ. The kiln dated from about AD 100. A tessellated pavement has been exposed at TQ6178 (railway). *Rodwell, KA, EAH (1983) 15,11. Couchman, C, EAH (1979) 11, 50. VCH Essex (1968) iii, 188.*

57. Great Baddow. Bronze Age enclosure. *OS* map 167. TL7305. Immediately north of A414 Great Baddow-Sandon Bridge road at Manor Farm.

Excavations in 1990 found a circular enclosure surrounded by a ditch 2.1m deep crossed by a 1.5m wide earth causeway. Pottery dated the enclosure to the Bronze Age about 1000 BC. There was no evidence for a gateway or a timber rampart. This enclosure lies on the opposite side of the valley of the River Chelmer to the roughly contemporary Springfield Lyons enclosure (qv), perhaps identifying two territories whose boundaries were the river. *Brown, N, Lavender, NJ, EAH (1994) 25, 3.*

58. Great Chesterford★. Roman fort and town. *OS* map 154. TL 5143.

An Late Iron Age settlement lay to the south of the south gate of the first century AD Roman fort on which roads converged from Radwinter (south-east), Cambridge (north) and Braughing (south-west). The fort, of about 13 hectares (32 acres), possibly built in response to the Boudican Revolt of AD 60/61, was protected on the west by the River Cam. The eastern defence, to the east of Newmarket Road, was a double bank and ditch with an internal timber rampart. When the army withdrew from the fort, native civilian settlement extended into it. The buildings were of timber with colour wash walls, internal plaster, thatched or shingled roofs and some mosaic floors. Postulated buildings include the rectangular villa with a pillared portico, a tax-collector's office, a bone-working shop, weaving and spinning house (Greyhound Public House site), a warehouse (in Braughing Road) and a smithy (next to the churchyard). A large octagonal stone, perhaps surmounted by a column of Jupiter, carved with figures representing the days of the week and later used as a water trough, is now in the British Museum.

In the fourth century the town (about 36 acres centred on the road junction) was enclosed with a mortared ragstone, flint and brick wall, 8-12ft thick, and a ditch of which the south-eastern extent is at the north-west end of Church Street, with the north gate just inside the northern defences of the fort. Geophysical survey east of the railway has shown the grid-pattern of the Roman streets and property boundaries (5). The northern road, after entering the town, deviates eastwards round a central pre-existing feature (?*principia*, the headquarters building or the *forum*, market-place). Towards the west is a large octagonal feature, 30m in diameter, which may be the theatre or a temple enclosure. Cemeteries were to the north, south-west and south outside the town walls.

1 km (0.6 mile) north-east (east of the Stump Cross-Little Chesterford road, TL5144) was a Late Iron Age rectangular timber shrine with a surrounding bank. About AD 70 it was replaced by a new square temple with a precinct and porch where was found a silver mask with lentoid eyes and a moustache.

Crossan, C., EAH (1990) 21, 11. Brooks, H, EAH (1991) 22,38. Burnham, BC, Wacher, J, Small Towns of Roman Britain, Batsford, 1990. Rodwell, WJ, Britannia (1972) 3,290. Miller, TE, Proc Cambridge Antiq Soc (1996) 84, 15. Wardill, R, Gt Chesterford Geophysical Rep, Essex Co Cncl, 1997. Medlycott, M, Gt. Chesterfield, EAA (forthcoming 2010). VCH (1963) 3, 72. Gadd, EAH (2001) 32, 238.

59. Great Dunmow. OS map 167. TL 6222.

In the Middle Iron Age (350-50 BC) there was a settlement enclosed with a bank and ditch immediately to the west of Newton Green (TL 6222) from which at least two round wattle-and-daub timber houses were excavated in 1993. The Roman town of about 10 hectares (24 acres) developed west of the junction of Stane Street (A120, Colchester-St Albans) with the road (B184) from *Londinium* and Chigwell (qv) and from Chelmsford (*Caesaromagus*, qv) on the ridge above the river Chelmer. The main road leaves the Stane Street alignment from both west and east deviating north round what may have been the Roman enclosure bank and ditch. Excavations in the town at Chequers Lane, New Street and Redbond Lodge have identified the settlement. At Church End (TQ 6323), to the north of the town, a second settlement developed.

Wilson, DR, Britannia, (1973) iv, 304. Lavender, NJ, EAH (1997) 28,47. Wickenden, NP, East Anglian Archaeology (1988) No 41. Brooks, H, EAH (1995) 26, 243.

60. Great Hallingbury, Wallbury ★. OS map 167. TL 4918. Little Hallingbury-Spellbrook road.

A double-ditched oval enclosure, overlooking the River Stort on the west, occupies 12.4 hectares (31 acres) dating from about 400 BC with a resettlement about 25 BC. This may be one of the line of Iron Age forts built by the Trinovantes guarding their western flank (with Loughton, Ambresbury and Ring Hill, qv). It has been proposed as the place where the leader of the Britons, Cassivellaunus, was encamped when Caesar was accepting the surrender of the Trinovantes in 54 BC.

VCH Essex (1903) i, 282. Archaeologia, xix, 411. Gould, IC, Trans EAS (1903) ns viii, 139. Black, EW, EAH (1990) 21, 8. Morris, S et al, EAH (1978) 10,1.

61. Great Horkesley, Pitchbury Ramparts★. Iron Age fort. OS map 168. TL 9629. North-east of Scarlets Farm.

An oval enclosure of about 5 acres (2 hectares), surrounded by a double ditch and banks, which remain on the north-west in Pitchbury Wood, is protected by a stream on the west. Excavations in 1933 and 1973 suggest a date 100-25 BC. Little evidence was found of prolonged settlement within it; it may have been used only as a temporary refuge.

Archaeologia, xxix, 250. Laver, H, Trans EAS (1898) ns vii, 109. Holmes, TV, Essex Naturalist (1882) i, 82. Hawkes, FC, Crummy, P, Camulodunum Two, Colchester Archaeological Report No 11, p 138. Rodwell, W, in Oppida, British Archaeological Reps (1976) S11,181. Crummy, P, City of Victory, 1997, Colchester Archaeological Trust, p 18.

62. Great Sampford. OS map 154. TL6436. North of road to Radwinter, B1053, at Shillingstone field.

Excavations have shown the area has been farmed since at least the Late Iron Age (first century BC) and revealed a droveway and Roman field boundaries. Roman material including roof and box-flue tiling, tesserae, painted brick and iron slag suggest a villa or farmstead is nearby.

Garwood, A, EAH (1998) 29, 33. Neale, K, Essex Journal (2000) 35(ii), 56.

63. Great Tey. OS map 168. TL 8925. 500m east of Walcotts Hall.

Excavations have revealed a Romano-British villa from first century AD. At Teybrook Farm, TL89102464, 200 yards north of where the modern road deviates eastwards, ditches and a metalled Roman road 6m (19.6ft) wide were excavated in 1990-1.

VCH Essex (1963) iii, 186. Fawn, J, Colchester Arch Gp Ann Bull (1991) 34, 29. Colchester Arch (2003) 16, 5.

64. Great Totham, Lofts Farm. OS map 168. TL 869093. West of Heybridge-Little Totham road.

On the low lying gravels north of the Blackwater estuary was a rectangular double-ditched and banked enclosure about 42x48m, with rounded corners (**21; colour plate 10**). The ditches were about 0.5m deep and up to 1.5m wide. The entrance was through the east side. In the centre of the enclosure was evidence of an oval building 10m diameter with a porch facing south. The roof (probably of thatch) had been held up by a circle of posts with an outer ring of posts for the wattle wall. Other buildings such as a rectangular long house (part for animals, part for humans) and granaries were sited around the central building. Between the buildings were several pits which contained flint implements such as axes, knife blades and scrapers (for hides). The finding of a spindle whorl indicated a spinning industry. Food had included wheat, barley, oats and beans, of which grains and seeds were recovered. The single metal object found was a bronze axehead. Eighty-four metres south was a well about 2m diameter which had been lined with oak; it contained a large amount of pottery. Although bones had not survived, the inhabitants may have pastured their cattle and sheep on the surrounding marshes and grassland. Radiocarbon dating suggests the enclosure was in use about 800-700 BC, towards the end of the Bronze Age.

Brown, N, Proceedings of the Prehistoric Society (1988) 54, 249.

64. Great Totham, Slough House Farm. OS map 168. TL 8709. By Heybridge-Little Totham road.

From a rectangular enclosure, about 30x12m, surrounded by a ditch up to 0.8m deep (and probably a bank), were excavated Neolithic or early Bronze Age (about 1500 BC) pottery. The enclosure seems then to have been abandoned in favour of a new enclosure several metres northwards in the late Bronze Age (about 800 BC) where there was a cattle watering pond, 15m across. Later, around 300 BC, there was a settlement which consisted of several roundhouses, one probably a smithy with evidence of a furnace. In the Roman period, a trackway crossed the site (?from Heybridge) towards the north-east, perhaps the forerunner of the present road towards Little Totham. Nearby was a well, 2m in diameter, shored with timber held by wooden pegs at the corners.

Wallis, S, Essex Journal (1989) 24 (ii),39. Wallis, S, EAH (1989) 20, 163. Wallis, S et al, East Anglian Archaeology (1998) 85.

65. Great Wakering. OS map 178. TQ 9487. 0.5km south-east of Great Wakering police station, east of the lake, at the south end of Alexander Road (new housing estate).

Field boundary ditches of Bronze Age date contained pottery, a flint scraper and blades. Roman pottery dated from first to third century AD. East of St Nicolas church (TQ9587) in the cemetery excavations in 2000 revealed a Middle Iron Age droveway, and a Roman infant buried with an oyster shell.

Reidy, K, EAH (1997) 28, 1. Trans Southend Antiq Hist Soc(1933) 2(iii), 206.

66. Great Waltham, Broads Green. OS map 167. TL 685122. North of Margret Woods Farm, Fanners Green.

An unenclosed settlement (?farm) was excavated in 1986 revealing cremation burials, a possible four-sided hut, storage pits (for grain) and copper working. The site is dated to about 700 BC and is significant as it shows that the heavier Boulder Clay areas of Essex were being

exploited by this date as well as the easier-worked sand and gravels.

Brown, N, EAH (1988) 19, 1 and (1989) 20, 147.

67. Hadleigh, Essex. OS map 178. TQ 8187. 830ft south of High Street, 1130 ft WSW of the church on Salvation Army land.

Aerial photography shows a rectangular enclosure 250ft square with a ditch, a military construction, fort, administrative base or collection point which dates from the first century AD.

VCH Essex (1963) iii, 135. Rodwell WJ, Southend Museum Publication No 16 (1971).

68. Hadstock. OS map 154. TL 5746.

Excavations in 1826 in Red Field revealed a Romano-British villa on the south bank of the River Granta, 22 yards north-east of the church. The mosaic pavement with a blue and white diaper pattern was relaid in Audley End House.

VCH Essex (1963) iii, 135.

69. Halstead. OS map 168. TL 8032. South-west of Hepworth Hall.

In the bank of the River Colne has been found building tile, a vase and flagon, probably fourth century.

VCH Essex (1963) iii, 137.

70. Harlow★. Roman Temple. OS map 167. TL 468123. 1km (0.6 mile) west of A414 junction with A1184 Bishops Stortford road, in the park north of the railway, approached by turning north at the Elizabeth Way roundabout into River Walk.

20ft above the floodplain of the River Stort has been marked out (not quite in alignment) the ground plan of the first century AD Roman temple. There was a previous Iron Age sanctuary from which offerings of coins of the British kings Addedomaros, Dubnovellaunus, Amminus, Andocomius, Tasciovanus and Cunobelinus (Cymbeline) dating from *c*.50 BC to AD 40, many in mint condition, rings and brooches have been recovered. These offerings suggest that people were coming from or trade was active as far afield as Norfolk, Leicestershire and Dorset. The Romano-British temple dates from about AD 80. A cella (central shrine) 18ft 9in square of flint and mortar with 2ft 10in thick walls, and an ambulatory 48ft 6in square were approached along a cobbled pathway from the south. About AD 120 a wooden palisade was built around the site, and a tessellated floor, gateway and an altar were added about AD 200. A carved limestone head of the goddess Minerva complete with helmet over curly hair suggests the temple was dedicated to her. The temple was in decay by AD 400. Quantities of broken tile, painted wall-plaster and worked stone were found. The site was probably venerated from early times, since Bronze Age urns containing cremations were also recovered from under the Iron Age sanctuary.

Wheeler, M, Antiquaries Journal (1928) 8, 300. France, NE, Goble, BM, Romano-British Temple at Harlow, West Essex Archaeology Group (1985). Bartlett, R, London Archaeologist (1988) 23, 9. Bartlett, R, Current Archaeology (1988) 112, 163. Haselgrove, CC, Oxford Journal of Archaeology (1989) 8, 73.

70. Harlow, Church Langley. OS map 167. TL 4810. Old House.

At Church Langley, Netteswell (TL4510) and Brenthall Park (TL4709), fieldwalking has produced flint implements and burials from the Palaeolithic, Mesolithic, Neolithic

and Bronze Ages. At Perry Springs Wood (TL473095) there was an Early Iron Age (about 700-350 BC) settlement. That paganism was still being practised in the third and fourth centuries AD at Church Langley (Old House TL483096) is suggested by the finding of a Romano-Saxon cremation pot with burial of animal bones.

Harold, R, EAH (1990) 21, 132. Ecclestone, J, EAH (1994) 25, 253. Bartlett, R, EAH (1988) 19,266. Medlycott, M, EAH (2000), 31, 33.

70. Harlow, Holbrooks. OS map 167. TL 470128. Immediately south-west of A1184 (Harlow-Bishops Stortford road) crossing of River Stort. Reached from River Walk via the Edinburgh Way roundabout A414.

Excavations in 1970 found a Late Iron Age (about 10 BC) and Roman settlement which probably extended over 30 acres. Two hundred pieces of bronze sheet, some with leaf and other decoration, were recovered. A 'curse tablet' (*defixio*) 54x72mm contained a message invoking Mercury. The settlement was apparently engaged in making religious offerings such as bronze leaves and lead dedicatory plaques, for the pilgrims to take to the nearby temple (qv, TL 4712). One house had a mortared flint wall, painted plaster and a red tessellated floor. Another was a smithy. Bronze and bone pins, bracelets and rings were recovered.

Conlon, RFB, Essex Journal (1973) 8 (ii), 31. Wright, RP, Britannia (1973) 4, 325.

70. Harlowbury. OS map 167. TL 4812. North of Gildas Way.

Evaluation suggests a Romano-British villa, mainly of timber and tile.

Essex Sites & Monuments Record, County Hall, Chelmsford.

71. Harwich, Dovercourt. *OS* map 169. TM 2431. Pound Farm, Gants Pit, at junction of Harwich Road and Parkeston Quay road, now a school.

In 1908 Acheulian handaxes (see Glossary) and remains of elephant, rhinoceros, deer, ox and mammoth were discovered. Three years later a hoard of Bronze Age axes was found. A Roman villa with tessellated floors has been traced at Dovercourt vicarage (TM2632). Harwich was a source of much of the septaria stone used in Roman building.

Wymer, JJ, in Barringer, C (ed) (1984) Aspects of Anglian Prehistory, Geo Books. Wymer, J, Prehistoric Sites in East Anglia (1985) Geo Books, p237. VCH Essex (1963) iii, 144. Medlycott, M, Historic Towns Survey, 1998, ECC.

72. Hatfield Broad Oak, Matching Barns. Map 167. TL 5513. 1km (0.6 mile) north of Manwood Green.

A hoard of 74 bronze pieces including a bucket, spearheads and axes dating from the eighth century BC found here in 1893 is now in Colchester Castle Museum.

Davies, DG, in Burgess, C et al, British Archaeological Reports (1979), 67, 149. Laver, H, Trans EAS (1896) ns 6, 172. Butcher, CH, Trans EAS (1923) ns 16, 262.

72. Hatfield Broad Oak, Portingbury Hills★. *OS* map 167. TL 532204. In north-west Hatfield Forest, 3km (1.9 miles) north-east of Great Hallingbury (**34**).

Excavations in 1964-5 near to Port Lane (from Wallbury to Stane Street, A120) sampled a four-sided mound about 100ft in diameter and 3.5ft high surrounded by a ditch 6ft deep. On the east is a causeway and an irregular four-sided area partly enclosed by a ditch 40mx14.5m. Pottery

was of Iron Age date (600 BC-AD 50). The earthwork may be a short-lived farmstead or woodmen's settlement.

Wilkinson, P, EAH (1978) 10, 221. Rackham, O, The Last Forest, Phoenix, 1998. p161.

73. Hempstead. *OS* map 154. TL 6540. North of Hillside Farm, a Romano-British villa.

Rodwell, W. in Todd, M (ed) (1978) Studies in the Romano-British Villa. Leicester University, p31.

74. Hockley, Plumberow Mount★. *OS* map 178 TQ 840938. 0.5km south-east of Lower Hockley Hall, west of Plumberow Avenue at the south edge of Plumberow Wood.

The earthen mound excavated in 1913 is 4m high and 25m in diameter overlooking the valley of the River Crouch. A coin of Emperor Domitian (AD 81-96) and a small amount of Roman pottery makes it likely to be of Roman origin, but its purpose is unclear. It appears not to be a burial but may have been a beacon or boundary mark. The Domesday Book name *Plumberga* (plum-tree hill) could indicate a man-made or natural mound.

Francis, EB, Trans EAS (1873) old series, v, 224. Francis, EB, Trans EAS (1915) ns 13, 225. Heppell, E, EAH (1998) 28, 269. EAA (1981) 12, 5. Kemble, J, EAH (2004) 34, 155.

75. Hornchurch. *OS* map 177. TQ 5587. South of Woodhall Crescent.

The railway cutting made in 1892 exposed the boulder clay deposits of the extreme southerly extent of the Anglian ice sheet, and the early terraces of the diverted Thames.

Lucy, G, Essex Rock, 1999, Essex Rock & Mineral Society.

75. Hornchurch. OS map 177. TQ 5183. Askwith Road, 300 yards south-east of Mardyke Farm.

In 1928 a Roman coffin with skeletons of a woman and a child was found.

VCH Essex (1968) iii, 148

75. Hornchurch South, Rainham Road. OS Map 177. TQ520 831. 500m north of A13-Rainham Road (A125) junction (Dovers Corner) at Lessa sports ground. A field system of boundary ditches and a well excavated in 1998 suggest a nearby late Iron Age or early Roman hamlet.

Holder, N, London Archaeology (1999) vol 9 suppl 1, 13. Sankey, D, London Archaeologist (2000) vol 9 suppl 2, 48. Proc Prehist Soc (2002) 60, 319.

76. Ickleton, Cambs. OS map 154. TL 5043. 400m south-east of the church.

A villa and barn dating from second century AD were excavated in 1880s. It measured *c.*30mx20m, and had at least 17 rooms, with painted plaster depicting dancing nymphs.

Fox, C, Archaeology of the Cambridge Region (1923) 183. Taylor, A, Archaeology of Cambridgeshire (1997), I, 73, Cambridgeshire County Council.

77. Ilford, Buttsbury Road. OS map 177. TQ 4585. Between Loxford Lane to the north and Buttsbury Road to the south.

Excavations in 1992-4 showed the area was frequented by mesolithic man (about 6000 BC) using flint tools. The area was occupied in the Bronze Age (about 2000-1000 BC) by fenced and ditched fields and stock enclosures. Domestic activity is suggested by four fire pits or hearths containing ash. It seems likely that the River Roding was fordable at this point. The site lies only

300m from the strategically important Iron Age Uphall Camp, Ilford (qv).

Lawrence, D, et al, London Archaeologist (1997) 8,98.

77. Ilford, Ilford Lane/Uphall Road/ High Road area. OS map 177. Around TQ 4486.

Excavations in the nineteenth century, particularly by amateur geologist, archaeologist and civil servant, Sir Antonio Brady, and during road construction in the 1980s have produced bones of mammoth, rhinoceros, giant ox, straight-tusked elephant, bear, lion and giant deer. These probably date to a warm period in the late Wolstonian stage from 200,000 to 150,000 years ago. [In the Natural History Museum, South Kensington]

Walker, H, Trans Essex Field Club (1880) i, 27 and (1884) iii, 94. Rednap, M, and Currant, A, Essex Journal (1985) 20(i), 8. Wymer, J, Palaeolithic Sites in East Anglia (1985) Geo Books, p 299.

77. Ilford, Uphall Camp. Iron Age fort. OS map 177. TQ437850. South of the Romford-Stratford road A118, Ilford Lane to Barking A123 runs east of the fort, now sealed under buildings. Uphall Road runs north-south through the centre, with Wingate Road just inside its north-eastern bank and Victoria Road just outside its south-eastern bank. The Ilford-Barking parish boundary followed the southern rampart (**26**).

On the east bank of the River Roding, one of the largest Iron Age defended settlements in the country of about 550x440m, 48 acres (19.5 hectares) was surrounded by a bank topped by a palisade and a ditch, doubled on the west. A plan of it was drawn about 1735, showing the enclosure to be roughly rectangular. At the north-west was 'a high keep of earth', possibly for a mill or beacon of the sixteenth or seventeenth century, subsequently called Lavender Mound. In 1978 a remnant of the northern bank still existed at the rear of houses on the south side of Baxter Road, and the western (riverside) slope of the camp at its northern corner was still clear. Within the enclosure have been excavated the bases of round timber houses. The largest, about 14.4m diameter, had partition walls. One was a smithy and another possibly a granary in which were found burned cereal grains. Soil samples produced spelt and emmer wheat grains, barley, oats and vegetable seeds. Other rectangular buildings may have been for farm animals. Pottery and coins recovered suggest a date to the Middle Iron Age (*c*.350-50 BC). The size of the enclosure and the houses indicate a permanent or at least semi-permanent settlement, and its position suggests its use as a port (an entrance on the riverside seems to have been at the north-west corner), and as a guardian of the river passage.

Crouch, W, Trans EAS (1903) ns ix, 408 and (1906) ns x, 19. Wilkinson, P, EAH (1978) 10, 220. Greenwood, P, Essex Journal (1988) 23,19. London Archaeologist (1989) 6,94 Merriman, N, Prehistoric London, HMSO,(1990) p41. Sidell, J et al, London Archaeologist (1999), 9(iii), 70.

78. Ingatestone★. *OS* map 167. TQ 6599. Stock Road, 250m east of the railway line. Mesolithic activity (about 8000-4000 BC) was found here in the form of a flaked flint adze, 20x6x3.5cm, possibly used as a woodworking tool (**43**).

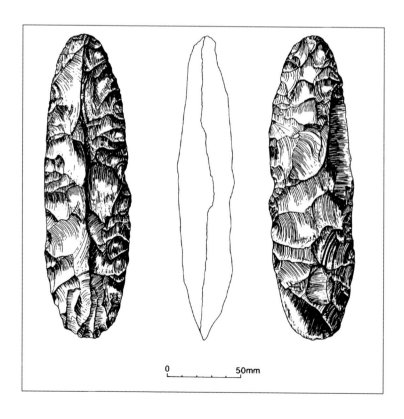

43   Mesolithic tranchet adze from Ingatestone

0 _____ 50mm

It appears more sophisticated than a similar tool 9.9x5x2.5cm found in Byron Road, Chelmsford (TL7207). Large sarsen stones, one found under the north-east chancel (now at the south porch of the church) and two at the junction of the Roman road with the road to Fryerning, are glacial erratics of sandstone. Their position at the church (TQ 651997) raises the query as to whether this was an early ritual site. The presence of a Romano-British villa is suspected at Mill Green at Box Wood (TL 6502). A ditch about 2m deep, 6m wide with lateral banks extends from Stoneymore Wood to Box Wood for about 650 yards (Moores Ditch, TL6401). Without sure dating evidence, it is possibly prehistoric.

Drury, P, Trans EAS (1970), third series, 2(iii), 335. Austin, L, EAH (1996) 27, 304. Kemble, J, Essex Journal (1993) 28(i) 14. Christie, M, Trans EAS (1915) ns 14, 49.

79. Kelvedon. OS map 168. TL 8619.

About 400,000 years ago, Kelvedon was at the edge of the great glacial ice cap which covered Britain in the Anglian Ice Age. A hundred thousand years later it was at the shores of a large lake from whose banks have been found handaxes left by early man. North of Doucecroft School, excavations revealed a probable round timber house 12m in diameter indicating a settlement (?farm) dated about 200 BC. A Late Iron Age settlement (50 BC-AD 50) developed on a north-east south-west trackway (now the main street) at which an enclosed Romano-British settlement was formed. A *mansio* (travellers' hostel) was built at Docwra Road school. A possible fort or field boundary (TL862186) may be responsible for the two right-angle bends of the road at the south-west end of the High Street. From a temple at the rear of

Lawson Villas, High Street (TL864189) were found a votive bowl, a lead 'curse tablet' (*defixio*) and a chalk figurine (now in Colchester Castle Museum). In the later Roman period (?late second century), the main road swung north of the enclosure to cross the River Blackwater at Easterford to Colchester. Kelvedon has been identified as *Canonium* of the second/third century Antonine Itinerary. Burials in the Roman period (some rich, with stone and lead coffins) in the cemetery on the east continued into the Saxon period.

Rodwell, KA, Britannia (1972) 3,333. Rodwell, K, W Current Archaeology (1975) 5, 25. Rodwell, W, Rowley, RT, Brit Arch Reps (1975), 15. Rodwell, KA, CBA Res Rep (1988) 63. Wilson, DR, et al, Britannia (1973) iv, 305; (1974) v, 442. Eddy, MR, Essex Co Council, occ paper 3 (1982). Jnl of Roman Studies 48, 150. Clarke, CP, EAH (1988) 19, 15; (2001) 32,102; (2002) 33, 63. EAA (2007) 118.

80. Langdon Hills Park. Late Bronze/Early Iron Age fort. OS map 177. TQ 677862.

On a spur overlooking the Thames plain, in 1978 lengths of banks and ditches remained amongst gravel extractions. These suggest a defensive hillfort, dating to about ?700 BC, protecting from a riverborne invasion. The flint-gritted pottery is in Thurrock Museum.

Couchman, C, EAH (1976) 8,149. Morris S, Buckley DG, EAH (1978) 10,1.
Buckley, DG, Brown, N EAH (1984-5) 16, 105. Isserlin, RMJ, EAH (1995) 26, 46.

81. Langley, Rumberry Hill★. OS map 154. TL 4635. 1km (0.6 mile) east of Langley (Harmcamlow Way) beside the Roman road.

The barrow 120ft in diameter and 8ft high

when excavated in the nineteenth century produced Roman glass, tile and Samian ware.

Neville, RC (1858) Trans EAS, old series i, 194. VCH Essex (1963) iii, 152.

82. Latchingdon, Crouch estuary.
OS map 168. TQ 8997. In Bridgemarsh Creek.

A prehistoric wooden platform (?jetty), 10x15m, of squared ash and oak timbers, extended out into the water (see also Althorne).

Wilkinson, TJ (ed) East Anglian Archaeology (1995) 71, 139.

83. Lawford★. Neolithic long barrow. OS
map 168. TM 0830. Lawfordhouse Farm. Lawford-Burnt Heath road.

Some 60ft long and 14ft wide, a barrow of Neolithic appearance. The long mound was usually higher at the eastern end where was the interment, and was accompanied by a ditch either side, sometimes joining in a horseshoe round the ends (see Glossary) (*Essex Sites & Monuments Record No 2723*) (**17**).

In Lawford Park, 600m west of Lawford Hall (TM 0832), a round barrow opened in 1812 produced 'two urns' and Late Bronze Age pottery *(Sites & Monuments No 2710)*. South of the church (TM0830) a ring-ditch 21m in diameter, until recently with a central barrow mound, was a Neolithic domestic site which produced Grooved Ware pottery, late third-early second millennium BC. At TM 0907 3000 is the Roman road from Colchester to Manningtree, 20 paces wide, which cuts through a ring ditch (*Sites & Monuments Record No 2770*). *Jones, Rev CA, A History of Dedham, 1907, p3. Priddy, D, East Anglian Archaeology (1981) 12, 95. McMaster, I, Colchester Archaeology Group Annual*

Bulletin (1971) 14, 18. Erith,FH, Colchester Archaeology Group Annual Bulletin (1971) 14, pp35, 38. Shennan, SJ, Healey, F, Smith, IF, Archaeological Journal (1985) 142, 150.

84. Layer Breton. OS map 168. TL
9418.

Fieldwalking suggests a Roman villa.

Beckett, D, Colchester Archaeology Group Annual Bulletin (1983), 26, 31.

85. Layer Marney. OS map 168. TL 9017.
South of Pods Wood.

A Bronze Age hoard of four axes and a razor was found by a metal detector and reported to the museum. They date from about 900 BC. One axe is incomplete suggesting the hoard was scrap, perhaps to be recycled.

Sealey, PR, EAH (1997) 28, 273.

86. Littlebury, Ring Hill★. Iron Age fort.
OS Map 154. TL 515382. On private land in Audley End Park.

An oval banked and ditch fort encloses 4.3 hectares (10.6 acres) with an internal rampart. On the north-east and south-west sides are steep scarps. The bank is 0.3m high, 10m wide, and is separated from the ditch by a flat space (berm) up to 8m wide. The original entrance is unknown. In 1741 a Temple of Victory designed by Robert Adam after the temple at Tivoli (Italy) was erected within the enclosure. The fort has not been excavated but is almost certainly dated between 600-100 BC, though the names *Sterberry (1719, now Strawberry), and Lyttlanbyrig (AD 1004)* suggest it may have been reused in the Saxon period .

VCH Essex (1903) i, 280. Laver, H, Trans EAS (1900) ns vii, 109. Royal Commission for Historic Monuments of England Survey, 1995.

87. Little Dunmow. OS map 167. TL
6621. Felsted old railway station, Little
Dunmow-Felsted road.
Samian pottery, tiles and a millstone have
been excavated.
VCH Essex (1963) iii, 126.

88. Little Hallingbury. OS map167. TL
4916. West of South House.
Site of a Romano-British villa with first
century burials nearby.
VCH Essex (1963), iii, 136.

89. Little Laver. OS map 167. TL 5409.
East of Church Farm.
Excavation has revealed a Romano-British
villa.
VCH Essex (1963) iii, 153.

90. Little Oakley. OS map 169. TM
2229. South of Foulton Hall.
The plan of a Romano-British villa has
been found.
*VCH Essex (1963) iii, 164. Farrands, RH,
Colchester Archaeology Group Annual Bulletin
(1958) 1(iv), 43. Essex Journal (1980) 15(i),
6. Barford, P, EAA (2002) 98.*

91. Little Sampford. See Finchingfield.

92. Little Waltham. OS Map 167. TL
707128. Junction of A130 Broomfield-
Great Leighs road with the Little Waltham-
Minnow End road.
At a junction of roads, 18 round timber
houses from the Middle Iron Age (350-
50 BC), about 12m in diameter, were
excavated prior to road building; no
enclosure ditch was identified (**colour
plate 30**). A possible Roman road
penetrating through a pre-existing Iron
Age field system towards the north-east
has been suggested. The name of nearby
Chatham Green (Hall) is derived from

Cet-ham, a mixture of Celtic *cet* with
Saxon *-ham,* suggesting a Romano-British
community remained here into the Saxon
period.
*Reaney, PH, Place-Names of Essex (1935),
Cambridge. Drury, PJ, Council for British
Archaeology Research Reports (1978) No 26.*

93. London.
**The following are now in the British
Museum and Museum of London:**
Tombstone of Julius Classicanus,
procurator (chief finance officer) in Britain
after the Boudican rebellion of AD 60/61,
found in 1852 and 1935 in a bastion of
London wall. RIB 12: 'To the spirits of the
departed and of G(aius) Iul(ius) Alpinus
Classicanus son of G(aius), of the Fabian
voting tribe, procurator of the province of
Brit(ain). Iulia Pacata I[ndiana], daughter
of Indus, set (this up)'.
Bronze plate found on south side of
Colchester in 1981. RIB 191. Around AD
222-35: 'To the god Mars Medocius of
the Campeses and to the Victory of our
emperor Alexander Pius felix, Lossio Veda,
descendant of Vepogenus a caledonian,
set up this gift from his own resources'.
Lossio Veda and Vepogenus appear to be
Celtic names.
A headless statuette with horses' hooves
found at Martlesham, Suffolk inscribed
around the rim. RIB 213. Undated.

**The following is now in the Ashmolean
Museum, Oxford:**
Tombstone with a figure holding a scroll
found in St Martin's Church, Ludgate
Hill, London, in 1669. RIB 17. ?Third
century AD: 'To the spirits of the departed
and to Vivius Marcianus, centurion of the
Legion II Augusta. Ianuaria Martina his
most devoted wife set up this memorial'.
The following is now at the Society

of Antiquaries, Burlington House, London:

Tomb found in Goodman's Fields, the Minories, east of the Roman city wall, in 1787. RIB 11. ?Third century AD: 'To the spirits of the departed, Fl[avius] Agricola, soldier of Legion VI Victrix, lived 42 years 10 days. Albia Faustina had this made for her peerless husband'.

Further details of the above inscriptions are to be found in *Maxfield, VA, Dodson, B, 1995. Inscriptions of Roman Britain, London Association of Classical Teachers 4* and *Collingwood, RG, Wright, RP, 1965, Roman Inscriptions of Britain, Oxford.*

94. Loughton.★. Iron Age fort. *OS* map 177. TQ 411975. From Loughton, junction of Rectory Lane A1168 and Church Hill A121 take Church Hill south-westwards. Turn right into St Johns Road. Well-defined paths westwards from Baldwins Hill in Epping Forest lead to Loughton Camp.

Standing on the southern headland of an elevated plateau at 310ft above sea level, an oval enclosure of about 6 acres (2.6 hectares) is surrounded by a bank and external ditch 13.7m wide and 2.4m deep. The southern and western sides are protected by a steep ravine. Being only 3.4 km (2 miles) south-west of Ambresbury Banks (qv), it may have succeeded it. The original entrance has not yet been detected. Along with other similar embanked enclosures (such as Wallbury and Ring Hill, qv), it would have been a place of refuge in time of attack from neighbouring Iron Age tribes such as the Catuvellauni. It has the advantage of a spring arising within it.

Morris S, Buckley, DG, EAH (1978) 10,1.
Warren, SH, Essex Naturalist (1928) 22,117.
VCH Essex(1903) i ,277

95. Maldon★. Iron Age fort? *OS* map 168. TL 8507. The circuit of the rampart approximately follows St Peters Hospital Spital Road, West House London Road, Gate Street, Beeleigh Road, Dykes Chase and Highlands Drive estate.

A ditched and banked enclosure, with an inner space of 220x290 yards, was illustrated in 1775 by Joseph Strutt. London Road runs through the centre towards All Saints' Church. Excavations have produced Iron Age pottery (about 300 BC) and evidence of occupation. It is, however, still unclear whether the defences were built then or by Alfred the Great's son Edward the Elder as a burgh against the Vikings (AD 916). As at Danbury (qv) and Witham (qv) it possible that he reinforced an already existing Iron Age fort.

Strutt, J, Horda Angel-Cynnan, (1775) vol I, London. Brown, PN, The Maldon Burgh Jigsaw, Maldon Archaeology Group, 1986. Bedwin, O, EAH (1992) 23, 10.

95. Maldon, Osea Road. *OS* map 168. TL 8907. East of the road leading from the Maldon-Goldhanger road to the River Blackwater causeway to Osea Island.

Excavations in 1971-2 of a 'red hill' produced seawater evaporation briquetage (burnt clay and pottery shards of the evaporation pots and tanks), Late Iron Age and Roman shards. It appears that this was an early salt-production site; it has been radiocarbon-dated to within 63 years of 239 BC. [See also Glossary, Red Hills].

Brisay, K de, (1972) Colchester Archaeology Group Annual Bulletin,15, 24, and (1973) 16, 20.

95. Maldon, Elms Farm, Heybridge. *OS* map 168.TL 850086. North of the Maldon northern bypass roundabout

Heybridge to Langford, now occupied by Bovis houses.

On low ground, beside the former course of the River Blackwater, about 2500 BC, there was a farmstead from which flint tools and pottery were found. The people were hunters too, as flint arrowheads were also discovered. Some 1,000 years later, two people were buried under an earth mound surrounded by a ditch. Then about 50 BC there developed an Iron Age village, eventually occupying perhaps 25ha (60 acres), dependent on farming and maybe as a small port. It was excavated from 1993-5 in one of the largest-ever archaeological exercises in Essex. There was a main north-south road (?linking to Witham and Colchester) with three side-roads running east. The northern side appears to have had domestic and market-place activity, the central a temple site and, to the south, industry. Weights have been found, indicating measurement of merchandise. Because it was so low-lying the village often flooded and the villagers dumped layers of gravel to try to raise the level. The dead of the village were buried in the cemeteries to the north and east. One was buried with nine brooches, one with his stone gaming counters like draughts. The temple was first built in the Iron Age (?AD 10). A small square shrine was later replaced by a large circular building, 11m in diameter, enclosed within a rectangular fence. Close by were other buildings, perhaps for priests or worshippers. Around AD 150, the shrine was replaced by a new circular building 15m in diameter, at the rear of which was an altar, at first of mortared flint, later of wood. About AD 250 the wooden temple wall was rebuilt with a masonry foundation. The town's greatest prosperity declined after the end of the first century AD. In the second century AD several houses were burned down, but the roads were maintained into the third century, and perhaps into the fourth when it was abandoned, not to be occupied again until the new inhabitants of 1996.

Wickenden, NP, EAH (1986) 17,6. Atkinson, M, Current Archaeology (1995) 144, 452. Langton, B, Holbrook, N, EAH (1997) 28,12. Atkinson, M, Preston, SJ, Britannia (1998) 29, 85; EAH (2001) 32,42. Hidden Heybridge, Essex Co Council (1999).

96. Mersea Island★. Cudmore Grove cliffs, East Mersea. OS map 168. TM 0715. From under the beach gravels have been excavated the bones of elephant, rhinoceros, hyaena and hippopotamus dating to a warm stage in the Wolstonian period. On the shore at West Mersea (TM0513) was found a Late Bronze Age sword (Ewart Park type) with rivets in the grip, dated seventh to sixth century BC.

Lucy, G, Essex Rock, 1999. Wymer, J, Lower Palaeolithic Occupation in Britain (1999), English Heritage, p 99. Bridgland, Quaternary of Thames, p. 369. Brown, N, EAH (1984-5) 16, 104.

96. Mersea Island★. Romano-British barrow. OS map 168. TM 023144. By the East Mersey road, 1km (0.6 mile) from the island causeway.

A circular mound, 110ft (34m) in diameter, 22½ ft (7m) high with a flat top 16ft (5m) wide, contained a tiled chamber 18x18x 21in high (45x45x53cm). A casket made of five lead plates½in thick measured 12½in square, 13in deep, joined by the blow-pipe method (not soldered). In it was a glass urn. A bowl 11⅜in high, 12-⅔in diameter of sea-green blown glass with a small mouth and beaded rim held

cremated adult human bone, and is now in Colchester Museum. It was dated AD 100-20 and attributed to the tomb of a Romanised Briton
Warren, SH, Trans EAS (1873) old series v, 116.
Warren, SH, Trans EAS (1915), ns xiii, 116.

96. Mersey Island. Roman villa. OS map 168. TM 0112. In West Mersey church, churchyard and Hall garden.
Overlooking the Blackwater estuary, two masonry buildings with mosaics and a private cemetery have been dated to the first/second centuries AD. *VCH Essex (1963) iii, 158. Rodwell W, in Todd, M,(ed) Studies in the Romano-British Villa, Leicester University (1978), p29.*

96. Mersey Island. Wheel tomb. OS map 168. TM 0112, 200 yards east of West Mersey church.
Investigated in 1896, a Roman mausoleum. A circular mortared ragstone wall 3ft thick, 65ft in diameter, contained a hexagonal chamber 5ft across from which six walls radiated.
VCH Essex (1963) iii, 159.

97. Messing. OS map 168. TL 8919. 1km (0.6 mile) north-west of the church.
The site of the excavated Romano-British villa with bathhouse.
VCH Essex (1963) iii, 162.

98. Mistley. Roman fort. OS map 168. TM 1231.
Supply of the Roman garrison at Colchester may have been through a port at Mistley along a two-track road, which may be partly represented at Crockleford Hill (TM 033262) and Lawfordhouse Farm (TM091300, qv).
Farrands, RH, Colchester Archaeological Group Annual Bulletin (1975) 18, 5. Holbert, PR, ibid (1976) 19, 13.

99. Mucking. Bronze Age enclosure (North Ring). OS map 177. TQ 675811. West of Mucking church.
A substantial ditch surrounded a circular enclosure with an entrance on the east (**20**). A visitor entering would have been faced with a wide wooden screen that separated off the west side of the ring. The round central timber building was 5m in diameter and around it were other round and rectangular buildings. The community inhabitants were self-sufficient, raising their own cattle, sheep and goats, grinding their own corn with saddle-shaped querns, weaving and spinning and making bronze implements which they cast in clay moulds. The settlement was dated to about 900 BC.
Bond, D, East Anglian Archaeology (1988) 43. Jones, MU, Essex Journal (1972) 7,67.

99. Mucking. Ancient Landscape between Mucking and Chadwell St Mary. OS map 177. TQ 6781.
Aerial photography in 1965 showed many features which have proved to be from the Bronze Age through Iron Age, Roman and Saxon periods, to the Nissen huts of the Second World War, sited above the Thames valley at a strategically dominant bend in the river (**4**). Included amongst the many features are an Iron Age hillfort, smithy and houses, cemeteries, Roman pottery kilns and wells. In 1886 a burial flask and bowl were excavated 100 yards north of the church (TQ6881).
Jones, MU, et al, Antiquaries Journal (1963) 48(ii), 210. Jones, MU, EAH (1973) 5, 6. VCH Essex (1963) iii, 162. Jones,MU, Panorama(1980) 23,47. Clark,A, English Heritage Archaeological Report, Excavations at Mucking, (1993) vols 20, 21.

100. Navestock, Fortification Wood★.
OS map 167. TQ 5598. 1km (0.6 mile) east
of Navestock church, south of Dudbrook
Road.

Four acres are enclosed by a bank and
ditch, with a pond at the south end.
*Gould, IC, Trans EAS (1903) ns, viii,
327. VCH (1903) i, 279. Hore, SC, Essex
Naturalist (1894) 8,222.*

**101. Nazeingbury, Great Blacklands
field.** *OS* map 166. TL3907. West of
Nursery Road, 500m north of its junction
with Nazeing Road.

Here was a late Iron Age (50 BC-AD 50)
farm at which rectangular and circular
buildings were excavated in 1975 and
1976. Animal bones such as ox, sheep,
pig and deer found in a midden show
the likely diet of the farmer. Weaving
is evidenced by the finding of loom-
weights. A bronze coin of Cunobelin
(died *c.*AD 40), leader of the Trinovantes
tribe, was recovered. The earlier farm
buildings seem to have been destroyed by
a fire and were replaced by the Romano-
British farm. The drainage ditches were
dug 120 Roman feet or one *actus* or furrow
apart, suggesting the fields were ploughed
rather than purely pastoral. Wells were
sunk to give a water supply; they were
made from hollowed-out tree trunks cut
into sections, each tapered to fit into the
next. Roofing tile and brick from a nearby
building had fallen into the well. The
farm seems to have fallen into decay by
the third century, and the land was used
later as a Saxon cemetery from which 186
burials were recorded. As most were of
females this may have been a nunnery.
Radiocarbon dating suggests burials from
the seventh century AD.
Huggins, PJ, EAH (1978) 10, 29.

102. Newport★. Great or Leper Stone.
OS map 154. TL 521349. On the east side
of the Great Chesterford-Cambridge Road
north of the public house at north end of
Newport.

This large stone brought here by glacial
action may have been a Neolithic/Bronze
Age monument mirroring standing stones
found in Cornwall, Wessex and elsewhere
(See also Stansted, chapter 4). Being poor
in stone, such survivals in the county are
rare, though timber monuments (which
have not survived) may have had a similar
purpose. In a private garden (Shotgrove
House, TL 526351) a flat-topped earthen
mound 4m high, 13x10m at the summit,
may be a Roman burial mound (or an
ornamental garden feature).
*Rudge, L, Pagan Stones & Essex Churches,
Essex Countryside (1957) vol 5, xix. Andrews,
D, et al, EAH (1989) 20, 84. Essex Sites &
Monuments Record (County Hall) No 225.*

103. Ockendon, South★. *OS* map 177.
TQ 6083. 'The Mount', 200m north-east
of The Hall.

The barrow 150ft in diameter and 17ft
high produced Roman pottery including
a *mortarium* and the rim of an Iron Age
vessel. At TQ582831 a first century AD
Romano-British site.
*Thompson, MW, Trans EAS (1945-60) ns
xxv, 271. Barton, KJ, Thurrock Local History
Society Journal, (1961), 6,54. Chaplin, RT,
Brooks, RB, Trans EAS (1966) third series,
2(i), 83.*

104. Orsett. Causewayed enclosure. *OS*
map 177. TQ 653806. 1.5km (0.9 mile)
north-east of Chadwell St Mary, 700m
south of Orsett Cock A13 flyover.

Overlooking the Thames valley, an oval
enclosure surrounded by three concentric
ditches was excavated in 1975 (**colour**

plate 7). The innermost ring was about 80-95m in diameter. There was a space about 35m between inner and middle rings, and 10m between middle and outer rings. Within the middle ditch was a trench which probably contained a timber palisade. The ditches were crossed at three places by earthen causeways. The south-east side of the rings was interrupted by a rectangular ditched enclosure. The enclosure dates to the Neolithic (about 2500 BC). Uses of similar monuments found in Wiltshire, Dorset, Oxfordshire, etc suggest a stockade or tribal meeting centre. The Orsett causewayed enclosure was the first shown to have a palisade. There was probably a Neolithic settlement 800m to the south-west. In the Early Iron Age (700-350 BC) the southern part was occupied by huts. Within the enclosure was found a $1\frac{1}{2}$in long bronze fibula pin with a six-coil spring (to pin a garment), dating to the Late Iron Age (first century BC-first century AD). Thereafter it reverted to grazing until it was used as a Saxon cemetery.

Hedges, JD, Buckley DG, Proceedings of the Prehistoric Society (1978) 44,219

104. Orsett Cock (Public House) Iron Age enclosure. *OS* map 177. TQ654813. Immediately south-west of Barrington's Farm on the west side of the old Bulphan and Brentwood road A128, in the north-west angle of this road with the old Stanford-le-Hope-Grays road A1013. The shifting of the old Bulphan and Brentwood road westwards and building of a roundabout here in 1960 damaged the western side. The site was further engulfed about 1982 when the new A13 flyover was built north of the older Stanford-Grays Road A1013.
A triple ditched Late Iron Age/early Roman double rhomboidal enclosure 140x80m

contained Iron Age spearheads (?as a ritual deposit). The enclosure was divided across the middle by a shallow east-west ditch. Subsequent occupation included Roman pottery kilns. Interpreted as a native Romano-British farmstead (**44**).
Rodwell W, EAH (1974) 6, 13. Hedges, J, Buckley, D, Britannia (1978) 44, 224. Toller HS, Britannia (1980) 11, 35. Milton,B, EAH (1987) 18,16. Carter, GA, East Anglian Archaeology (1999) 86. Sealey, PR, in Bedwin, O (ed), The Archaeology of Essex, Essex County Council (1996), p58.

105. Panfield. OS map 167. TL 7426. East of Great Priory Farm.
A Romano-British villa from which flue-tiles have been recovered.
Rodwell, W. in Todd, M (ed) (1978) Studies in the Romano-British Villa. Leicester University, p 31.

106. Pleshey. Plesheybury Roman villa. OS map 167. TL 6614. $\frac{3}{4}$km (half a mile) west of Pleshey village.
In 1750 human bones, a coffin, a glass urn containing cremated ashes and a mosaic floor were found with a brick vault, 3ft square, on the south side of the road in Stitch Field, indicating a Roman cemetery and possible villa. Of reasonably comfortable status, the villa may have been the home of an affluent Romano-British farmer.
VCH Essex (1963), iii, 166. Williams, F, British Archaeological Reports (1977) 42,1. Rodwell, WJ in Todd, M, (ed,) Studies in the Romano-British Villa (1978), 11. Medlycott, M, Historic Towns Survey, Essex County Council, 1998

107. Purfleet, Thurrock. OS map 177. TQ 5779, TQ 5678. Bluelands Quarry north of North Road, west of Stonehouse

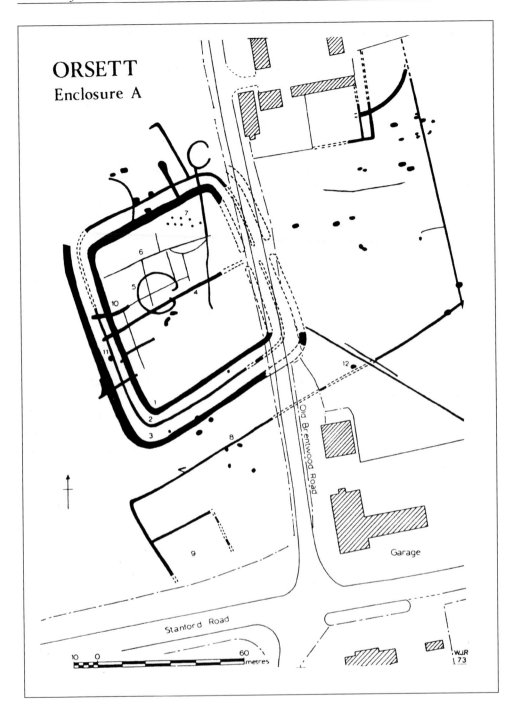

44   *Triple-ditched enclosure at Orsett (after Rodwell, 1974)*

Lane. Greenlands Quarry, south of North Road, west of Stonehouse Lane.

Excavation produced Palaeolithic, Mesolithic and Neolithic flint tools deposited in an old branch of the River Thames, scrapers, cutting tools and handaxes (Acheulian type). Earlier flint implements were found at Globe Pit, Little Thurrock, TQ6378, (of Clactonian industry) dating to about 320,000 years old.

Bridgland, DR, et al, Proceedings of the Geological Association (1993) 99,315. Palmer S, EAH (1975) 7, 1. Wymer JJ, Palaeolithic Sites of East Anglia (1985) Geo Books, Norwich, p307-311.

108. Rainham. OS map 177. TQ 521823. Bridge Street, south bank of Ingrebourne river (Tesco petrol station).

A brushwood trackway surviving in the bank silts had been laid over an area of marsh; it was made of overlapping bundles of coppiced alder cut with a metal tool, axe or adze, dated to the Early/Middle Bronze Age (2000-1000 BC).

Meddens, F, London Archaeologist (1990) 6(ix) 242. Meddens, F, (1995) Current Archaeology, 143, 412.

108. Rainham. Iron Age enclosure. OS map 177. TQ 548821. 5 km (3 miles) east of A13 Dovers Corner, 200m east of Launders Lane, 500m south of the watercourse. In 1977-81, on a gravel spur overlooking the Thames, excavations revealed a Late Bronze Age (eighth-seventh centuries BC) cremation cemetery containing burials in urns placed in pits. Two hundred metres to the south-west was a Late Iron Age (50 BC-AD 50) square enclosure surrounded by triple ditches (and banks), measuring 78x84m, enclosing 1,360 square metres. The entrance faced east. There were probably earthen ramparts within the bank, and a wooden palisade on top. A well, 2m deep, was sited in the south of the enclosure. The strength of the defences and the small area suggests the enclosure was a place of defendable refuge rather than a settlement.

Passmore Edwards Museum, Essex Jounal (1982) 17(ii), 6. Greenwood, P, London Archaeologist (1982) 4(vii), 185.

108. Rainham, old football ground. OS map 177. TQ 523819. South of Wennington Road, east of Viking Way, east of the station and Ferry Lane.

Pottery dating from the Early Bronze Age (c.2000 BC), Iron Age and Roman period shows activity here over more than 2000 years.

Costello, MP, EAH (1997) 28, 93.

109. Rawreth. Map 178. TQ 7793. London Road, A127 (verges), $2\frac{1}{4}$km (1.4 miles) south-east of Wickford church, 300m west of Chichester Hall.

A Romano-British farm dating to the third and fourth centuries and continuing into the early Saxon period was found in 1968. At least one timber building was enclosed by ditches (and banks). Pottery finds suggested it was reasonably affluent.

Drury, PJ, EAH (1977) 9,20.

110. Rayne. OS map 167. TL 7122. Junction of Rayne bypass and former A120 to Rayne, west of Broadfields Farm.

A farm occupied this, near to Roman Stane Street, (Colchester-Great Dunmow) site from the first century AD. It may be close to a villa, and part of an estate. Coins of the emperors Gallienus, Postumus, Septimius Severius and Faustina the Younger were

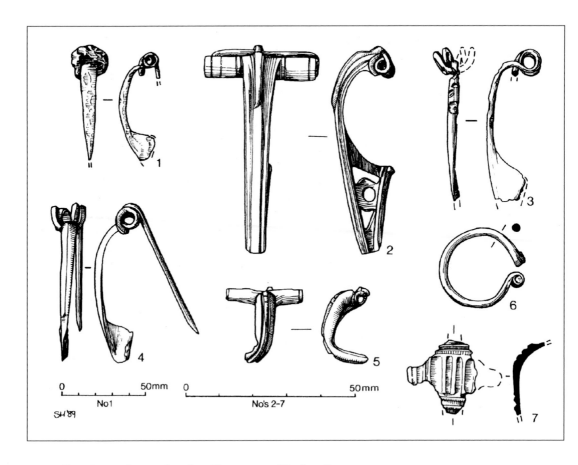

45   *Iron and copper brooches, First century AD, from Rayne*

found together with a ring, a glass flagon and copper-alloy brooches (**45**).
Smoothy, MD, London Archaeologist (1988) 23(iii), 59. Smoothy, MD, EAH (1989) 20, 1.

111. Redbridge, Romford. *OS* map 177. TQ 464910. 2km (1.2 miles) north of Goodmayes Hospital, 400m NW of Hainault Farm, west of Hainault Road, 300m south of its junction with Forest Road.

In one of two Bronze Age ring-ditch enclosures (?once barrows) were an urn containing a human cremation and another cremation not in an urn. Ash, cremated bone and charred timber from the second barrow suggested a pyre. Close by was found a Middle Bronze Age bronze palstave axehead (**19**) and a late Bronze Age timber post structure (?shrine/hut) with large amounts of pottery in a pit. Other barrow remains indicate this was a Bronze Age cemetery, the site of which was used again in the Late Iron Age/Roman period for cremations in urns.
Gibson, S et al, London Archaeologist (1999) vol 9, suppl 1, 19.

112. Ridgewell. OS map 155. TL 7340. West of Ridgewell — Great Yeldham road, 500m south-west of Ridgewell.

A Roman villa consisted of three wings around a court. On the north side was a veranda with a tessellated pavement 60ft long and 9ft wide, with six column bases 3ft square, 7ft apart, which may have supported timber columns.

Neville, RC, Trans EAS (1858) old series i, 197. VCH Essex (1963) iii, 170. Rodwell, W, Roman Essex (1975), Colchester Borough Council.

113. Rivenhall★. OS map 168. TL8318. From the northbound A12 north of Witham, signposts for Silver End. In the churchyard.

Roman villa. In 1848, east of the church, a Celtic bronze mirror with an etched back was found, and in 1971 the west wing of a large villa which extended beneath the chancel was discovered. Building I faced a courtyard with a large central room and a range of rooms enclosed on the north side of the yard. Building II (partly under the church) is 182ft (55m) long; it has an east-facing corridor backed by a subsidiary range of rooms. The walls are of coursed, mortared flints with painted plaster, some highly decorated with birds, and the floors are of black and white *tesserae*. The villa, built AD 70-80, was the residence of a well-to-do native Briton or a Roman official.

VCH Essex (1963), iii. Rodwell, W and K, Britannia (1973), iv,115. Rodwell, W, Roman Essex (1975) Colchester Borough Council. Rodwell, W, in Todd, M (ed), Studies in the Romano-British Villa, Leicester Univ (1978), 29. Rodwell, W, Antiquaries Journal (1973), 53. Rodwell, W and K, Council forBritish Archaeology Res Reps (1985) 55; (1993) 80. Clarke, R. EAH (2004) 35, 26.

113. Rivenhall End. OS map 168. TL 846167. 800m east of junction A12 with Rivenhall-Great Braxted road, 200m west of River Blackwater, 30m south-east of A12 at Colemans Farm, in a field named 'Lowes' (Old English *hlaw*=barrow).

Excavated in 1986 was an oval enclosure 49x16m with a continuous surrounding double-ditch. The ditch was 1.7m deep and 2m wide at its top. It may have had a central mound or a central flat area for burial practices. The enclosure was dated to the Neolithic (about 2000 BC) from finds of pottery, scrapers and blades. Rivenhall End is one of over 12 similar burial enclosures, mostly sited near rivers or estuaries. *Buckley, DG, Major, H, Milton, B, Proceedings of the Prehistoric Society (1988) 54, 77.*

114. Rochford. OS map 178. TQ874908. At Rochford Hospital, immediately south-east of the junction of Ashingdon Road with Dalys Road.

Roman building material suggest the remains of a major Roman building ?villa. *Medlycott, M, Historic Towns Survey (1998), Essex County Council. Essex Journal (1977) 12(iv), 96.*

115. Romford, Havering. OS map 177. TQ5185. Lower Palaeolithic handaxes and other flint flakes were retrieved during gravel extraction near to the Thames. At TQ 493892, north of A12 between it and the west end of Marlborough Road (off Mawney Road), excavations produced an early Mesolithic site, a sixth century BC fortified settlement about 100m in diameter, an early Roman road with a building beside it and a late Iron Age or early Roman (50 BC-AD 100) four-sided enclosure surrounded by up to three ditches to which the road led.

153

*Couchman, CR, EAH (1979) 11, 32.
Greenwood, P, London Archaeologist (1989)
7(iii),74.*

116. Runwell. *OS* map 167. TQ7694.

In the nineteenth century, three fields to the south of the road from Runwell to Woodham, a stone coffin $8\frac{1}{2}$ ftx$2\frac{1}{2}$ ft was uncovered dating to the Roman period. It contained the bones and tooth of a middle-aged man. Excavations along the route of the new A130 showed Middle Iron Age stockades, roundhouses and cremation burials.

*Roberts, E, Trans EAS (1863) old series ii, 69.
Dale, R, EAH (2005) 36, 10.*

117. Saffron Walden. *OS* map 154. TL 534384. Gibson Close.

On rising ground above the River Slade, ditches on the west and south some 480 and 500ft long, south of Abbey Lane, mark the medieval town enclosure, possibly dug in the thirteenth century. In the south-west corner, in the area of Gibson Close, (named after the landowner when excavated in 1876), was a cemetery which yielded Romano-British and Anglo-Saxon burials. It seems probable that there was a Romano-British settlement west of the present town. The name 'Walden' (Anglo-Saxon for 'Valley of the Britons') is evidence of an enclave of Romano-Britons living here into Saxon times. A catapult bolt suggests a Roman military fort. A Neolithic skull from a female was found in the old river bed of the Cam on the Audley End estate. [Material in Saffron Walden Museum].

Maynard, G, Essex Naturalist (1914) 17, 244. Bassett, SR, Saffron Walden to AD 1300, Chelmsford Archaeological Trust, 1982. Ravetz, A, et al, Trans EAS (1962) third series, 1, 141. Smith, HE, Trans EAS (1884) ns, 2, 311.

118. St Osyth. *OS* map 168. TM 1217, TM 1117. 1km (0.6 mile) south of Martins Farm. Two Romano-British stone buildings with a tessellated pavement (?villa) and a timber building 11x13ft with a cobbled floor.

VCH Essex (1963) iii, 176. Blake, B, Trans EAS (1965) third series, i, 259. Farrands, RH, Colchester Arch Gp Ann Bull (1981) 24, 24. At TM 1315, a causewayed enclosure, pond barrow, MIA settlement. EAA (2007) 117.Essex Jnl, (2003) 38(2) 39.

119. Shelley. *OS* map 167. TL5505. On Shelley Common, west of the church.

Tumuli up to 9m in diameter of possible Bronze Age, Roman or Saxon date.

Lawson, AJ, Priddy, D, EAA (1981), 33, 89. Milton, B, EAH (1982) 14, 117.

120. Shoebury, North. *OS* map 188. TQ 929859. Supermarket site, north of Poynters Lane, south of the church and Shoebury Hall Farm. (**colour plate 8**). Two unurned cremation burials of a child and a woman dated *c.* 1855–1100 BC, Middle Bronze Age enclosures and pits were excavated. Iron Age storage pits or wells and three ovens or kilns with clay fragments including a pedestial were found. A field system dated to the late Roman period.

Crowe, KL, EAH (1992) 23, 115. Wymer, J, and Brown, N, East Anglian Archaeology (1995) 75. Brown, N, EAH (1984-5) 16, 100.

121. Shoeburyness★. *OS* map 178. TQ 939845. Iron Age fort. At south end of Shoeburyness High Street and Gunners Park. Rampart Street marks the northern line of an embanked and ditched enclosure. The western rampart and ditch 40ft wide, just south-west of Chapel Road, and the southern rampart and ditch, just east of

Warrior Square Road, are visible. The eastern rampart has been eroded by the sea. Dated to the Iron Age/Romano-British with roundhouses, hearths and salt-manufacture, perhaps similar to that at Gun Hill, West Tilbury, qv, though it is now known as Danish Camp. Dating to about 10,500 BC, a stone blade (now in Colchester Museum) was found on the beach.

Laver, H, Trans EAS (1898) ns vi, 97. VCH Essex(1903) 1, 286. Jacobi, RM, in Bedwin, O, (ed), The Archaeology of Essex, Essex County Council (1996) p10.

122. Southchurch. Map 178. TQ 9085. North of the railway.
A hoard of 48 bronze pieces including knives, axes, spearheads and swords is now in Colchester Castle Museum.
Davies, DG, in Burgess, C et al, British Archaeological Reports (1979) 67, 166. Laver, H, Trans EAS (1898) ns 6, 173.

123. Southend. OS map 178. TQ 9188. Fox Hall, west of the Southchurch-Little Wakering road. The edge of a settlement dating from about 600-500 BC had cattle corrals and field boundaries, with remains of sheep, horse, ox, pig and red deer antler. The salt marsh offers good grazing. Loom-weights suggested a weaving industry close by. A greensand saddle quern had been traded from Kent. Prittlewell IA camp occupied 8 acres. At Cherry Orchard Lane, Prittlewell, TQ8787, a Roman cemetery.
EAH (1995) 26, 24. Essex Jnl (1977) 12(iv), 96. Trans Southend Antiq Hist Soc (1930) 2 (i), 29.

124. Stansted. OS map 167. TL 5322. The Airport.
The proposal in 1985 to enlarge the airport allowed an exceptional opportunity to carry out archaeological survey over 600 hectares (1,500 acres) of Essex. Before the survey just four sites were known, afterwards over 25. By about 800 BC, there was a Bronze Age settlement with huts and a cattle droveway. By 50 BC there was an Iron Age village containing several round timber houses and a granary around a central building, possibly a shrine, all surrounded by a ditch, 80x80m (**colour plate 32**). Near the 'shrine' were found brooches and an onyx ring-stone carved with the Greek hero Diomedes. A hoard of 51 potin coins had been buried in the gully of one of the houses by 40 BC. Of the Roman period were found five bronze vessels, two jugs, a glass bowl and cup and a Samian dinner service made near Lyons, France around AD 140, all with a cremation burial (**colour plate 19**). Nearby with a lady's burial were a bronze mirror, a perfume container and a pair of sandals.
Archaeology at the Airport,Stansted, English Heritage (1990). Brooks, H, Current Archaeology (1989) 10, 322, Essex Jnl (1989) 24, 6. Havis, R, Brooks, H, The Stansted Project 1985-1991, EAA (2004), 107. Cooke, N. Huntergatherers. Framework Arch mono 2 (2008)

125. Stansted Mountfichet. OS map 167. TL5224.
Under the churchyard at Stansted Hall, a Romano-British villa.
VCH Essex (1963) iii, 181 Rodwell, W, in Todd, M, (1978) Studies in the Romano-British Villa, Leics Univ, p31.

126. Stanway. OS map 168. TL 9522. A Romano-British villa.
VCH Essex (1963) iii, 182. Rodwell, W (1975) Roman Essex, Colchester Borough Council, p20.

127. Stapleford Abbotts. *OS* map 177. TQ 5194. East of Stapleford Abbotts-Lambourne Road.

A bronze palstave axe (*see* **19**) weighing 267g, 14cm long, the blade 5.3cm wide, which would have been hafted, dated to the Middle Bronze Age about 1500 BC.
Brown, N, EAH (1996) 27, 305.

128. Stebbing Green. *OS* map 167. TL 6923. North of road junction of road to Stebbing Green from A120.

Roman malt house and villa. Building 1 was thatched or shingle-roofed; a dog was buried under the floor. Building 2 contained the base of a timber or lead tank (now gone) which may have been used for soaking grain. The floor was cobbled and there were three pairs of flues. Pieces of millstone grit suggested a milling industry. The building was interpreted to be a malthouse, preparing mead for the villa or the native estate workers. A villa 200m north-west of the malthouse (TL6923), dating from the early second to end of the fourth century, was excavated in 1947. It had three or four rooms fronting to the south onto a corridor, with one or two crosswings. Excavations produced window glass, blue and white wall plaster, floor tesserae (small stone cubes), an iron key and a copper alloy brooch. Another villa with bathhouse and courtyard has been recorded north-west of Yew Tree Farm (TL6824).
VCH Essex (1963) iii, 183. Bedwin, O, EAA (1988), Occasional paper 6. Essex County Council. Britannia (1978) 9, 452.

129. Steeple Bumpstead. *OS* map 154. TL 7143. 200 yards north of Watsoe Bridge.

A Roman encampment.
VCH Essex (1963) iii, 59.

130. Stifford. *OS* map 177 TQ 595800. Ardale School, north-west of Clock House Lane.

An unenclosed settlement stood here at the lowest fording point over the Mar Dyke in about 200 BC. About 50 BC rectangular enclosures were dug with ditches (and banks). The houses were of chalk cob and wattle, and the dead were buried in a small cemetery to the south. The settlement seems to have gone out of use around AD 150 but the ford was still recognised by the Saxons who called it *Stig-ford* (path-to-the-ford).
Wilkinson, TJ, East Anglian Archaeology (1988) 42, 24.

131. Stock★. *OS* map 167. TQ 6999. South side of Mill Lane, off Billericay to Chelmsford road.

A bank and hedge define the south side of a four-sided enclosure in which Romano-British pottery has been found. This may have been a small settlement (? farmstead) or a cattle enclosure.
VCH Essex (1963) iii, 184. Eddy, MR, EAH (1980) 12, 57.

132. Stumble, Goldhanger. *OS* map 168. TL 9007. North shore of Blackwater estuary.

South of the salt marsh were found 11 oak and hazel poles about 3m long between which had been woven a lattice of thin oak branches. This 'hurdle' was radiocarbon dated to about 516-390 BC when it had formed a bridge across a marshy area on the foreshore.
Wilkinson, TJ, East Anglian Archaeology (1995), 71, 150.

133. Sturmer★. *OS* map 154. TL 688443. ⅗ km (0.4 mile) north-west of Red Lion Inn, 30m south of Cambridge/Bury St

Edmunds roundabout, Haverhill bypass.
A round barrow about 6ft (2m) high and 150ft (50m) diameter, formerly dated as Romano-British from a nearby coin hoard and Roman road, is now interpreted as a Bronze Age bowl barrow (**colour plate 4**).
VCH Essex (1963) iii, 185. Lawson, AJ et al, East Anglian Archaeology (1981) 12,105. Abbott,C, EAH (1998) 29,294.

134. Takeley. OS map 167. TL 5521. 1km (0.6 mile) east of the church.
In 1849 a human skeleton was found with a wooden chest measuring 3x1ft and having a brass hasp (Roman).
VCH Essex (1963) iii, 185.

135. Thaxted. OS map 167. TL 6133. North-west of Boyton End.
Surface finds suggest a Romano-British villa.
VCH Essex (1963) iii, 187. Rodwell, W, in Todd, M (1978) Studies in the Romano-British Villa, Leics Univ, p31.

136. Thurrock. OS map 177. TQ 6680. 1½km (0.9 mile) north-west of East Tilbury station (Rainbow Wood).
Excavations at gravel quarries produced several postholes of a building 2.9m square interpreted as a granary, and Darmsden-Linton type pottery (see Glossary) dating from 400-200 BC.
Potter, TW, EAH (1974) 6, 1. Proc Prehist Soc (2006) 72, 21. Levallois Site.

137. Tilbury (West), Gun Hill. OS map 177. TQ 6578.
On a gravel spur overlooking the Tilbury floodplain two rectangular enclosures, surrounded by a bank and ditch. Excavations from 1969 showed field boundary ditches dating from about

800 BC (**46**). On the summit of the hill, three massive timber posts had been sunk 1.75m into the ground, the postholes packed with gravel, and in the bottom were some teeth from the head of an ox; these may have been a monument which would have been visible from several miles around. The smaller (eastern) enclosure, B, constructed about 100 BC has been explained as a stock pen. It was approached by a droveway track from the north, which crossed Turnpike Lane and continues north of Muckingford Road to High House (TQ657793). The larger (western) enclosure, A, dating from about AD 50, measuring 62m east-west by *c.*55m north-south, seems to be a military defence though whether a defence against the Roman invasion or by a Roman corps as a protective encampment is unclear. Its entrance was from the east through the earlier enclosure. As the enclosure ditches silted up in the latter years of the first century AD, they were used as a pottery kiln factory. Thereafter the site was ploughed over. A Saxon house was found north-east of the two enclosures, which may have been part of a village, the precursor of West Tilbury.
Drury PJ, Rodwell W, EAH (1973) 5,48.

138. Tollesbury. OS map 168. TL 9481. Rolls Farm.
Bronze Age trackway. On the Blackwater estuary foreshore was found a brushwood bundle 1.9x0.5m with branches and a twiggy infill of hazel, oak and field maple. It had lain in a depression in the creek over a wet or muddy hollow and was dated to 1000-850 BC. Under the churchyard (TL 956104) is the site of a Romano-British villa. *Wilkinson, TJ, East Anglian Archaeology (1995) 71, 145. VCH Essex (1963) iii, 192.*

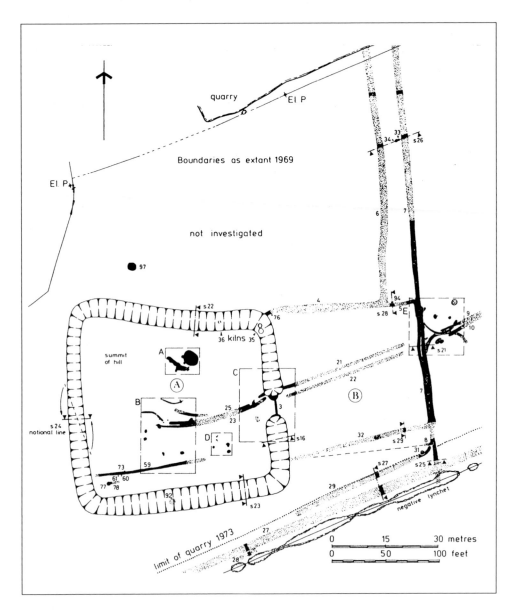

46   *Iron Age and Roman enclosures (A, B) and 'droveway' (6 ,7), West Tilbury*

139. Tolleshunt Knights. OS map 168. TL 9315. Barn Hall.

A Romano-British villa from which tessellated pavements have been recorded. *VCH Essex (1963) iii, 192.*

140. Upminster. OS map 177. TQ 563831. Hunts Hill Farm, Upminster-Aveley Road

Double-post ring houses and Bronze Age pottery, round houses dating to about 300 BC, and a later four-sided banked and ditched enclosure of about 100 BC were excavated up to 1996. Roman wells, some with timber lining, and large amounts of Roman pottery have been found at the quarry.

Greenwood, P, EAH (1995) 26, 251 and (1997) 28, 221.

141. Vange. OS Map 178. TQ 716882. Swan Mead School, north-east of junction of Clay Hill Road with Church Road.

In 1953 excavations produced from a single deposit (perhaps originally in a bag) a hoard of bronze axes (**47**), spearheads, a hammer, an adze, sickle, gouges, ingots and sword blades, in all 174 pieces. Only three other adzes of a similar type in this country are known. They date from about 1000-700 BC and may have been lost, deposited as a ritual offering or abandoned. [Southend and Colchester Museums].

Brown, N, EAH (1998) 29, 1.

142. Waltham Abbey, Town Mead. OS map 166. TL 3800.

A hoard of an Iron Age blacksmith's tools was recovered from the former course of the River Lea in 1967, including tongs, an anvil, hammers and poker, a sword and a linchpin. It has been dated *c.*25 BC-AD 43. Several of the tools have been deliberately bent making it likely that they were cast into the river as a ritual offering to the gods.

Sealey, PR. in Bedwin, O (ed) The Archaeology of Essex, Essex County Council (1996). Manning WH, in Oddy, W (ed) British Museum Occasional Paper No 17, p87.

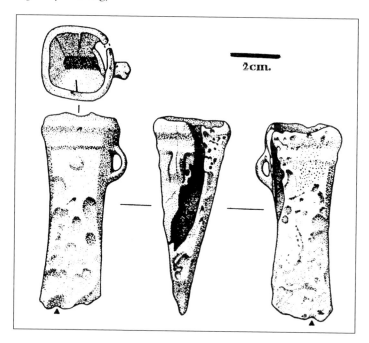

47 *Late Bronze Age socketed axe from Vange*

2cm.

142. Waltham Holy Cross, Fishers Green. OS map 166. TL3600.

Human activity has been dated by the radiocarbon method to around 7,000 years ago. A 'toothed' antler point was found beside a gravel pit in 1974. *Hedges, REM, et al, Archaeometry (1989) 31(ii), 207. Jacobi, R, in Bedwin, O(ed), The Archaeology of Essex, Essex County Counci (1996), p13.*

142. Waltham Holy Cross, Sewardstone Road. OS map 166. TQ 3898. 3.2km (2 miles) south of Waltham Abbey at Northfield Garden Nurseries.

A probable Roman farm excavated in *c.*1970 revealed a coin of Emperor Constantius (AD 324-37), beakers, bowls, flagons, jars and a bronze brooch. The farm seems to have been abandoned in the fourth century AD. *Huggins, RH, EAH (1978) 10,174.*

143. Walton-on-Naze★. OS map 169. TM2623. Cliffs and beach, The Naze to Stone Point.

Fossil bones including elephant dating to a warm phase in the Wolstonian stage have been recovered since the thirteenth century. Flint punches, burins and points have been eroded from the beach, dating to the Mesolithic, and reported to museums for recording. *George, WH, Essex Field Club Newsletter (1997) 20, 3. Lucy, G, Essex Rock (1999), Essex Rock & Mineral Society. Jacobi, RM, Council for British Archaeology Research Reports (1980) 34, 20.*

144. Wanstead. OS map 177. TQ 4187. Wanstead Park, north-west of Heronry Pond.

In 1715 a pavement with a Racchaeus mosaic was uncovered, with a roof tile and a brass coin of Valens (AD 364-78). *VCH Essex (1963) iii, 198.*

144. Wanstead Flats. OS map 177. Around TQ 4088.

Handaxes and Levallois flint flakes (see Glossary) have been found. [British and London Museums]. *Wymer, J, Palaeolithic Sites in East Anglia (1985) Geo books, p293.*

145. Wendens Ambo, near Saffron Walden. OS map 154. TL 5136. Beside M11 motorway.

A small Iron Age hamlet with at least two round houses, cooking hearths, bones (mainly beef) from meals refuse, and a probable stock compound here dates to about 200 BC. Nearby (TL5136) is a Roman villa, which was excavated in 1853. It had a double corridor, underfloor heating system (hypocaust), plastered walls painted white with a red border with an apse-shaped dining room. An infant had been buried in a room east of the apse, and two more under the apse. Outside were corn-drying kilns and a granary. The finds are in Cambridge University Museum. *Britannia (1972) iii, 335 & (1975) vi, 265. Hodder, IA and Halstead, P, Archaeology of the M11 (1982) vol2, pp 4-64*

146. West Bergholt, Chitts Hill. Bronze Age cemetery. OS map 168. TL 9626. 700m south of West Bergholt village, 250m south-east of Chitts Hill bridge, south of the River Colne.

Seven circular ditches (?formerly with central mounds) were investigated. Cremation burials in urns, some upright, some inverted were found within and between the ringditches. Ten cremations were found without urns. Five cremations were of children. Neolithic (and possibly Mesolithic) flints were excavated, representing scrapers, blades and (cutting) flakes. The pottery resembles that of the Ardleigh cemetery, qv, dating to the Middle Bronze Age (about 1500-1000 BC). About 50 BC a triangular enclosure with bank and ditch was dug, using Gryme's Dyke as the western boundary. *Crummy, P, EAH (1977) 9, 1. Petchey, MR, EAH (1977) 9, 17.*

147. White Colne. *OS* map 168. TL8729. 1.5km (0.9 mile) south-west of the church from a gravel pit.

8ft (2.5m) below the surface, under a Mesolithic site, a flint bifacial leaf-point blade (Solutrean type, see Glossary) made by modern humans with remains of mammoth, ox, ibex and bison, about 30,000 years ago (Oxygen Isotope stage 3). This securely-dated artefact to the Devensian iceage (from its stratigraphy immediately above Pleistocene faunal remains) is rare evidence for human occupation at this period.
Layard, N, Antiquaries Journal (1927) 7, 513. Wymer, JJ, in Bedwin, O (ed), The Archaeology of Essex, Essex County Council (1996) p8.

148. White Notley. *OS* map 167. TL 7818.

Near the Hall, a stone building complex with flue tiles and painted wall plaster (?villa) dating from the first century AD has been excavated. Near the vicarage, a circular brick tomb 8ft across with a tiled central chamber contained a toilet set, glass and a second century coin.
VCH Essex (1963) iii, 164. Dunnett, R, The Trinovantes, Duckworth, 1975, p 101.

149. Wickford. *OS* map 168. TQ 762937. School, formerly Beauchamps Farm, north of Wickford-Rayleigh road and the railway, now built over.

A villa-farm dating from the Iron Age and Roman period was excavated in 1966-8. A ditched enclosure had an entry from the east and possibly north. The road from the east was metalled 15ft (5m) wide with a flint kerb and side-ditches. Within the enclosure were several timber domestic and agricultural buildings dating to the second-fourth centuries AD and which burned down in the latter part of the fourth. Some of the fine fourth century pottery had been made in the Rettendon kilns. Occupation had begun *c*.300 BC as evidenced by pottery in pits. The foundations of the villa of chalk flints and septaria nodules had been largely robbed out in the twelfth/thirteenth century AD (?for the nearby church or manor house). Several blue-painted timber planks had been preserved in a waterlogged ditch close to three late Roman pedestal pots containing blue, white and red pigment. The villa had had a tiled roof, one tile being impressed with a Christian symbol, plaster and heating flues. Domestic items included glass, coins, ivory pins, a shale bracelet and pewter plate. A dog skeleton was unearthed. Around the villa were a granary and a corn-drying oven.
Rodwell, WJ, Trans EAS (1970) third series, 2(iii), 330. Rodwell, W, Antiquaries Journal (1972), 52, 338.

150. Witham★. Chipping Hill Iron Age fort. *OS* map 168. TL 818153. Centred approximately on the road bridge by the station over the railway; the scarp to the ramparts is best appreciated from Armond Road looking north up across the River Brain.

The construction of the railway cut through several burials and the centre of the fort. In 1844 three Late Iron Age pokers were found, probably a set, part of a ritual burial. Two concentric banks and ditches, constructed in the Middle Iron Age (about 350-50 BC) surround 3.5 hectares (8.7 acres). The circuit follows approximately White Horse Lane, Albert Road, crosses the railway north of the station, The Avenue and Collingwood Road/Guithavon Valley junction. The domestic activity seems to be concentrated on the west and south sides of the fort. Rodwell (1993) holds the fort is, on strategic grounds, unlikely to have been the burh reinforced by Edward the Elder in AD 913 in his battles against the Danes; this may be at Wulvesford (TL8214, recreation ground between Maldon Road and the river).

Lucas, WJ, Trans EAS (1884), ns ii, 208. Spurrell, FCJ, Essex Naturalist (1887) i, 19. Cottrill, F, Antiquaries Journal (1934) 14, 190. Rodwell, W, The Origins of Witham, Oxbow Monograph 26 (1993). Medlycott, M, Witham — Historic Towns Project, Essex County Council, 1998.

150. Witham. OS map 168. TL 810136. Ivy Chimneys, Allectus Way, 2km (1.2 miles) south-west of Newland Street. A banked and ditched enclosure, approximately bounded north-east by Howbridge Road/Spinks Lane, north on Stevens Road, south on Witham Lodge, south-east on Maltings Lane/Town End Field/Wickham Mill west of the stream, in all about 56 hectares (140 acres) (**colour plate 21**).

Excavations in 1970-80 found six round houses and a possible Iron Age temple. The settlement from about 400 BC, enclosed by two or three ditches and bank 3.5m wide surrounded by fields and stock enclosures. About AD 80, two timber buildings, probably part of a Romano-British temple complex, were erected. In the late second century a pond was dug close by, supplied by springs. In the late

third century a large square timber temple, 18x22m, was separated from the pond by a fence. It had a double entrance on the east, and the size of the posts suggests a substantial roofed building. Around the mid-fourth century, the square temple was replaced with a rectangular one 20x10m, to the east of the pond. Two infant burials and a large number of votive offerings were close by. These included carved double-sided soft septaria figurines (?of rustic deities) 10cm high x 8cm wide x 3cm thick (*Frere, 1970*), a bronze female head, coins, 37 palaeolithic axes, gold and silver jewellery and a clay phallus. The axes, regarded as 'thunderbolts' and thousands of years old when deposited, may indicate the worship of Jupiter. By the late fourth century there is evidence of Christian worship. An immersion font and a ?chapel were built on opposite sides of the pond. The font was an octagonal tile basin 60cm tall and 2m wide with a tiled floor set in mortar. The chapel was about 1.9m square with walls of mortared septaria and a tiled floor.

Brooks, RT, Stokes, AH, Essex Journal (1975/6) 10(iv), 107. Turner, R, Ivy Chimneys, East Anglian Archaeology (1999) 88. Frere, SS, Britannia (1970), I, 267. Rodwell, W, (1993) Origins of Witham, Oxbow monograph 26. Medlycott, M,Historic Towns Survey, Essex County Council, 1998. Turner,R, Wymer, J, Antiquaries Journal (1988) 67, 43.

151. Woodford. OS map 177. TQ 4190. M11 motorway slip, 500m west of the River Roding.

Excavated in 1975 were four handaxes lying in their mint condition, dated to the Wolstonian Stage about 250,000 years ago. Nearby were flints which had been crazed in a fire.

Wymer, J, Prehistoric Sites in East Anglia (1985), Geo Books, p298.

152. Woodham Walter. *OS* map 168. TL 8106. Oak Farm.

In 1991, three bronze torcs found by metal detectorists were reported to the British Museum. An excavation revealed pottery and worked flint. They are dated 1200-1000 BC. They consist of twisted bronze rings with a gold alloy (thought to have been worn around the arm) about 38gm in weight and 5cm in diameter [Colchester Castle Museum].

Brown, N, EAH (1992) 23, 113. Meeks, ND, Varndell, GL, EAH (1994) 25, 1.

152. Woodham Walter. *OS* map 168. TL 812081. In the angle formed by Hoe Mill Road and Manor Road, immediately east of Hoe Mill Barns in Brook field.

A rectangular ditched enclosure dating from the Middle Iron Age and another to the west open on the north side dating to the Late Iron Age (abandoned in the second century AD) produced pottery and querns, possibly a 'rite of termination' feast to local gods.

Priddy, D, Buckley, DG, East Anglian Archaeology (1987) 33. Wallace, CR, EAH (1989) 20, 172.

153. Wormingford. *OS* map 168. TL 9333. Wormingford bridge 700m (0.4 mile) north of the church.

A 'mattock' of antler beam perforated at one end for a wooden handle dates from the Mesolithic and was recovered from the river Stour during the building of the bridge. (Also see Bures).

Smith, WG, Essex Naturalist (1898) 10, 312.

154. Wrabness. *OS* map 168. TM 1632 and 1732. On the banks of the River Stour estuary.

In 1701 John Luffkin discovered 'diverse bones of extraordinary bigness... 16ft below the surface of the earth'. Subsequent excavations have produced bones of straight-tusked elephant and mammoth from brick-earth of Pleistocene deposits dating to the Ipswichian interglacial about 120,000 years ago. Also were found bison, hippopotamus, red deer, horse and whale.

Luffkin, J, Philosophical Transactions Royal Society (1701) 22, 924. Christy, M, Essex Naturalist (1907) 15, 102.

Wymer, J, Prehistoric Sites in East Anglia (1985) Geo, p236. George, WH, Essex Field Club Newsletter (1997) 21, 4.

155. Writtle★. Birch Spring, Highwood. *OS* map 167. TL 6202. South-east of the Blackmore-Highwood road.

A four-sided enclosure with a surrounding ditch and bank, entrance from the south-east, occupies about 0.56 hectares (1.4 acres). The ditch is 5-9m wide and the longest side (north-west) 96m long. Dated to the Late Iron Age (50 BC-AD 40) from the pottery. It may have been used for short periods of domestic occupation (loom-weights suggest a weaving industry). A probable Roman trackway (Fryerning, Mapletree Lane, qv) lies 600m south-east.

Gobold, S, EAH (1996) 27, 1.

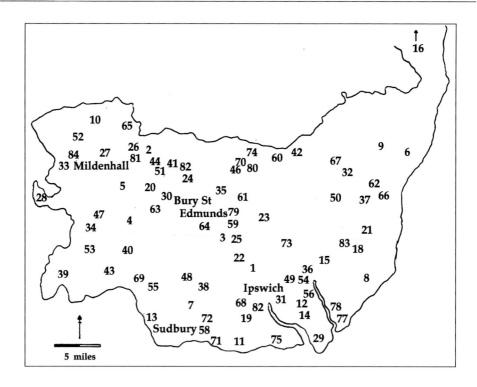

48   Suffolk, Site location map

SOUTH SUFFOLK

1. Barham. *OS* map 156. TM134514. 500m north-west of the church, and in the churchyard.

The site east of the River Gipping was occupied from the third to the beginning of the second millennium, and again, after an apparent gap, about 850 BC from which period a round house 11m in diameter containing Darmsden type pottery (?fifth-third century BC) was excavated.

Martin, E, East Anglian Archaeology (1993) 65, 23.

2. Barnham. *OS* map 144. TL 875787. East Farm, south of the barn.

A flint-tool knapping site was excavated about 1934 and in 1979, dating to the Clactonian Stage (see Glossary). Axes,

scrapers and cores were being made here about 400,000 years ago.

Paterson, TT, Proceedings of the Prehistoric Society of East Anglia (1937) 3, 87. Wymer, J, Prehistoric Sites in East Anglia (1985), Geo Books , p116. Martin, E, PSIAH (1994) 38(ii), 208.Antiquity (1994) 68, 585.

2. Barnham. *OS* map 144. TL 868791. East of the nineteenth-century windmill.

A Bronze Age tumulus 60ft diameter, 6ft high, contained a skeleton, head to the east, buried with legs contracted and arms crossed. Nearby was an incense cup 2.2in high, base diameter 3.7in with a banded decoration. Dated 1700-1400 BC (**49**).

Edwardson, AR, PSIAH (1958) 27(iii), 186.

2. Barnham. *OS* map 144. TL 8777. An Iron Age double-ditched four-sided

49   *Barnham*
      tumulus, plan
      and section

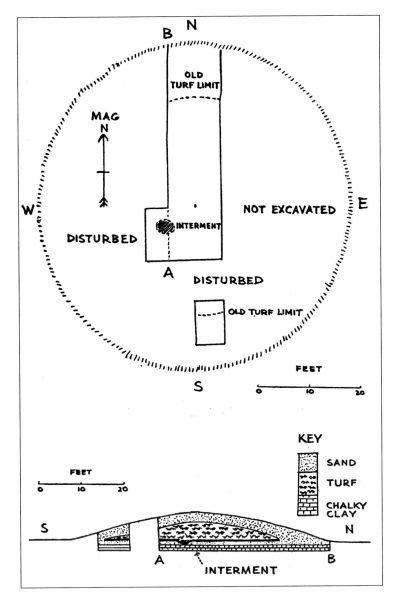

enclosure of about one hectare. The ditches are 7m wide by 3m deep. Carbon-dating shows 180 BC–AD 20. Icenian coins were recovered.

Martin, E, East Anglian Archaeology (1993) 65, 1.

3. Barking. OS map 155. TM0753.
Found near Barking a bronze statuette of Emperor Nero dressed for battle,

18in high, possibly taken as booty from Colchester in the Boudican Revolt of AD 60/61. [In British Museum].

Moore, IE, (1988) Archaeology of Roman Suffolk, Suffolk County Council, p20.

4. Barrow*. Map 155. TL 7664. 500m west of the village south of Barrow-Higham road.

Two iron spear heads resembling Bronze

Age types were excavated from the tumulus
Clarke, RR (1963) East Anglia, Thames & Hudson, p 96.

5. Barton Mills★. Map 154. TL 7172. Beacon Hill.
Excavation of the tumulus has produced a cremation burial and a bone necklace dated to the Bronze Age. From one of four barrows excavated in 1869 was recovered an unburnt contracted skeleton and three flint scrapers.
Cawdor, Earl, Fox, C, Proceedings of the Cambridge Antiquarian Society (1925) 26, 19. Fox, C, Archaeology of the Cambridge Region (1923) p31.

22. Baylham. *OS* map 155. TM1153. See Coddenham.

6. Blythburgh. *OS* map 156. TM 4575. Flint choppers and scrapers of the Neolithic period.
VCH Suffolk (1911) i, 256.

7. Boxford. *OS* map 155. TL 9739. Whitestreet Green.
In 1966 was discovered a Belgic cemetery which contained a female buried with two bronze brooches, the bones of a child and a woman with an iron buckle and two iron brooches, dated ?AD 10-60.
Owles, E, Smedley, N, PSIAH (1968) 31(i), 88.

8. Boyton. *OS* map 169. TM 3747.
In 1835 a Bronze Age gold torc 5in diameter weighing 20oz 4dwt was found. [In British Museum].
Stodart, E, Archaeologia (1836) xxvi, 471. VCH Suffolk (1911) i, 269.

9. Brampton, Westhall. *OS* map 156. TM 4281.
Iron Age hoard of horse tack contained enamelled bronze harness mounts, bridle terret rings and linch pins.
Clarke, RR, East Anglia (1963) Thames & Hudson, p103.

10. Brandon. *OS* map 143. TL 7687. South of Hockwold-cum-Wilton, dredged from Little Ouse river.
A lead plaque (*defixio*), 57x40mm, scratched with a Latin curse 'Whoever whether male slave or female slave whether freedman or freedwoman whether man or woman has committed theft of an iron pan(?) he is sacrificed to Lord Neptune with hazel(?)'.
Hassall, MWC, Britannia (1994) 25, 293. EAA (2004) occ paper 19. Bronze Age Settlement.

11. Brantham. *OS* map 168. TM 1233. Brantham Hall, Marsh Farm.
Three Bronze Age Beaker graves, one of a woman with two infants. Five cremation burials in urns. [In British and Ipswich Museums].
Gilmour, RA, PSIAH (1975) 33(ii), 116.

12. Brightwell★. Map 169. TM 2545. Devils Ring, on Brightwell and Martlesham Heaths.
A Bronze Age barrow cemetery.
Clarke, RR, (1963) East Anglia, Thames & Hudson, p78.

13. Brundon. *OS* map 155. TL 863417. Ballingdon, Brundon, 500m north-west of Sudbury church.
Acheulian flint handaxes and Levallois handaxes dating to the Hoxnian and Wolstonian periods (see Glossary) in the River Stour valley. Bones of horse,

mammoth, lion, bear and giant deer have been recovered. Uranium dated 230,000 to 174,000 years ago.

Wymer, JJ, in Barringer, C (ed) (1984) Aspects of Anglian Prehistory, Geo Books. Wymer, J, Prehistoric Sites in East Anglia (1985), Geo Books, p 198. Moir, JR, Hopwood, AT (1939) Proceedings of the Prehistoric Society, 5, 1.

14. Bucklesham★. OS map 169. TM 2241. Seven Hills.

Between the railway and A45 a barrow cemetery.

Lawson, AJ et al, East Anglian Archaeology (1980) 12, 14.

15. Burgh-by-Woodbridge★. OS map 156. TM 2252. St Botolph's church, Drabs Lane.

Overlooking the River Lark a four-sided double banked and ditched enclosure surrounds 7 hectares. Pottery had been imported from Camulodunum and Gaul of Late Iron Age (50 BC-AD 40) date. In a pit in 1975 the skull of a young man, dog and raven bones were found, suggesting a ritual burial. Later soon after AD 43 a Roman military presence is attested by a *pilum* (spearhead) and *ballista* bolt. A Romano-British villa with tiled roof, hypocaust (underfloor heating) and tessellated floor occupied the site until the end of the fifth century, now a medieval church.

Martin, E, East Anglian Archaeology (1988) 40.

16. Burgh Castle, Norfolk★. OS map 134. TG 475046. 4.8km (3 miles) west of Great Yarmouth. Turn west off Gt Yarmouth-Beccles road, A143, along New Road towards Belton. At the entry to Belton turn right along Step Short and Butt Lane. At the T-junction turn left into Church Lane.

Gariannum, a Roman fort of the Saxon shore, probably built in the third century AD. The east and most of the south and north walls, of flint and lacing courses of brick and tile, are still present, the west having been eroded by the river Yare. Bastions were later added. In all about 6 acres are enclosed.

VCH Suffolk (1911) i, 301. Morris, AJ, PSIAH (1949) 24, 100. Johnson, JS, Roman Forts of the Saxon Shore, 1979. EAA (1983) 20. Martin, EA, (1988) EAA, 40. Maxfield, V, (ed), The Saxon Shore (1989), Exeter. Cleary, ASE, Britannia (1997) 28, 430. Breeze, A, PSIAH (2006) p. 227.

17. Bury St Edmunds. OS Map 155. TL 835644. Westley Road.

About 1850 a human skeleton was uncovered 2.3m below the surface and, in 1882, the frontal and parietal bones of a human skull which was believed to be of Pleistocene date. Handaxes and flakes have been recovered in addition to mammoth molars and an elephant tusk.

Baden-Powell, DFW, and Oakley, KP, Proceedings of the Prehistoric Society (1952) 18, 1. Wymer, J, Palaeolithic Sites in East Anglia (1985) Geo Books, p139.

18. Butley, east of Woodbridge. OS map 156. TM 3651.

A Bronze Age metalworking industry making winged axes, of which a hoard was found.

Clarke, RR (1963) East Anglia, Thames & Hudson, p88.

19. Capel St Mary. OS map 169. TM 0838. West of the church.

A Romano-British villa dates from the first century AD. Excavations in 1938 and 1950 produced glass and mosaic tesserae.

Maynard, G, PSIAH (1950) 25, 209 and (1966) 30, 278 and (1967) 31, 74.

20. Cavenham, Black Ditches★. *OS* map 155. TL 7769 and TL 7672. 700m south-east of Cavenham crossroads and 500m south-west of Icklingham church on Cavenham Heath.

Crossing the Icknield Way, 5½km (3.4 miles) of bank and ditch in two sections run from the River Lark to Risby Poor's Heath. In 1992, excavation produced a Late Iron Age (50 BC-AD 40) pottery rim of a Belgic jar. This appears to be a prehistoric boundary mark. To the east on Risby Poor's Heath and at Cuckoo Hill are several tumuli (at TL787679, TL794684, TL785695).
Caruth, J, 1992, Suffolk County Council Archaeology Service excavation report CAM022.

21. Chillesford★. *OS* map 156. TM 400531. Money Hill, in Tunstall Forest.

Two tumuli. 'Hill' is used in East Anglia for a mound/barrow. Excavation produced an urn 13½in tall, 13½in in diameter, with a whipped cord decoration and a cremation of a male, about 30-40 years old, who had had arthritis in his lower spine [In Ipswich Museum].
Lawson, AJ, et al, East Anglian Archaeology (1981) 12, 13. Owles, E, Smedley, N, PSIAH (1968) 31(i), 108.

22. Coddenham. *OS* map 155. TM 1153. On the east side of the River Gipping at Baylham House Farm. From the B1113 Great Blackenham-Needham Market Road, turn east along Mill Lane just north of the turn-off to Baylham.

Air photography showed two rectangular enclosures (?forts) as crop marks, surrounding the Farm house. The enclosures, one inside the other, are surrounded by ditches on the north, east and south sides with the river on the west.

The outer enclosure has triple ditches, the inner (enclosing 2.43 hectares, 6 acres) quadruple. Limited excavation has produced the base of a masonry wall, Roman pottery and a coin of Commodius (AD 180-92). A bronze statue of Nero suggests a Roman shrine (*Clark, 1963*). At this Romano-British settlement of *Combretovium* five roads converge. At Baylham Mill north of the ford a gravel streak in the field marks the line of the road to Stoke Ash which was excavated in 1953 to show it to be *c.*32ft wide of rammed gravel. The line of the Roman Road is marked by the paddock walkway in the Farm. [Finds in Ipswich and British Museums].
West, SE, Antiquaries Journal (1956) 36, 73. Clark, RR, (1963) East Anglia, Thames & Hudson, pp117, 230. Smedley, N, PSIAH (1968), 28, 91. Martin, E, PSIAH (1989) 37(i), 72. Farrands, RH, Colchester Archaeology Group Annual Bulletin (1979) 22, 10.

23. Creeting St Mary. *OS* map 155. TM 0956. South-east of Stowmarket.

An urn with cord-like decoration contained a cremation, dating to Early or Middle Iron Age.
Clarke, RR, Archaeological Journal (1939) 96, 1.

24. Culford★. *OS* map 144. TL 8471. North of Brockley, a tumulus 'Hill of Health'.
Lawson, W, et al, East Anglian Archaeology (1981), 12, 13.

25. Darmsden. *OS* map 155. TM 1053. Part of a ring ditch 19.1m diameter contained a probable roundhouse 7m diameter with a hearth containing burnt clay at its centre. Pottery was sand-tempered of Middle to Late Iron Age date.

Darmsden-Linton pottery forms a style type of shouldered bowl and jar form with flared rims, flint or sand temper and horizontal line or groove decoration. Dated to the Early Iron Age eighth-fourth centuries BC.

Abbott, C et al, (1996) Excavations at Suffolk 1994, Suffolk County Council, report no 96/26. Martin, E (1999) in Davies, J et al, Land of the Iceni, University of East Anglia, p 74.

26. Elveden. *OS* map 144. TL 8380.

In 1888 was found a two-handled bronze-plated wooden tankard with Celtic medallions of the Late Iron Age.

Evans, AJ, Archaeologia (1890) 52, 351,359. VCH Suffolk (1911) i, 270.

1146 Roman coins including 673 *denarii* and 173 *antoniniani* dated AD152 to AD248 were found in a pot in 1953. Its neck was stuffed with an unusual double-thread plain-weave textile, possibly wool. At TL8080, Brickyard Pit, were found organic lake muds dating to the Late Anglian Ice Age, 400,000 years ago, containing worked biface flint tools.

Briscoe, G. PSIAH (1957) 27(ii), 120. Numismatic Chronicle, 14 (44), 204. Martin, E, PSIAH (1997) 39(i), 92. Proc Prehist Soc (2005) 71, 1.

27. Eriswell★. North of Barton Mills. *OS* map 143. TL 747769. Upper Chamberlains Farm, south-east of farm buildings, 250 yards north-east of B1112.

A partly ploughed-down bowl barrow 90ft diameter, 13in high, surrounded by a circle of chalk soil and a ditch contained four burials, a cremation of a young adult male under an inverted urn, two other inverted urn cremations and an inhumed female skeleton, aged 25-35 years lying south-east-north-west, head to the south-

east, dating to the Bronze Age. Beneath the barrow was Neolithic pottery.

Dymond, DP, PSIAH (1974) 33(i), 1.

28. Exning, Landwade, north of Newmarket. *OS* map 154. TL 6363.

Bronze Age burials dated 1570 +/- 80 bc included an adult male with 5 juveniles and an infant, and an adult female (**50**). At Roman Farm (TL6165), excavations in 1959 showed timber huts of *c*.AD 70 had been replaced *c*.AD 115 by an aisled stone building. A small bathhouse was added later that century. A mosaic floor was laid in the early third century. The buildings were destroyed by fire in the early fourth century.

Martin, E, Denston, CB, PSIAH (1986) 36(ii), 131. Greenfield, E, Journal of Roman Studies (1960) 50, 228.

29. Felixstowe. *OS* map 169. TM 3134.

A hoard of swords and metal, dating from the Bronze Age. On the coast, now eroded but still visible in the eighteenth century, Walton Castle was probably one of the Saxon Shore Forts, built in the third century AD.

Clarke, R.R, (1963) East Anglia, Thames & Hudson, pp89, 126. Johnson, JS, Roman Forts of the Saxon Shore, 1979. Maxfield, V, (ed) The Saxon Shore (1989), Exeter. Cleary, ASE, Britannia (1997) 28, 430.

30. Fornham All Saints. *OS* map 155. TL 8367. North-east of Bury St Edmunds.

Detected from air photography, a cursus monument about 1580m long, aligned roughly north-west/south-east with three direction changes, overlies two ditched enclosures.

St Joseph, JK, Antiquity (1964) 38,290. Hedges, J, Buckley, D, 1980, Springfield Cursus, Essex Co Council occasional paper

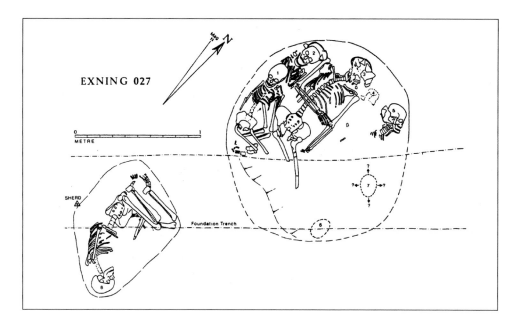

50   *Bronze Age graves at Exning*

no 1. Loveday, R, Current Archaeology (2000) 167, 439. Buckley, DG, Hedges, JD, Brown, N, Proceedings of the Prehistoric Society (2001) 67, The Neolithic Cursus Springfield..

31. Foxhall. OS map 169. TM 2343. East of Ipswich.
Pits 4m long and 1m deep contained Neolithic Grooved Ware pottery (see Glossary). A defended rectangle of 0.3 hectares, 65x55m, enclosed by a bank and ditch containing a single round house overlooks a tributary of the River Deben. The entrance was to the east. At least two buildings lay outside the enclosure. Pottery finds suggest an Early to Middle Iron Age (700-100 BC) date, reinforced by thermoluminescence dates averaging 395 BC +/-110 and 360 BC +/-80. In 1855 at Crag Pit (TM230434) was found a human jaw (now lost) at a depth similar to Palaeolithic flint tools.

The double *foramina* (openings) in the jawbone are a primitive feature. At Pole Hill, TM237443, is a tumulus.
Martin, E et al, PSIAH (1992) 37(iv), 371, 384. Clarke, RR, (1963) East Anglia, Thames & Hudson, p 39.
Spencer, HEP, East Anglian Magazine, April 1965.

32. Framlingham. OS map 156. TM 2862. Kettleburgh road, on spur above River Ore, west of (disused) railway.
Excavations in 1986 produced Iron Age fine ware with top or edge decoration.
Martin, E, East Anglian Archaeology (1993), 65, 59.

33. Freckenham. OS map 154. TL 6672.
In 1998 were found a Bronze Age knife, coins of the Iceni tribe and of Cunobelin, and a coral or enamel La Tène brooch (see Glossary).
Martin, E, PSIAH (1999), 39(iii), 356.

34. Gazeley. *OS* map 154. TL 724673. Pin Farm, 300m north of Icknield Way, on Breckland.

In 1969 was excavated a Bronze Age barrow 60cm high, surrounded by a deep ditch 29m diameter. 7 individuals (3 cremated, 4 inhumed) were found including a 10- to 12-year-old child. Associated were sheep humerus, an amber bead.

Petersen, F, PSIAH (1974) 33(i), 19.

35. Great Barton. *OS* map 155. TL 885653. 1.5km west of East Barton.

A tumulus was called Catteshull ('wild cat hill'), now Cattishall.

Lawson, W, et al, East Anglian Archaeology (1981) 12, 12.

36. Great Bealings. *OS* map 169. TM 249482. South-west of Seckford Hall. [Also Little Bealings].

Neolithic pottery indicates a settlement which was then abandoned to be reoccupied in the Iron Age where spinning was being done in round houses in the unenclosed settlement

Martin, E, East Anglian Archaeology (1993) 65, 41.

37. Hacheston. *OS* map 156. TM 3159.

A large Romano-British settlement. Flint-footed buildings, iron-smelting and pottery kilns have been excavated. Nearby the cremation cemetery. At TM 3157 (A12 junction) was found an oak-lined well 5m deep in which were preserved leather, wood and a metal bucket handle, dating first-second century AD.

Moore, IE (1988) Archaeology of Roman Suffolk, Suffolk County Council, p39. Owles, EJ, PSIAH (1975) 33(ii), 216.

38. Hadleigh. *OS* map 155. TM 0441. Ipswich-Hadleigh railway track, south of Town House Farm.

In 1954-8 a Romano-British villa was partly excavated. It had a mortar floor and a hypocaust.

Rodwell, W. in Todd, M (1978) Studies in the Romano-British Villa, Leicester University, p29. Moore, IE (ed) (1988) The Archaeology of Suffolk, Suffolk County Council, p47 PSIAH 27, 43 and (1961) 28, 91.

39. Haverhill. *OS* map 154. TL 6745.

A hoard of Gallo-Belgic gold coins dated 100-75 BC. (Also see Sturmer, Essex).

Clarke, RR, (1963) East Anglia, Thames & Hudson, p 105.

40. Hawkedon. *OS* map 155. TL 7954. Hawkedon House.

In 1965 was found a Roman bronze helmet. A reversed S stamp on the chin piece suggested it was Etruscan-made. Its heavy weight indicated its use in practice by a gladiator. Possibly booty brought from Colchester after the Boudican Revolt of AD 60/61 [In British Museum].

Painter, KS, PSIAH (1968) 31(i), 57

41. Hengrave. *OS* map 155. TL 816679. Stanchil's Farm.

This was an ancient riverbed before the Anglian Ice Age 470,000 years ago; it contained a black flint flake, possibly made by early *Homo*.

Rose, J, Wymer, J, PSIAH (1994) 38(ii), 119.

42. Hoxne. *OS* map 156. TM 1877. Oakley Pit in a field of Home Farm (now a private residence) on east side of the road to Eye.

In 1797 John Frere of Roydon Hall, Diss, noticed workmen extracting clay for brick-making and uncovered handaxes of which at that time only one was known in Britain (from Kings Cross, London). He dated them to a period 'even beyond that of the present world'. Excavations here from 1896 and in 1970s, beside what was a lake, have shown evidence for a relatively warm (interglacial) period dating from about 400,000 years before present (Oxygen Isotope stage 11) in which grew hazel, oak, elm and alder. Bear, wolf, horse, bison, wild cattle, straight-tusked elephant, giant beaver, rhino and lion shared the land with flint toolmakers of Acheulian industry of black flint and ovate handaxes and flakes, used, as determined by microscope examination of the cutting edge, for animal butchery, bone-chopping, hide-cutting and scraping and wood-wedging and adzing. Smashed elephant bones and a fork tool of antler attest to human activity.

Frere, J (1800) Archaeologia, 13, 204. West, RG, Proc Prehist Soc (1954) 20. Philosophical Trans of Royal Soc (1956) B239, 265. Wymer, JJ, PSIAH (1983), 35 (iii), 169. Wymer, JJ, Palaeolithic Sites of East Anglia (1985) Geo Books, Norwich, p149. Wymer, J, Lower Palaeolithic Occupation of Britain (1999), English Heritage. Brit Arch (2000) 56,8. PSIAH (2002) 40 (2), 226.

42. Hoxne. *OS* map 156. TM 1877.

In November 1992 over 14500 coins including over 500 gold *solidi* dating from the fourth/fifth centuries AD were found by a metal detectionist and reported to the museum. They came from mints in Trier, Arles, Milan, Lyons, Rome, Ravenna and Antioch. The hoard which also contained gold and silver tableware (ladles and spoons inscribed Aurelius Ursicinus and with Christian crosses), necklaces (one inscribed with the wearer's name Juliana), rings, bracelets, an amethyst and garnets had been buried in a wooden chest after AD 407 [British Museum].

Jones, C, Minerva (1993) 4(ii) 3; Bland, R, Minerva (1993) 4(iii), 15. Current Archaeology (1993) 136, 152.
Jones, C, Bland, R, Britannia (1994) 25, 165. The Hoxne Treasure, British Museum, 1993.

43. Hundon. *OS* map 155. TL 7548. 600 yards north-west of Chilton.

In 1928 was found, with a skull, the earliest known copper tanged dagger in Britain, 18.2cm long its tip missing. Early Bronze Age, about 2000 BC [In British Museum].

Moore, N, PSIAH (1973) 32(iii), 274.

44. Icklingham *OS* map 144. TL 7872. South-east of village.

Since the nineteenth century three lead tanks of the Roman period have been found, the last in 1971, 87cm diameter, 37cm high. On the sides, omega, alpha and chi-rho symbols indicate Christian use, dating from about AD 350, possibly as a ritual bath. It was later used in a workshop to hold hinges, nails and saw blades. The site was a cemetery from which 47 burials were analysed; diseases included osteoarthritis, bone infections and fractures. Tesserae suggest the presence of a building ?temple or church. Coins stamped ECE and ECENI show the site was at least at some time before the Roman conquest in Iceni territory. Roman temple bronzes of a cheetah, a face mask and metal figures were found by the farmer on his land. The Christian site was abandoned about AD 420. At London Bottom (TL 7774) from a Late Upper Palaeolithic (Magdalenian, see Glossary) site have been recovered flint scrapers, long blades and borers.

Bunbury, HE, Proceedings Bury & West Suffolk Archaeological Institute (1853) 7, 250.

West, SE, East Anglian Archaeology (1976) 3, 63. Minerva (Jan 1990), p 10. Owles, EJ, PSIAH (1975) 33(ii), 217; (2001) 40 (I), 100. Sturge, WA, Proc Prehist Soc of E Anglia (1912) i, 210. Wymer, J, Palaeolithic Sites in East Anglia (1985), Geo Books, p131.

45. Ipswich, Bobbitshole. OS map 169. TM 1642. Belstead Brook
The 'type-site' for the Ipswichian interglacial stage (see Glossary) during which silt and clay was deposited containing remains of hippopotamus and straight-tusked elephant.
West, RG, Philosophical Transactions of the Royal Society of London B (1957) 241, 1.

45. Ipswich, Bramford Road. OS map 169. TM 140455. To the east of a loop of the River Gipping.
Mousterian handaxes and Levallois flint flakes, blades and leaf points, elephant, rhinoceros, whale and reindeer found here indicate human and animal habitation in Devensian Stage (see Glossary).
Wymer, J, Prehistoric Sites in East Anglia (1985) Geo Books, p213.

45. Ipswich, Belstead Hill. OS map 169. TM 1443. Belstead Hills estate, north of Holcomb Crescent.
In 1958 and in 1970, six gold torcs (neck-rings) were found by a farmer and reported to the museum. They weighed from 858-1044g, of twisted gold with ornamented circular terminals. They were worn by Iron Age nobility and regarded as regalia [Replicas in Ipswich Museum, originals in British Museum].
Brailsford, JW, PSIAH (1969) 31(ii). Brailsford, JW et al, Proceedings of the Prehistoric Society (1976) 38, 219.

45. Ipswich, Castle Hill, Whitton. OS map 169. TM 1446. Chesterfield Drive.
Excavations in the nineteenth and twentieth centuries found two Roman buildings dating to third-fourth centuries with a bathhouse having painted plaster walls. A mosaic pavement found in 1854 and a jet plaque of a figure wearing a Phrygian (pointed) cap, indicate a Mithraic cult [In Ipswich Museum]. An outbuilding was for corn-drying or malting.
VCH Suffolk (1911) i, 319. Clarke, RR, 1963, East Anglia, Thames & Hudson, pp 128,230. Moir, R, Maynard, G, PSIAH (1933) 21, 240. Martin, E, PSIAH (1990), 37(ii), 160.

45. Ipswich, Foxhall Road. OS map 169. TM 185439. Formerly Valley brickyard (Derby Road). Engineering works.
Bones of mammoth, deer, ox and a rhinoceros tooth, handaxes and a scraper of Acheulian industry (see Glossary) have been recovered, dating to the early Wolstonian Stage about 350,000 years ago.
Layard, NF, Journal of the Royal Anthropological Institute (1906) 36, 233. Wymer, J, Palaeolithic Sites of East Anglia (1985) Geo Books, p220.

45. Ipswich, Stoke Tunnel & Maidenhall. OS map 169. TM 1643. Railway tunnel through Stoke Hills.
Mammoth (*Elephas primigenius*) trapped in the mud, deer, wolf, cave bear, giant ox (*Bos primigenius*) and horse, dating to a warm episode in the late Palaeolithic period about 100,000 years ago (Oxygen Isotope stage 5, qv) [In Ipswich Museum]. Levallois tools (see Glossary) include a side-scraper and blades.
Layard, N, (1920) Proceedings of the Prehistoric Society of East Anglia, 3 (ii), 210. Wymer,

JJ, in Barringer, C (ed), (1984) Aspects of Anglian Prehistory, Norwich, Geo Books, p37. Wymer, J, Prehistoric Sites in East Anglia (1985), Geo Books, p227.

46. Ixworth. OS map 155. TL 9469. ½ mile south-east of Ixworth on the road to Stowlangtoft.
In 1849 was excavated a Roman hypocaust house with painted plaster walls.
Warren, J, PSIAH (1853), 1, 74.

47. Kentford. OS map 154. TL 7267 (railway) and TL 7268 (west of Icknield Way Path).
In 1891 were found remains of giant ox, mammoth, horse, hippopotamus and rhinoceros. Tools include handaxes and scrapers of Acheulian industry (see Glossary).
Wymer, J, Palaeolithic Sites of East Anglia (1985) Geo Books, p96.

48. Kersey, near Hadleigh. OS map 155. TM 0145. Ivy Tree Farm.
Excavation of a crop mark of a round barrow, 57ft in diameter with a 7ft wide surrounding ditch, 1½ ft deep, produced a collared-shaped urn with a cremation of a child 11-15 years old, with Samian pottery. Roman.
Corbishley, MJ, PSIAH (1975) 33(ii), 109.

49. Kesgrave. OS map 169. TM 2145. East of Ipswich.
The 'type-site' for the geology of the pre-Anglian glaciation course of the River Thames (see Glossary, Anglian Ice Age). The sands and gravels here and under the middle of Essex from Harlow towards Norfolk were brought down by the proto-Thames more than 500,000 years ago, later to be covered by the boulder clay (till) deposited by the Anglian ice sheets.

Some deposited rocks suggest that the proto-Thames once drained from as far west as Wales. Few human artefacts have been found in the Kesgrave layers though artefacts at Dartford (Kent), Sheringham (Norfolk), Wallingford (Oxford), Boxgrove (Sussex) and Mildenhall (Suffolk) attest to occasional human occupation in the Cromerian Interglacial Stage.
Lucy, G, Essex Rock (1999) Essex Rock and Mineral Society. Bridgland, DR, Quaternary of the Thames (1994), Chapman and Hall.

50. Kettleburgh. OS map 156. TM 2660. Home Farm.
Late Bronze Age/Early Iron Age pottery of 'Hallstatt B' type resembling that found at Marne, France, and Early Iron Age pottery of 'Darmsden' type (see Glossary).
O'Connor, B, PSIAH (1976) 33(iii), 231.

51. Lackford★. OS map 155. TL 789711.
Here Icknield Way crosses the River Lark. At TL786696 (Cuckoo Hill), a tumulus.
Lawson, W, et al, East Anglian Archaeology (1981) 12, 12. PSIAH (2001) 40 (I), 75.

52. Lakenheath. OS map 143. TL 7384. A large grey urn, 14in high and 11in diameter, with a whiskered face decoration, third-fourth century AD. At Lackenheath Industrial Workshop (TL7380) were excavated Late Iron Age and Roman pottery, two round houses, a 2.5m deep well, and three burials with a bronze cosmetics grinder.
Briscoe, G, PSIAH (1953) 26, 71 and (1958) 27(iii), 176. Martin, E, PSIAH (1994) 38 (ii), 217.

53. Lidgate. OS map 154. TL 7258. Air photographs in 1971 showed the crop mark of a Roman winged-corridor villa with an outbuilding.

Moore, IE (ed) 1988. The Archaeology of Roman Suffolk, Suffolk Co Council, p47.

53. Little Bealings. OS map 169. TM 233467. North of Kesgrave Hall, Beacon Hill quarry.

Excavations have produced Neolithic sherds, Beaker pinch-decoration pottery, and an eighth-ninth century BC cordon-decorated Iron Age bowl.

Martin, E, East Anglian Archaeology (1993) 65, 51.

55. Long Melford. OS map 155. TL 8646.

At the confluence of Roman roads from Cavendish, Hartest, Rougham, Coddenham, Colchester and Braintree. A Roman road crosses the NW corner of Chapel Field (TL8645) going NE to SW. Air photographs in 1971 to the east of the town have shown a Roman villa with a winged corridor and an outbuilding. Excavations in 1958 in Listers Lane by Long Melford Place north of the Post Office found a Roman tessellated pavement.

Journal of Roman Studies (1959) 44, 124. Smedley, N, PSIAH (1960), 28, 272. Avent, R et al, PSIAH (1980), 34, 229. Moore, IE, The Archaeology of Suffolk (1988), Suffolk County Council, p47.

55. Long Melford. OS map 155. TL 8654, Gardeners Garage, Little St Marys.

Six Roman skeletons, five adults and one child, were buried, head to west. One was in a stone coffin and one in a plaster-like substance, a Christian practice. Dated fourth century AD.

Martin, E, PSIAH (1998) 39(ii), 236

56. Martlesham Heath★. OS map 169. TL 2545. SE corner of Spratts Plantation

A tumulus (at TM256454) 25m diameter 1.8m high was excavated in 1974 with two other flattened mounds (which showed on air photographs at TM2245 and TM2545). They produced sherds of Beaker pottery and evidence of postholes suggesting a Bronze Age building. At the bypass (TM2648) Neolithic Grooved Ware and Iron Age pottery have been found (see Glossary).

Maynard, G, Suffolk Archaeology (1947). Martin, E, East Anglian Archaeology (1976) 3,17 and (1993) 65, 49.

57. Mildenhall, High Lodge. OS map 143. TL 7475. In the Nature Reserve, 4km north-east of Mildenhall.

This classic Lower Palaeolithic site lies on the south-east of chalk escarpment. Further excavations in 1988 in clay silts predating the Great Anglian Ice Age (500,000 years BP) have revealed the extinct rhinocerous *Dicerorhinus etruscus* (which has not been found later than the Cromerian Stage, see Glossary) and flint knapping debris of Lower Palaeolithic, hide-scrapers, wood-planers and hammers which compare with those found at Boxgrove, Sussex.

Marr, JE, Moir, JR, Smith, RA, Proceedings of the Prehistoric Society of East Anglia (1931) 3, 353. Wymer, J, Palaeolithic Sites of East Anglia (1985), Geo Books, p86. Cook, C, Aston, N, Current Archaeology (1991) 123,133. Wymer, J, Lower Palaeolithic Occupation of Britain (1999), Wessex Archaeology/English Heritage, p138. PSIAH (2003) 40 (III).

57. Mildenhall, Hurst Fen. OS map 143. TL 7377. 1.5km north-east of Mildenhall, west of Eriswell Lode and A1065.

Flint scrapers, leaf-shaped arrowheads, burins (borers), celts (axes) and pottery dating to the Middle Neolithic period (about 2500 BC) indicate a flint knapping site. Of antler and bone were bodkins and chisels. Pottery had emmer wheat grains imprinted into the wet clay. The finds are in Cambridge University Archaeological & Anthropology Museum.

Clark, JGD, Antiquaries Journal, (1936) 16, 29. Clark, JGD, Proceedings of the Prehistoric Society (1960) 27, 202.

57. Mildenhall, Thistley Green. OS map 143. TL 6676. 4 km west of Mildenhall.

In 1932 were excavated two rooms of a Romano-British house with hypocaust. A Roman hoard contained evidence of spoons with a Christian motif [In British Museum].

Moore, IE (ed) (1988) The Archaeology of Roman Suffolk, Suffolk County Council, p47.

57. Mildenhall, Three Hills, Warren Hill. OS map 143. TL 7474. Icklingham — Wisbech road, now plantation.

A number of ovate handaxes have been found at this site since the nineteenth century, of pre-Anglian, Clactonian and Acheulian industry (see Glossary).

Wymer, J, Palaeolithic Sites of East Anglia (1985), Geo Books, p90. Wymer, J, Lower Palaeolithic Occupation of Britain (1999) Wessex Archaeology/English Heritage.

58. Nayland. OS map 155. TL 9734. 2km south-west of Stoke-by-Nayland.

A Bronze Age urnfield cemetery unmarked by mounds.

Clarke, RR, (1963) East Anglia, Thames & Hudson, 86.

59. Needham Market. OS map 155. TM 0954. Needham Lake Recreation Area.

A circular ditch dating to the Early Bronze

Age 25.5m in diameter. Evidence for earlier activity were Mesolithic worked flint tools.

Martin, E, PSIAH (1993) 38(i), 94.

60. Oakley. OS map 156. TM 1478. Scole-Stuston bypass, A143.

Roman occupation in the form of four wells and ditched plots aligned along a first-/second-century road were found. A cobbled street ran east-west to a junction with the main north-south road.

Martin, E, PSIAH (1995), 38(iii), 356.

61. Pakenham, Barton Mere. .OS map 155. TL 9167. East of Beyton Green to Gt Barton road.

In the Mere were found bronze spear heads lost in a wattle-built 'lake house', dated to the Bronze Age.

Clarke, RR, (1963) East Anglia, Thames & Hudson, p84.

61. Pakenham, Red Castle Farm. OS map 155. TL 9069. East of Great Barton to Great Livermere road.

Excavations in 1776 and 1953 found a decorated mosaic floor and a building with an apsidal central room, painted plaster walls, window glass, dating from second-fourth centuries AD.

Moore, IE, (ed) (1988) The Archaeology of Roman Suffolk, Suffolk County Council, p47.

62. Rendham near Saxmunden. OS map 156. TM 3564.

From the River Alde was recovered by a boy in 1907 the bronze head of Claudius, 13ins high, probably booty from the Boudican sack of Camulodunum in AD 60/61, ?part of an equestrian statue, a leg of which was found at Ashill, Norfolk. (Head now in the British Museum).

Macdonald, G, Journal of Roman Studies (1926) 16, 3. Clarke, RR, (1963), East

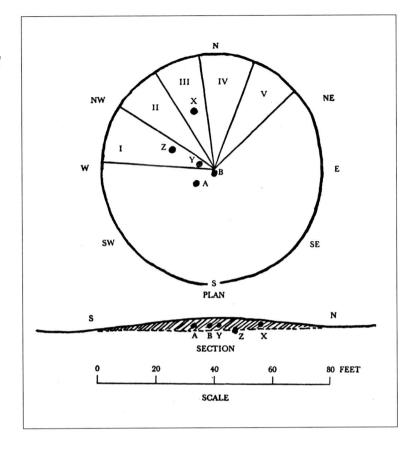

51 Risby
tumulus.
Y = sherd
of Bronze
Age urn

Anglia, Thames & Hudson, pp 113, 228. Toynbee, JMC, Trans Essex Archaeological Society (1955) 25(i), 10. Sealey, PR, The Boudican Revolt, Shire, p29.

63. Risby, **Poors Heath**★. OS map 155. TL 794685. Round barrow beside old road from Risby to Lackford.

The mound 24x23m, 1m high contained an adult male buried in the contracted position with a beaker and, to one side, a child lying on its left side (**51**). The burials were dated 2000-1400 BC. Several barrows on the Heath, excavated in the nineteenth century and again in 1959, contained urns, inhumations and cremations (TL7868). On the line of the A45 in 1975 a tumulus was excavated prior to destruction 10m east of a tributary of the River Lark (at

Barrow Bottom, TL 774661). It contained a central crouched burial of a male 40-45 years old, 5ft 4½in tall, with beads of jet and a collared urn. The jet was analysed as being from East Yorkshire. In the silted ditch was a burial of a young adult man the back of whose skull had been split with a sharp blow. At Risby Barrow Bottom (TL 7766) is a Late Upper Palaeolithic open site from which some 20 blades and flakes have been found.

Fox, C, Archaeology of the Cambridge Region (1923) p33. Vatcher, F de M, Proceedings of the Prehistoric Society (1976) 42,263. Edwardson, AR, PSIAH (1961) 28, 154. Martin, E, East Anglian Archaeology (1976) 3, 43. Wymer, JJ, Council for British Archaeology Research Report 22 (1977) p431.

64. Rougham ★. *OS* map 155. TL 9062. Eastlow Hill at the junction of Rougham Green and Little Welnetham roads.

A villa with an *opus signinum* (mortar & crushed flint) floor, tiled roof, tesserae and painted walls. Four tumuli produced samian pottery and a lead coffin.

VCH Suffolk, (1911) i, 279-323. PSIAH (1929) iv, 256. Clarke, RR, (1963) East Anglia, Thames & Hudson, p124.

65. Santon Downham. *OS* map 144. TL 8187.

In 1869 was found a hoard of 109 Iron Age coins, 12 inscribed ECEN, 19 with ECE, 4 with AESC, 14 with ANTED.

Numisatic Chronicle, ns ix, 326. VCH Suffolk (1911), i, 274.

66. Saxmunden. *OS* map 156. TM 3863. Flint scrapers dated to the Neolithic period.

VCH Suffolk (1911) i, 261.

67. Saxtead Green. *OS* map 156. TM 2665. Roman road to Peasenhall, south-west of Wood Hall.

The Roman road had flanking ditches either side 21ft apart, 3ft wide, 2 ½ ft deep.

Owles, E, PSIAH (1973) 32(iii), 273.

68. Sproughton. *OS* map 169. TM 1343443. Devils Wood Pit, south of Chantry Cut.

In the floodplain of the River Gipping were found two barbed points, one of bone 19.5cm long with 17 barbs cut with a sharp flint, and one of antler, broken but with two barbs, with a horse skeleton (?hunted), dating to the end of the Last Glacial period or Mesolithic, radiocarbon date 9420 to 7930 bc. They may have been used as fish-spears. Here was a flint industry producing magnificent long blades, flakes and scrapers.

Wymer, JJ, Jacobi, RM, Rose, J, Proceedings of the Prehistoric Society (1975) 41, 235. Wymer, JJ, East Anglian Archaeology (1976), 3,1.

69. Stanstead. *OS* map 155. TL 8449. A Roman villa with flint footings, seven courses high, a hypocaust, tesselated floors and crushed wall plaster.

Martin, E, PSIAH (1995) 38(iii), 359.

70. Stanton Chare. *OS* map 144. TL 9574.

Excavations in 1935-9 found a courtyard building started before *c.*AD 130, with a hypocaust. From coin evidence the villa, which is 300ft (100m) long, was in use until the end of the fourth century AD.

Clarke, RR, (1963) East Anglia, Thames & Hudson, p120. Moore, IE (ed) (1988) The Archaeology of Roman Suffolk, Suffolk County Council, p47.

71. Stratford St Mary. *OS* map 155. TM 0534.

Air photographs suggest a Neolithic henge monument and cursus with double ditch arrangement. (See also Chelmsford Springfield, Essex).

Clarke, RR (1963) East Anglia, Thames & Hudson, p 66. Hedges, J, Buckley, D (1980) Springfield Cursus, Essex County Council occasional paper no 1. Loveday, R, Current Archaeology (2000) 167 (xi), 439.

72. Stoke-by-Nayland. *OS* map 155. TM 010350. Thorington Street, Wick Farm.

A 3m-long mammoth tusk was excavated from 5m below the surface. Also from 5m down has come an unusual thin flint axe.

Engleheart, FHA, Trans Suffolk Nat Society (1955) 9, 226. Engleheart, FHA, PSIAH (1962) 29, 217.

73. Stonham Aspal. *OS* map 156. TM 1359. East of the *Combretovium* to Stoke Ash Roman road (A140)
Excavations in 1962-5 revealed a Roman bathhouse dating to the third century AD.
Smedley, N, et al, PSIAH (1966) 30, 221.

74. Stuston. *OS* map 156. TM 1478. Scole-Dickleburgh road, A140.
A semicircle of postholes 5.75m in diameter, and Roman timber rafters spanning a leet suggested a mill, and gave evidence of Roman carpentry techniques.
Martin, E, PSIAH (1994) 38(ii), 220.

75. Stutton. *OS* map 169. TM 150330. Stour estuary and Ness.
The most south-easterly extent of the Anglian ice sheet in Suffolk. From here have been found Acheulian handaxes and Levallois flint tools (see Glossary), as well as mammoth, straight-tusked elephant, rhinoceros and lion.
Wymer, JJ, in Barringer, C (ed) (1984) Aspects of Anglian Prehistory, Geo Books. Wymer, J,

Prehistoric Sites in East Anglia (1985), Geo Books, p209.

76. Sudbury★. *OS* map 155. TL 8741. Stour House, Gregory Street.
The rounded street pattern by St Gregory's church on the hilltop above the River Stour suggests an Iron Age enclosure measuring *c.*270x350m (**52**). Excavation 190m south of the church found Neolithic pits, fired-clay sling bullets, weaving combs and a bronze button-and-loop fastener. In the Iron Age it was a high-status settlement.
Martin, E, et al, PSIAH (1990) 37(ii), 162.

77. Sutton★. *OS* map 169. TM 3346. North-east of Shottisham.
A tumulus east of Sawpit Covert; another at TM3448.

78. Sutton Hoo★. *OS* map 169. TM 2949. From Wilford Bridge over River Deben, the B1083 in 400 yards passes Tranmer (Sutton Hoo) House south of which are the Anglo-Saxon ship burial mounds. Access

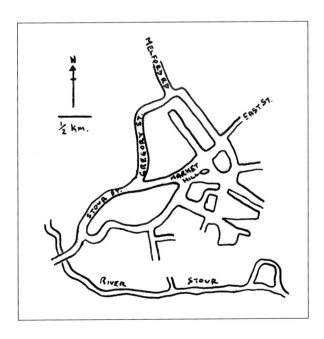

52   Sudbury centre

179

by foot from the B1083 at the Sutton Common and Hollesley road junction at TM298491. 'Howehills' (*haugr*=mound, Old Norse, *Hoh*=spur, Old English), later Sutton Mounts.

Evaluation and excavation in the 1960s and 1980s revealed beneath the mounds Bronze Age (about 2000 BC) roundhouses with timber posts 1 foot diameter, a south-east entrance, a central hearth and beautifully decorated Beaker pottery. The land was divided up into fields by 3m wide ditches. In the Iron Age (*c.*500 BC) the soil was ploughed with an ard, the criss-cross ploughmarks of which were seen beneath the mounds. But soil erosion due to loss of tree-cover and over-cultivation rendered what was left infertile by the middle Roman period. The Anglo-Saxon ship burials at Sutton Hoo are dated from the seventh century AD.

Bruce-Mitford, RLS, The Sutton Hoo Ship Burial, 1975-83 (3 volumes) British Museum. Lawson, AJ et al, East Anglian Archaeology (1981), 12, 14. Care-Evans, A, The Sutton Hoo Ship Burial, British Museum, 1986. Carver, M, 1998. Sutton Hoo, Burial Ground of Kings. British Museum. Arnott, W, 1946, Placenames of the Deben Valley Parishes, p70.

79. Thurston. OS map 155. TL 9265.
Copper alloy bracelets with diagonal and curving decoration dating from the Bronze Age.
VCH Suffolk (1911) i, 277.

80. Wattisfield. OS map 155. TM 0074.
Neolithic style decorated beakers continued to be made into the Bronze Age about 2000 BC. Over two millennia later the Romano-British were producing pottery in over 20 kilns here.
Maynard, G, Brown, B et al, PSIAH (1936) 22,178. Clarke, RR, (1963) East Anglia, Thames & Hudson, pp65, 123.

81. West Stow. OS map 155. TM8071.
On the north bank of the River Lark, excavations in 1965-72 produced evidence of a Mesolithic flint industry, a late Neolithic cemetery, an Iron Age settlement and nine kilns of a Romano-British pottery industry (TL8270). Subsequent excavations at Beeches Pit (TL7971) produced Lower Palaeolithic biface flint tools, some with evidence of burning, thermoluminescence and uranium dated (see Glossary) to soon after the Anglian Glaciation, 400,000 years ago.
West, S, East Anglian Archaeology (1990) 48. Martin, E, PSIAH (1994), 38(ii), 224 and (1997) 39(i), 100.

82. Wherstead. OS map 169. TM 1640.
The excavated skeleton of a long-headed (dolichocephalic) youth dated to the Neolithic period.
Clarke, RR, (1963) East Anglia, Thames & Hudson, p 66.

83. Wickham Market. OS map 156. TM 3055.
Flint tools of the Neolithic period. Iron Age coin hoard.
VCH Suffolk (1911) i, 263. Rudd, C, (2009) Current Archaeology, 227, 12

84. Worlington. OS map 154. TL 6973.
Swales tumulus in Swales Plantation..
A tumulus 35ft in diameter contained evidence of fire and cremated bones. An accessory burial at the edge contained charred wood (?coffin) and a flint Neolithic or Early Bronze Age axehead
Clarke, RR, (1963) East Anglia, Thames & Hudson, p57. Briscoe, G, Proceedings of the Cambridge Antiquarian Society (1957) 50, 101.

Visible sites and locations

Further details of the monuments are contained in the Gazetteer.
E = Essex, S = Suffolk.

Finds should always be reported to the local museum having accurately noted the find-spot, so that they can be identified and recorded to allow a better understanding of the context from which they come.

Palaeolithic/Mesolithic
Blackwater estuary, E.
Stutton, S, and Wrabness, E, Stour estuary.
Thames estuary, E.

Crouch estuary, E.
Thurrock quarries, E.
Walton-on-Naze, E.

Neolithic
Lackford, S.

Lawford, E.

Bronze Age
Barton Mills, S.
Bucklesham, S.
Eriswell, S.
Risby, S.

Brightwell, S.
Chelmsford, Springfield Lyons, E.
Martlesham Heath, S.
Sturmer, E.

Iron Age
Asheldham, E.
Billericay, Norsey Wood, E.
Burgh near Woodbridge, S.
Colchester, E.
Epping, E.
Great Horkesley, E.
Littlebury, E.
Maldon, E.
Shoeburyness, E.
Witham, E.

Barrow, S.
Brentwood, Weald Park, E.
Cavenham, S.
Danbury, E.
Great Hallingbury, E.
Hatfield Broad Oak, E.
Loughton, E.
Navestock, E
Sudbury, S.
Writtle, E.

Romano-British

Bartlow, Cambs/Ashdon, E.

Burgh Castle, Gt Yarmouth, Norfolk.

Chelmsford, Moulsham Street, E.

Fryerning, E.

Harlow, E.

Ingatestone, E.

Newport, E.

Rougham, S.

Bradwell-on-Sea, E.

Canvey, E.

Colchester, E.

Great Chesterford, E.

Hockley, E.

Mersea Island, E.

Rivenhall, E.

Prehistoric and Roman roads

While with some certainty a few roads can be attributed to Roman wholesale regional planning both on documentary grounds, archaeology and/or from topography (such as the road from London — Chelmsford — Kelvedon to Colchester), the native British will have continued to use the local trackways for as long they served a purpose. Many of these are now lost but some are preserved into the present either as roads, lanes, paths, bridleways or parish, estate and field boundaries. Rarely in Essex are the Roman *agger* and ditches still visibly extant (Ingatestone, Mapletree Lane may be an exception), though excavation can sometimes reveal them. More often they may be indicated from an understanding of how a settlement related to another or to a main road. A succession of parish boundaries lying along a road may indicate a landholding, perhaps originating from the Roman period, the boundary of which was determined by the pre-existing road (Davies, 2002).

Long tracks of pre-Roman ways are likely to have linked centres of occupation. Stane Street may be an Iron Age route joining *Camulodunum* with St Albans and Wheathampsted, the centre of the *Catuvellauni* tribe. It was subsequently incorporated into the Roman system but lacks the military precision of the road from London to Colchester which clearly postdates it since the London road joins it (at Marks Tey).

Long-distance routes were needed for trade. They may have originated in the Neolithic period or earlier but are difficult to date. Such a route would follow the easiest ground and that would vary not only with the season but also would deviate over the years until constrained by a territorial boundary or the application of stone or bitumen. The Icknield Way between Wessex and East Anglia crosses the north west corner of Essex. Its name alone attests to a pre-Roman origin. It may have linked with the Peddars Way (believed to be of Roman origin) to the northern coast of Norfolk.

Local investigation will reveal many more early routes than are at present known and documented. Some of the documented ways are appended. Not all are authenticated as pre-historic or Roman.

Miller Christy described and traced 28 such routes in a series of articles in the Transactions of the Essex Archaeological Society: 1921, ns xv, 190; 1923, ns xvi, 127; 1926, ns xvii, 83; 1926, ns xvii, 226.

Laver, H, Trans Essex Archaeological Society (1889) ns iii, 123 for Chesterford, and (1895) ns v, 33 for Dengie.

The Antonine Itinerary, a second/third century AD list of routes in the Roman Empire gives:

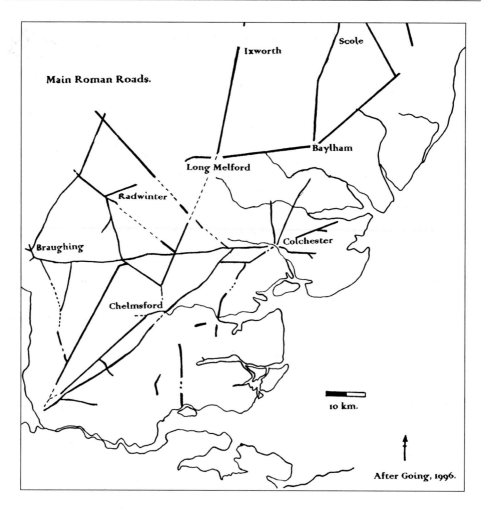

53   *Main Roman roads*

Route V: *Londinio* — *Caesaromago* (Chelmsford) — *Colonia* (Colchester) — *Villa Faustini* (?Scole, Norfolk).

Route IX: *Sitomago* (?Yoxford, Suffolk) — *Combretovio* (Coddenham) — *Ad Ansam* (Higham) — *Camoloduno* (Colchester) — *Canonio* (Kelvedon) — *Cesaromago* (Chelmsford) — *Durolito* (?Chigwell, Little London, qv) — *Lundinio*.

Rivet, AL, Smith, C, Place-Names of Roman Britain, Batsford, 1979. Rodwell, W, Britannia (1975) 6, 76. Steerwood, R, Proc Suff Inst Arch Hist (2003) 40 (3), 253

Air photographs suggest:

Harlow, Thornwood Common (TL4643 0500 to 4675 0335) to Hobbs Cross (TQ477992) to join the Dunmow-Chigwell road.

Wickham Bishops — Langford (TL8474 0931 to TL8472 0967) to TL8483 0818 to Maldon, Heybridge.

Wixoe (TL6853 4213 to 6880 4228, TL6778 4170 to 6563 4049 to TL6474 3945 to 6348) to Radwinter (TL6067 3737).
Couchman, C, Essex Archaeology & History (1979) 11,53. Charge, B, Journal Haverhill & District Archaeological Group (1986) 4.2, 46.

The Ordnance Survey 1:50000 maps show:
Abridge (TQ4697) — Moreton (TL5307) — Great Dunmow (TL6220).
Bradwell on Sea (TM0007) — Othona Roman fort (TM0308).
Bells Cross, Suffolk (TM1552) — Ottley Bottom (TM2054).
Bungay, Suffolk (TM3489) — Halesworth (TM3979).
Coddenham, Suffolk (TM1354) — Pettaugh (TM1659).
Coddenham, Baylham House, Suffolk (TM1153) — Stoke Ash (TM1170).
Colchester, Lexden Road (TL9725) — Coggeshall (TL8523) — Braintree, Rayne Road (TL7523 — Blake End (TL7023) — Stebbingford (TL6722) — Great Dunmow (TL6222) — Takeley (TL5612) — Bishops Stortford, Herts (TL5021). (Stane Street).

Margary, ID, Roman Roads in Britain, Baker, 1973. Christy, M, Trans Essex Archaeological Society, ns 15, 198.
Easthorpe (TL8921) — Stanway Hall, Colchester (TL9522).
Great Chesterford, Stump Cross (TL5044) — Worstead Lodge, Cambs (TL5352).
Hitcham, Suffolk (TL9851) — Poystreet Green (TM9857).
Holton St Mary, Suffolk (TM0636) — Capel St Mary (TM1038) — Sproughton (TM1243).
Icknield Way: Royston, Cambs (TL3640) — Lackford, Suffolk (TL7870).
Langley, Rocketts Farm(TL4736) — Brent Pelham, Herts (TL4331).
Little Waltham (TL7113) — Braintree (TL7623) — Gosfield (TL7829).
London, Mile End Road — Stratford (TQ3984) — Romford, London Road (TQ5088) — Brentwood, Brook Street (TQ5792) — Ingatestone (TQ6599) — Chelmsford, Moulsham Street (TL7006) — Boreham (TL7510) — Witham — Kelvedon — Marks Tey, Colchester (TL9123).
Long Melford, Suffolk (TL8646) — Cavendish (TL8046).
Long Melford (TL8646) — Ixworth, Suffolk (TL9370).
Long Melford (TL8646) — Coddenham (TM1153).
Pettaugh, Suffolk (TM1659) — Saxtead Green, Framlingham (TM2564) — Peasenhall (TM3569).
Scole (TM1579) — Norwich.
Sudbury, White Hall, Suffolk (TL9043) — Newton Leys (TL9140), *Colchester Arch Group Ann Bull, (1981), 24, 19.*
Weybread, Suffolk (TM2480) — Peasenhall (TM3569).
Several alignments are documented in *VCH* Essex (1963), vol iii, pp26-29.

Miscellaneous sources:
Abberton, south of the church
Doorne, AA, Colchester Archaeological Group Annual Bulletin, 21, 3.

Asheldham.

Britannia (1977) 8, 405.

Billericay, Norsey Wood (TQ6995)—Stock (TQ6999).

Going, CJ, in Bedwin, O, Archaeology of Essex, 1996, Essex County Council, p97.

Braintree town and environs (TL7523)

Drury, PJ, Essex Archaeology & History (1976) 8, 121.

Chelmsford—Horsefrith Park Farm (TL6204)—Norton Heath (TL6004)—Ongar (TL5603).

Going, CJ, in Bedwin, O, Archaeology of Essex, 1996, Essex County Council, p97.

Colchester, East gate — St Osyth (TM1215).

Going, CJ, in Bedwin, O, Archaeology of Essex, 1996, Essex County Council, p97.

Colchester — Mistley: A road is represented at Crockleford Hill (TM 033262) linking Colchester with Mistley.

Farrands, RH, Colchester Archaeological Group Annual Bulletin (1975) 18,5.

Colchester — Cambridge: Earls Colne, Chalkney Wood (TL8727) .

Margery, ID, Roman Roads in Britain, Baker, 1973. Rackham, O, History of the Countryside,Dent,1986, fig 12.3

Harley, LS, Colchester Archaeology Group Annual Bulletin (1981) 24, 19.

Danbury (TL7805) — Maldon, Heybridge (TL8508) — Langford (TL8309) — Colchester.

Wickenden, N, Essex Archaeology & History (1986) 17,7.

Dengie peninsula: Rectilinear roads and field boundaries around Asheldham (TL9601) and Tillingham (TL9903)

Laver, H, Trans Essex Archaeological Society (1889), ns v, 33. Drury, P, et al, Antiquaries Journal (1978) 58, 133.

Fairlop TQ4490—Horseman's Side (TQ5496) — Doddinghurst (TQ5999) — Fryerning, Mapletree Lane (TL6201, qv) — Writtle Park — Bumpsteads Farm (TL6704) — Chelmsford.

Great Chesterford, North gate (TL5043) — Icknield Way.

Going, CJ, in Bedwin, O (ed), Archaeology of Essex 1996, Essex County Council, p 95.

Ingatestone, Roman Road electricity substation (TQ644989) — Dodds Farm (TQ637997) — Woodbarns Farm (TL620008) joining to Mapletree Lane at TL618009.

Kemble, J, Essex Journal (1993) 28(i), 14.

Kelvedon area (TL8619).

Rodwell, WJ, in British Archaeological Reports (1978) 48, 89

Langley tumulus (TL4534) — ?Great Chishill (TL4239) — Icknield Way.

VCH Essex (1963) iii, 35.

Little Waltham area (TL7012). See also Braintree town and environs (above).

Drury, PJ, Council for British Archaeological Research Reports (1978) 26.

Rivenhall villa (TL8217).

Rodwell, K, et al, Council for British Archaeological Research Reports (1986) 55.

Roding: Iron Age and Roman field boundaries and roads (TL5713).

Rodwell, W, British Archaeological Reports (1978) 48, 87.

Saffron Walden, Audley End Park (TL5237).

Bassett, SR, Council for British Archaeological Reports (1965) No 45.
Thaxted (TL6131) — Elsenham (TL5326)
Goodburn, R, Britannia (1978) 9,430, 452.

Museums, Societies and Record Offices

Baylham House Rare Breeds Farm Museum, Mill Lane, Baylham, Suffolk (Site of *Combretovium*). 01437 830264.

Brandon Heritage Centre, George Street, Suffolk. 01842 813707.

Braintree Museum, Manor Street, Essex. 01376 325266.

British Museum, Great Russell Street, London, WC1B. 020 7636-1555.

Burgh Castle (Roman Saxon Shore fort) (English Heritage), Off A143 west of Gt Yarmouth. 0845 602 0121.

Bury St Edmunds, Moyse's Hall, Cornhill, Suffolk. 01284 757488.

Butser Ancient Farm, Waterlooville, Petersfield, Hampshire. 023 9259 8838.

Cambridge Archaeology & Anthropology Museum, Downing Street. 01223 337733.

Cambridge, Fitzwilliam Museum, Trumpington Street. 01223 332900.

Chelmsford & Essex Museum, Moulsham Street, Chelmsford, Essex. 01245 605700.

Clare Ancient House Museum, High Street, Suffolk. 01787 277662.

Cockley Cley Museum & Iceni Iron Age Village (reconstruction), SW of Swaffham, Norfolk. 01760 721331.

Colchester Castle Museum, Castle Street, Essex. 01206 282939.

Dagenham, Valence House Museum, Becontree Avenue, Essex. 020 8592 4500.

English Heritage, 62-74 Burleigh Street, Cambridge CB11DJ. 01223-582700.

Essex Record Office, Wharf Road, Chelmsford CM2 6YT. 01245 244644. www.essexcc.gov.uk/ero.

Grimes Graves, (Neolithlic flint mine), near Santon Downham, off A134 NW of Thetford, Norfolk. 01842 810656.

Harlow Museum, Muskham Road, CM20 2LF. 01279 454959.

Ipswich Museum, High Street, Ipswich, Suffolk. 01473 213761.

Maldon Museum, 47 Mill Road, Essex. 01621 842688.

Mildenhall and District Museum, King Street, Suffolk. 01638 716970.

National Monuments Record (English Heritage), Kemble Drive, Swindon, SN2 2GZ. 01793 414600.

Saffron Walden Museum, Museum Street, Essex. 01799 510333.

Sites and Monuments Record (Essex), County Hall, Chelmsford, CM1 1LF. 01245 437637 http://unlockingessex.essexcc.gov.uk.

Sites and Monuments Record (Suffolk), Suffolk Archaeological Unit, Suffolk County Council, Shire Hall, Bury St Edmunds, IP33 2AA. 01284 352000.

Southend Museum, Victoria Avenue, Essex. 01702 215131.

Southend Prittlewell Priory Museum, Priory Park, Essex. 01702 342878.

The Suffolk Record Office, 77 Raingate Street, Bury St Edmunds. 01284-352352. www.suffolk.org.uk.

Thurrock Museum, Orsett Road, Grays, Thurrock. 01375 383961.

Waltham Abbey, Epping Forest Museum, 39-41 Sun Street, Waltham Abbey, Essex. 01992 716882.

Essex Society for Archaeology & History library, available to the Society's members at Essex University, Wivenhoe Park, Colchester, houses a specialist collection of county, national and international books and journals. Details from the Secretary, c/o Hollytrees Museum, High Street, Colchester, CO1 1UG, tel 01206-282940. Proceedings of the Suffolk Institute of Archaeology & History: information from Flat 514, Neptune Marina, 1 Coprolite Street, Ipswich, IP3 0BN.

Glossary

Acheulian Industry (named after the excavation site at St Acheul, Amiens, France). A Lower Palaeolithic flint-tool industry typified by the handaxe; some may have been hafted (**11**; **colour plate 6**). The tool was fashioned with a stone- and then wood- or antler-hammer. Acheulian handaxes were found at the same levels as the skull at Swanscombe (Kent) which has affinities with early *Homo sapiens* and *Homo neandertalensis*. The technology overlaps with the Clactonian (See Hoxnian Interglacial).

Amino-acid Dating. Amino-acids, the building blocks of proteins, in living tissue are chemically structured in the L-form. After death they change to the D-form (a kind of mirror-image) at a rate which depends on temperature but takes thousands of years. If a temperature is known (or assumed) the ratio of L-form to D-form therefore is proportional to the time since death. The method is of use for a time scale about 1000 to 100,000 or more years.

Amphora(e). Large ceramic two-handled storage vessels are known from the Middle Iron Age in Britain. Analyses of residues have shown that contents included olive oil, fish products or wine. Camulodunum and Dressel numbers (after H. Dressel's classification) of shapes are widely quoted; Dressel Type 1A amphorae appear in Britain in the second-mid first centuries BC, Type 1B from about 50 BC.

Anglian Ice Age. ('The Great Ice Age', equated, in Europe, to Mindel, named after a river in southern Germany). The period approximately 475,000-425,000 years ago. On their retreat, the glaciers left behind the boulder clays of north-west Essex and over much of Suffolk except the south-eastern coastal strip, overlying the earlier Thames sands and gravels (Kesgrave sands) (**9**) (*Bridgland, 1994*).

Ard. Implements for breaking up the soil for cultivation are first found in the Neolithic period. Earth-breaking was done by human or animal-drawn wooden bow or the more primitive crook ards. The bow ard had the share point inserted through a hole in the beam (**colour plate 29**). The beam and sole of the crook ard was made from a single piece of T-shaped wood, to which the handle (stilt) was fixed. Both stirred the soil but did not turn a sod. The seed-furrow ard drills a furrow. Prehistoric fields were often furrowed criss-cross. Stone points to the share tip have been dated in Britain from *c*.2000 BC. Iron tips were later introduced. Sods could be turned over by the coulter (plough) from the Roman period. Roman iron shares have been found at Great Chesterford and Worlington (*Rees, 1991; Reynolds, 1987*).

Aurignacian Culture (named from Aurignac rockshelter in south-west France). A tool industry intermediate between Mousterian and Solutrean, qv, of the Upper Palaeolithic, when appears the first west European cave art, dated in France about 32,000 years ago. Bone points with split bases are a characteristic tool. The burial of the 'Red Lady of Paviland Cave' in Glamorgan, in fact a male, sprinkled with red ochre, has been dated to about 24,000 BC (*Sollas, 1913*; *Aldhouse-Green, 1998*).

Aylesford-Swarling 'Culture'. These sites in Kent excavated in 1886 and 1921 produced well-made wheel-thrown pottery and cremation burials. Similar pottery and burials have been found also in Essex, Hertfordshire, Bedfordshire and around London. Tall urns with pedestal bases and narrow-mouthed jars are typical, dating from around 50 BC. Cremation remains are often within urns containing also grave goods such as brooches, keys, jewellery and spoons.

Barrow. A mound of earth or stone over one or more burials, usually with surrounding ditch. **Long barrows** usually dating from the Neolithic period contained at one end (often the higher, east end) burials in the contracted (flexed) posture or as disarticulated bones, perhaps originally in a mortuary chamber. They may have been used for many generations since skeletons may be disturbed, partial or bones segregated from skulls, the remains of the earlier bodies being moved aside to make way for the new. Access to the communal burial chamber was usually from the end through a wood, turf or stone entrance, though occasionally this entrance was false. Some barrows have a forecourt in front of the entrance where ceremonies could have taken place. Dated to the Neolithic, about 2500 BC, are the barrows at Rivenhall End (Witham) and Slough House Farm (Maldon), qv. **Round barrows** are associated with Neolithic and Bronze Ages, Roman, Anglo-Saxon and Viking periods. They may contain a central burial with lateral, subsidiary (?servant) burials. Saxon pagan interments may be distinguished from Neolithic, Bronze and Early Iron Age by the body being often (but not invariably) in the extended, as opposed to contracted, position. Ploughed-out round barrows identified from aerial photographs as circular crop marks require differentiation from other causes of round marks, such as mill mounds. Place-names containing 'beorg', 'brough', 'borough', 'barrow', 'bury' may indicate a barrow site, but other originates are possible including natural mounds (*Darvill, 1987*; *Grinsell, 1979*).

Beaker Culture. The introduction of metal technology (copper and bronze) into the British Isles occured at about the same time as single burials under round barrows and flat-bottomed beaker-shaped pottery vessels, about 2500-2000 BC (**54**). 'Beaker' culture is found widely from Europe north of the Alps, Iberia to the Atlantic. Whether this represents a migration of peoples with metal technology westwards is debated. Copper technology seems to have first developed in eastern Turkey, Taurus mountains and northern Syria around 4000 BC.

Belgic pottery. A late Iron Age and Early Roman ceramic thrown on a wheel and usually tempered with crushed pottery (grog), earliest about 50 BC (**colour plate 15**). It appears

54   *Early Bronze Age beaker*
      from Stebbing

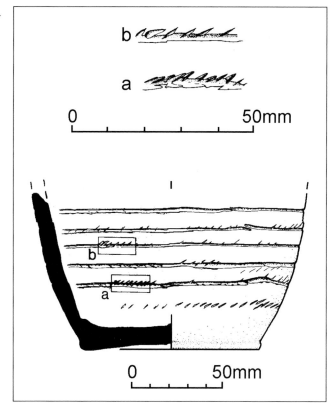

to be a newly imported style, not evolved from earlier British types. Pottery evolving from the British Middle Iron Age, not thrown on the wheel, continued to be made, often with shell-temper.

Carinate bowls. A pottery style with an angled profile, such as found at Clacton, Shoebury and Layer de la Haye, which has been shown to be the earliest ceramics in Britain dating from around 3100-2850 BC (**14**) (*Herne, 1988*). Contemporary with and subsequent to is Mildenhall ware, qv, a decorated bowl-style dating from from early to mid third millennium. From the mid- to late third millennium BC Peterborough, Grooved (Rinyo-Clactonian) and Beaker style pottery (qv) were produced (*Holgate, 1996*).

Causewayed Enclosure. Dating from the Neolithic and Bronze Ages, earthen enclosures encircled by embankment(s) and external ditch(es) with several uncut causeways across the ditch into the interior (**colour plate 25**). Lack of internal postholes suggest some were not used for habitation, hence possibly cattle corrals, meeting or trading places.

Clactonian Industry. Lower Palaeolithic. Simple flint tools were made during and after the Anglian Ice Age using blows from a hammer stone (**10**). Tools were core-choppers and rough handaxes, also found at Swanscombe (See Hoxnian Interglacial) (*Chandler, 1932*).

Coins, Roman (also see Potins). After the Claudian invasion of AD 43, Britain accumulated imperial coinage probably via the military who used it to purchase merchandise. Coins were 1 *aureus* (gold)=25 *denarii* (silver, later silver-plated)=100 *sestertii* (brass)=200 *dupondii* (brass)=400 *asses* (copper)=800 *semissess* (brass)=1600 *quadrantes* (copper). In AD 214 was introduced a silver *antoninianus*=1½ *denarii*, in AD 295 the *follis* (silver-alloyed bronze), in AD 309 the *solidus* (gold)= 3 *tremes*. The annual monetary pay to a legionary was, in the first century, 225 *denarii*, in the second century 300d, and at the beginning of the third century 675d (*Casey, 1980*).

Creswellian industry (see Magdalenian).

Cro-Magnon Man (named from the village Cro-Magnon in the Dordogne). In 1868 in a shallow rock shelter were excavated four skeletons deliberately buried with Aurignacian, qv, tools. Reindeer, mammoth, bison and horse bones were nearby. The best preserved skull was of a middle-aged man, brain capacity about 1600cc. This and other features ascribe the skeleton to early *Homo sapiens* and has been dated to the later part of the last (Devensian) ice age about 25,000 years ago.

Cromerian Complex. A series of warm and cold phases preceding the Anglian Ice Age, qv, in which the earliest evidence of *Homo* is found in Britain, before about 475,000 years ago. Skeletal remains of *Homo* have been found at Boxgrove, Sussex.

Cursus Monuments (plural, cursûs). Long earthworks with encompassing ditch, dating to the Neolithic (**colour plate 28**). The name derives from the eighteenth-century antiquary William Stukeley who supposed they were prehistoric chariot racetracks. Their function has been ascribed to ritual processional ways, mortuary monuments, astronomical alignments or boundary markers. Often they are associated with other nearby Neolithic and Bronze Age monuments (See Neolithic period).

Darmsden-Linton Pottery (named from sites in Suffolk and Cambridgeshire) (**55**). Dated from the Late Bronze/Early Iron Age (seventh-fourth century BC), burnished (shiny) jars and bowls found from the Wash to the Thames have a flared-out rim and a narrow shoulder, often decorated with transverse grooves. Pottery contains crushed flint or sand as temper (added to prevent cracking during firing of the clay).

Dendrochronology (Tree-ring dating). Trees grow in width by a series of annual rings, the thickness of which depends on the climate conditions of rainfall and temperature for each year. Rings counted from the bark inwards towards the centre represent the number of growing seasons (years). It follows that if bark is not present in the sample core an estimate of the number of absent outer rings has to be made. A minimum of 50 rings is usually necessary for an age to be calculated. The pattern of thick and thin rings in a core of tree-trunk is compared against the pattern in a core of known age for the same region of the country, and a 'best fit' (a statistical device) applied. For Essex and East Anglia a tree-ring chronology of wood cores of known

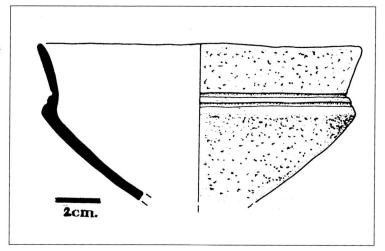

55 Darmsden-Linton style pot from Great Totham

2cm.

ages has been accumulated back to the medieval period with reasonable confidence of accuracy (*Andrews, 1999*). For earlier woods evidence is used from other parts of Britain and Ireland (with less confidence of accuracy), back to about 7000 BC for oak samples (*Aitken, 1990*).

Devensian Ice Age. ('The Last Glaciation' or, in Europe, Würm, the former name of the Starnberger See, Bavaria). A series of cold stages interspersed by warm interstadials dating from about 110,000-13,000 years ago. The furthest southern extent of the ice sheet was northern Norfolk. During much of this stage high sea levels left Britain an island. Fauna include reindeer, woolly rhinoceros and mammoth. Occupation by *Homo* during this Upper Palaeolithic period (beginning about 40,000 years ago) was sparse but occasionally attested by artefacts such as at White Colne and Ipswich.

Deverel-Rimbury Pottery (named after sites in Dorset where pottery styles may have diffused to and from Essex and Suffolk along the Icknield Way and/or round the south coast) (**56**). Dating is to the Middle and Late Bronze Age (generally about 1500-1000 BC). Cremation burials were in urns under barrows or in flat cemeteries. Characteristic pottery consists of bucket-shaped urns, coarse, thick, gritty and poorly fired (crumbly), flint or grog (crushed pottery) tempered. Globular urns are finer, better-fired, often finger-tip decorated with chevrons or triangles on the neck. Some have holes below the rim to which a leather cover may have been fitted. Essex styles are found at sites such as Ardleigh, Billericay and Shoebury (*Brown, 1995*).

Gipping Stage, named from the village and river near Stowmarket where gravels were deposited during a cold stage in the Wolstonian, qv.

Gravettian Industry (named from La Gravette in the Dordogne). An Upper Palaeolithic tool industry dated about 26,000 BC, of which small stone blades with flattened backs (like a knife) are typical.

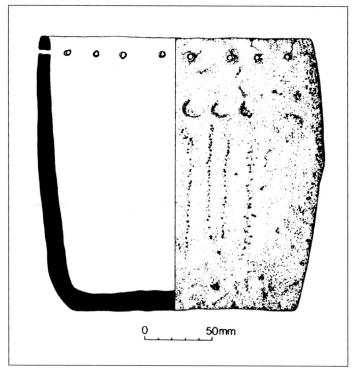

56 Deverel-Rimbury bucket urn from Great Baddow

Grooved Ware (Rinyo-Clactonian, named from the late Neolithic pottery sites on Rousay (Orkney Isles) and at Clacton Jaywick). A widely distributed pottery style, bucket-shaped pots with flat bases, incised groove decoration.

Hallstatt Culture (named from the cemetery 30 miles east of Salzburg found by Johann Ramsauer, a director of mining, in 1846). Natural salt deposits have preserved 3000 graves mostly dating from the Late Bronze and Iron Ages, eighth to fifth centuries BC. The characteristic weapon was the long bronze or iron sword, later daggers (*Collis, 1984*). Pottery was first thrown on the fast wheel in Europe in the sixth century BC. The culture was replaced by La Tène, qv, in the fifth century.

Hoxnian Interglacial (named from Hoxne, Suffolk), a warm period dating about 430,000 to 380,000 years ago. Two flint 'traditions' were being practised by *Homo*: (i) **Clactonian**, flakes struck off a flint core stone, and cores sharpened into bulky choppers. At Clacton golf course the landscape was open wood and grass land roamed by bison, fallow deer, horses, straight-tusked elephants and rhinoceros, (ii) **Acheulian**, stone nodules were flaked down into triangular handaxes or two-faced scrapers, choppers and cutters. Hoxne, then on a lake shore, was a temporary hunter-gatherer camp where horse, deer, bison, cattle and elephant were hunted or scavenged and butchered. The warmer climate encouraged oak, hazel, elm, alder and yew. A wide landbridge with the continent present until sea levels rose at the end of the Hoxnian allowed immigration.

Hypocaust. Roman underfloor heating. Hot air-filled ducts were supplied from furnaces burning below ground level outside the room. The floor was supported on columns of tiles stacked one on another. Wall heating could be provided (for example for the hot room of the bathhouse) through tile box flues.

Icknield Way. OS maps 144, 155, 154. The ancient prehistoric route which runs from Norfolk (where, near Thetford, it links with the Roman Peddars Way to the north Anglian coast). Westwards it crosses the River Lark at Lackford, the Black Ditches, Devils Dyke, Linton, Ickleton, Chrishall, Ivinghoe Beacon (Bucks), Goring, Vale of the White Horse Uffington Castle (known as The Ridgeway), West Kennet barrow in Wiltshire to Dorset. Before the Enclosure Acts of the eighteenth/nineteenth centuries it was a wide series of parallel tracks. Used for long-distance trading since Neolithic and possibly earlier times. The earliest documentary record is in AD 903 as '*Iccenhilde weg*'; its meaning is unknown. The name is not of Anglo-Saxon origin and may be pre-Celtic.

Ilfordian Interglacial Stage, named after sites at Ilford in the Lower Thames valley, dated from about 260,000-210,000 years ago, when lion, bear, horse and mammoth predominate in the fauna excavated. Sites also include Ipswich Stoke Tunnel and Stutton. A rarity of human sites suggests that high sea levels had cut Britain off from the mainland.

Ipswichian Interglacial (named after Bobbitshole, Ipswich) dates from about 130,000 to 110,000 years ago. Human occupation, probably cut off from the mainland by the English Channel, was sparse but may be represented by a handaxe and flakes at Stutton and Harkstead, Suffolk of flat-bottomed cordate (heart-shaped) form known as 'Mousterian of Acheulian tradition', MAT. Present were hippopotamus, red and fallow deer and straight-tusked elephant (*Wymer, 1985, 1996, 1999*).

Iron Age. (See 'Three Age System'). Iron technology was first developed about 1900 BC in Anatolia, Turkey possibly by the Hittites tribe (mentioned in the Bible). See Chapters 4, 5.

Kilns, Pottery and Tile (colour plate 31).
A summary of Roman sites for Essex is given in *Couchman, CR (ed), Essex Archaeology & History (1979) 11, 50* and *Rodwell, W, Essex Archaeology & History (1982) 14, 15*. Suffolk sites are summarised in *Moore, IE (ed) (1988) The Archaeology of Roman Suffolk, Suffolk County Council, p60*.

La Tène Culture (named from the site found by Hansli Kopp, a local collector, at the northern end of Lake Neuchâtel, Switzerland). Between 1857-1917 was discovered in the lake a huge collection of weapons and tools of bronze, iron and wood, dated from the mid-fifth century BC to the Roman conquest. The culture extended through Western Europe into Britain and Ireland (*Collis, 1984*). La Tène art is characterised by swirling patterns, forerunner of Celtic art.

Levallois Industry (After Levellois-Perret, a suburb of north Paris). A Lower and Middle Palaeolithic flint-tool technique which removed from the core flakes of predetermined size and shape by first knapping the core nodule into a tortoise shape (**12**). Used by some Mousterian communities. Levallois tools have been found at Brundon near Sudbury, Suffolk and at Lion Pit, West Thurrock (*Wymer, 1984*). (See Wolstonian Stage).

Lynchet. Prehistoric field boundaries may be preserved on hill slopes by the persistance of low earth banks. These are formed by the creep of plough-soil downhill (by rain and wind) whose progress is inhibited by a transverse fence- or hedge-line. Ploughing below the hedgeline removes soil from the downhill side of this hedge bank. When the hedge dies the line of the deposited soil creep is preserved as a lynchet.

Magdalenian industry (named from La Madeleine in the Dordogne). The final Late Upper Palaeolithic culture of Western Europe typified by cave art and by decorated bone, antler and ivory, and the barbed harpoon/fish hook, dated *c*.18,000-10,000 BC. In Britain Magdalenian-type flints, small backed-blades and trapezes and a bone engraved into the shape of a horse's head have been excavated at Creswell Crags, Derbyshire, dated about 7900 BC.

Maglemosian Culture (named from Maglemose in Denmark). The first Mesolithic culture dating from *c*.8000 BC, characterised by microliths, adzes and axes, fishing barbs and bone spear heads, as excavated from Star Carr, 5 miles south of Scarborough (*Clark, 1954*; *Legge, 1988*).

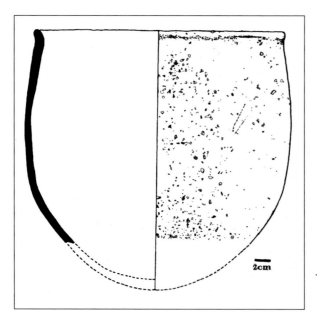

57   Mildenhall style urn from Orsett

Mildenhall Ware. The bowls of Mildenhall-style are wide, deep-sided, some with rolled rims, some without (**57**). Flint or sand temper is common, the bases rounded and the surface of the clay often smoothed. If decorated, the decoration often consists of vertical or diagonal lines incised on the neck of the pot, and finger-tip impressions. It dates from the early to middle Neolithic period, contemporary with or subsequent to carinate ware, qv (*Hedges, 1980, 1982*).

Mousterian Industry (after the excavation site at Le Moustier in the Dordogne, France). Dating to the Middle Palaeolithic period at the end of the Wolstonian Stage, tools were made from prepared cores typified by regular stone handaxes such as with the base flattened (**58**) rather than rounded as with Acheulian axes (qv). Occasional hide-scrapers, burins, barbed flakes and knives are found, traditionally associated with Neandertal Man (see Ipswichian Interglacial). The neanderthal skeleton excavated at Le Moustier in 1907 has now been dated to about 42,000 years old by Thermoluminescence dating and Electron Spin Resonance techniques (*Current Archaeology (1992) 131, 470*).

Neolithic Period. The first use of the term is credited to Sir John Lubbock (*Arch Camb, 1871, p168*) who excavated Parc-le-Brecos chambered tomb in Glamorgan. See Chapter 3.

Oxygen Isotope Time Scale. The sea and ocean floor contains calcium and silica skeletons of dead plankton. These plankton contain oxygen which occurs in three forms (isotopes), O^{16}, O^{17} and O^{18}. The relative amounts of these isotopes depends on the amount of water which was locked up in glaciers and the water temperature when the

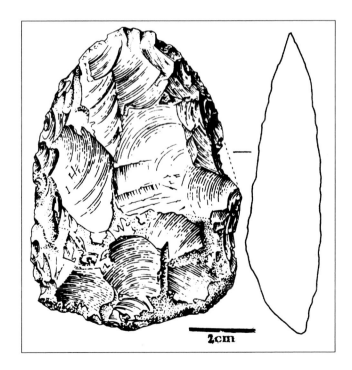

58   *Flat-butt axe of
      Mousterian Industry
      from Witham*

plankton were alive. Core samples taken from the ocean bed examined for the amounts of the different oxygen isotopes therefore indicate the degree of glaciation and temperature when the sediment was deposited. These cores are compared with soil samples from which analyses of pollen show predominance of cold-climate plants and trees (birch, pine) or warm (oak, alder) and comparison has been shown to correspond. Odd-numbered stages are warm, even are cold. Warm substages are lettered a,c,e, cold b,d. 5e corresponds to the last interglacial stage (Ipswichian) before the present Flandrian interglacial (*Aitken, 1990; Wymer, 1996*).

Palstave (19). A form of copper alloy axehead associated with the Middle Bronze Age (*c*.1550 BC) which was cast in a clay mould. Examples have been found mostly south of the line Waltham Abbey — Halstead. The form consists of a flared blade with marked stop-ridge flared shoulders and a metal loop to secure the haft. The blade may be patterned. Clay moulds have been excavated at Mucking and Chelmsford, Springfield. It may have evolved from the earlier flat and flanged axe. A later form, the socketed axe, introduced *c*.1400 BC, had a hollow into which the haft could be inserted; it remained in use until *c*.800 BC (**59**) (*Butcher, 1923; Sealey, 1991*).

Peterborough Ware. A pottery-type dating from the later Neolithic period, characterised by round-bottomed thick-walled vessels decorated with finger impression, stamped, combed and grooved ornamentation. Found at Shoeburyness and Chelmsford Springfield (*Brown, 1989*).

Pollen Record. Pollen and spores are often preserved in acidic soils and peat bogs. Identification of pollen types in soil samples gives an indication of the flora at the time of the soil deposition, an important caveat being the relative abundance of different species to produce different amounts of pollen (*Murphy, 1996*).

Querns (colour plate 16). Milling is attested from the Neolithic period from **saucer-**shaped querns on which grain was crushed with a rounded rocked stone 'rubber'. Querns from the Bronze Age were **saddle-**shaped with an elongated stone rider which was rubbed onto the grain placed onto the saddle. Two types were used in the Iron Age, the **saddle-**quern and the rotary '**beehive**' quern which had a notch in the centre of its upper surface for a wooden splindle and was capped with a beehive-shaped (centrally perforated for the spindle) top stone rotated by a side-handle; the grain was dropped into a central hole beside the spindle and fell between the two stones. Saddle and beehive querns continued in use in the Roman period but were complemented by **rotary** hand mills which had a metal or wood cap on the spindle supporting the upper stone making it easier to turn. Also rarely in use were **water-** and **donkey**-driven millstones. (Windmills are not known in Britain before the twelfth century AD).

Radiocarbon dates. The atmosphere contains 1 part per million million of radioactive carbon, C^{14}, as carbon dioxide. When plants respire they take in radio-carbon up to an amount equal to the concentration in the atmosphere, and when animals eat plants they acquire C^{14} too. On death plants and animals cease to acquire C^{14}. The C^{14} naturally

59   Socketed axe from Little Horkesley

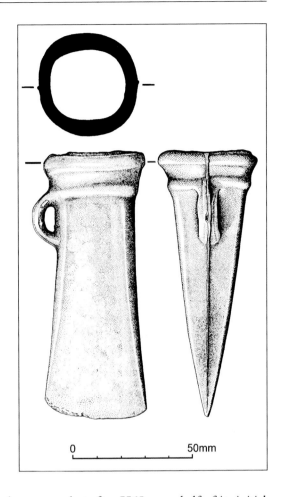

0   50mm

loses its radioactivity at a slow but steady rate, so that after 5568 years half of its initial radioactivity has decayed. Assuming the concentration of atmospheric C^{14} was the same in prehistoric times as now, the number of years ago of death can be calculated by measuring the amount of C^{14} still present in the specimen. In fact at least two factors make this simple calculation inaccurate. i. Atom bomb testing in the atmosphere in the 1950s greatly increased the amount of atmospheric C^{14} so all radiocarbon dates relate to 'before 1950'. ii. Prehistoric levels were not the same as in 1950 so that radiocarbon dates are too old by about 100 years at AD 500, and too young by about 900 years at 3000 BC. Radiocarbon dates therefore have to be 'calibrated' (corrected) against known tree-ring chronologies. By convention and usage, uncalibrated radiocarbon dates are written 'ad, bc or BP', i.e. before 1950, calibrated radiocarbon dates are written 'cal AD/BC' or 'cal ad/bc'. In each case an error of one standard deviation (68 per cent confidence limits) is usually quoted. The figure is followed by the initials of the calibrating laboratory and its unique laboratory reference number (eg HAR-6700=Harwell, Asheldham Camp cereal grain result 1980^{+}-80 years BP, cal BC 95-cal AD 75). For the British Iron Age, about 600-0 BC, radiocarbon dates have a wide range of standard error. Amounts of C^{14} remaining after about 40,000 years are too small to date samples much older than this (*Bowman, 1990*).

Red Hills★. Low reddish mounds or patchmarks are widely distributed along the coast in Ardale, Burnham, Great Clacton, Fambridge, Fingringhoe, Foulness, Goldhanger, Langenhoe, Little Oakley, Maldon, Mersea, Mucking, Pagglesham, Peldon, St Osyth, Salcott, Southminster, Steeple, Tilbury, Tillingham, Tollesbury, Virley, Walton-on-the-Naze, Wigborough and Woodham Ferrers. Excavation of a mound at Peldon, archaeometric dated 10 BC-AD 40 and radiocarbon dated 34 BC-AD 134, revealed three clay-lined tanks which would have received sea water at high tide from which clay pans were filled. The seawater was then evaporated to deposit the salt. The debris (briquetage) accumulated into red coloured mounds. Analysis suggests that the coloured material is charcoal flecks covered with a coat of fired or powdered clay, possibly resulting from burning turf or peat or salt-impregnated matter. *(VCH Essex 1903, 1963; Christy, 1928; De Brisay, 1978; Rodwell, 1979; Gurney, 1980; Fawn et al, 1990; Wilkinson, 1995; Sealey, 1995; Barford, 2000).*

Romano-British Villas in Essex are known or suspected at Abridge (TQ4798), Alphamstone (TL8835), Alresford (TM0620), Ashdon (TL5844), Berechurch (TL9920), Boreham (TL7609), Braintree (TL7824), Brightlingsea (TM0817, TM0819), Broomfield (TL6911), Chadwell St Mary (TQ6478), Chignall (TL6611), Chigwell (TQ4596), Colne Engaine (TL8731), Copford (TL9323), Daws Heath, Rayleigh (TQ1888), Felsted (TL6621), Finchingfield (TL6734, TL6932), Fingringhoe (TM0519), Fordham (TL9228), Gestingthorpe (TL8339), Great Sampford (TL6336), Grays Thurrock (TL6178), Great Tey (TL8925), Ingatestone (TL6502), Hadstock (TL5746), Halstead (TL8032), Harlowbury (TL4812), Harwich (TM2632), Hempstead (TL6540), Layer Breton (TL9418), Little Baddow (TL7807), Little Hallingbury (TL4916), Little Laver (TL5409), Little Oakley (TM2229), Messing (TL8919), Panfield (TL7426), Pleshey (TL6614), Ridgewell (TL7340), Rivenhall (TL8318), St Osyth (TM1117), Stansted Mountfichet (TL5224), Stanway (TL9522), Stebbing (TL6923, TL6824), Tollesbury (TL9610), Tolleshunt Knights (TL9315), Thaxted (TL6133), Wanstead (TQ4187)) Wendens Ambo (TL5136), West Mersea (TM0112) West Tilbury (TQ6377) and White Notley (TL7918).
(VCH Essex, 1963; Rodwell, W and K, 1973 and 1993; Rodwell, 1975 and 1978; Dunnett, 1975; Brooks, 1977).

Romano-British Villas in Suffolk are known or suspected at Burgh near Woodbridge (Castle Field, TM2351), Capel St Mary, Windmill Hill (TM0938), Earl Stonham (TM1058), Exning Landwade (TL6167), Farnham (TM3660), Hadleigh (TM0441), Hitcham (TL9852), Ipswich Castle Hill Whitton (TM1446), Ixworth (TL9369), Lidgate (TL7258), Long Melford (TL8645), Mildenhall Thistley Green (TL6676), Pakenham Redcastle Farm (TL9069), Rougham (TL9061), Stanstead (TL8449), Stanton Chair (TL9673), Stonham Aspal (TM1460). *(Moore, 1988).*

Samian Pottery Ware (*terra sigillata*). Fine red glossed tableware imported from the continent (mainly southern Italy and Gaul) was made by firing at 1000°C in an oxidising atmosphere. Relief was achieved by hardening the clay in moulds, by appliqué of preformed patterns, by trailing wet clay or rolling a patterned tool on to a plain vessel. The ware may be dateable from its potters' stamps and decoration style. Colchester had a small production industry from *c*.AD 160 (*Hull, 1963; Bedoyere, 1988*).

Sarsens, Basalts and Other Boulders in Essex. A survey of large exposed boulders in the county *(Salter, 1914)*.

Solutrean Culture (named from Solutré cave, near Mâcon in eastern France). A flint tool industry intermediate between the Aurignacian and Magdalenian, of the Upper Palaeolithic about 20,000 years ago, typified by bi-facial working (two-edged) which developed into slender pointed ?arrow and spear-heads by pressure-flaking. See Leaf-point.

Thermoluminescence dating. A method of dating pottery, burnt flint, baked brick and tile from the date when the interior of the clay or flint object was last exposed to sunlight. Pottery heated rapidly to 500°C gives off light which is detected by a photomultiplier. It is then reheated and the luminescence remeasured. The difference between the two readings represents the Thermoluminescence. This Thermoluminescence, TL, is derived from the radioactive impurities (potassium, uranium and thorium) in the clay which cause electrons to be trapped in luminescence centres. Heating expels these electrons releasing light in the process. The quantity of light released is proportional to the number of electrons trapped, which in turn is proportional to the length of time the clay has been exposed to the radiation from the impurities. When the clay was first fired by the potter, all the electrons were released setting the 'clock' to zero from which time trapping began (*Aitken, 1990*).

Three Age System. In 1848 J.J.A. Worsaae, a pupil of Christian Jurgensen Thomsen (1788-1865), published in English the system Thomsen used for classifying the collections of the National Museum of Denmark, stone objects, copper alloy (bronze) and iron. The Stone Age is subdivided into Old (Palaeolithic), Middle (Mesolithic) and New (Neolithic), respectively in Britain from about 500,000 years ago to 8000 BC, about 8000 BC to 4000 BC and about 4000 to 2200 BC. The introduction of metal (copper) technology in Britain dates from about 2200 BC and continued with the use of iron about 700 BC. Stone tools continued to be made well into the Bronze Age. The Iron Age is taken to end in Britain with the Roman conquest of AD 43 though clearly iron-working continued (*Davies, 1979*).

Uranium Dating. Teeth, bone and shell slowly take up uranium from the soil in which they are buried. The age of the sample relative to those buried in the same soil may be dated by measuring the amount of (radioactive) uranium acquired by the sample from the soil. A similar determination may be made by measuring the amount of **fluorine** (also absorbed from soil) or of **nitrogen** (which is lost into soil). Uranium slowly and at a constant rate loses its radioactivity as it converts to thorium and lead. An 'absolute' (as opposed to a 'relative') age may be given to sea sediments, calcium carbonate from spring waters, cave stalagmites and volcanics by measuring the uranium/thorium/lead ratios. The method may be applicable to samples between about 5000 to 350,000 years old.

Wolstonian Stage (named from Wolston near Coventry, equated, in Europe, to Riss, a tributary of the River Danube). Dating from about 380,000 to 130,000 years ago, several cold periods, the ice sheet reaching the Midlands and possibly north East Anglia, included warm interglacial periods. A new flint technique was developed termed '**Levallois**', qv.

Further reading

General topics

Blot, J.-Y., *Underwater Archaeology*. Thames & Hudson.
Chapman, H., *Landscape Archaeology and GIS*. Tempus, 2006.
Cunliffe, B. *Europe Between the Oceans: 9000BC-AD1000*. Yale, 2008.
Evans, J.G., *Land and Archaeology*. Tempus.
Fowler, P. *British Archaeology*, 2001, 62, 15. Reading the Land.
Gaffney, C., Gater, J., *Revealing the Buried Past*. Tempus, 2003. [Geophysics].
Hodges, H., *Technology in the Ancient World*. Pelican, 1970.
Hunter, J., Ralston, I., *The Archaeology of Britain*. Routledge.
Jones, M., *The Molecule Hunt*, Penguin, 2001. [DNA].
Parker-Pearson, M., *The Archaeology of Death & Burial*. Sutton, 1999.
Redd, M., *Landscape of Britain*. Routledge, 1990.
Renfrew, C., *Prehistory: Making of the Human Mind*. Weidenfeld, 2007. '
Renfrew, C., Bahn, P., *Archaeology*. Thames & Hudson, 1996.
Sykes, B., *The Seven Daughters of Eve*. Bantam, 2001. [DNA] '

Palaeolithic and Mesolithic

Bewley, R., *Prehistoric Settlements*. Tempus, 2003.
Carbonelli, E., et al., *Science* (1995) 269, 826. Lower Pleistocene Hominids at Atapuerca.
Conneller, C., Warren, G., *Mesolithic Britain & Ireland*. Tempus, 2006.
Huang Wanpo et al., *Nature* (1995) 378, 275. Early Homo in Asia.
Lewin, R., *Human Evolution*. Blackwell, 4th edition, 1999.
McKie, R., *Ape-Man*. British Broadcasting Corporation, 2000.
Pitts, M., Roberts, M., *Fairweather Eden*. Arrow, 1998.
Pollard, J., *Prehistoric Britain*. Blackwell, 2008.
Schrenk, F., Miller, S., *The Neanderthals*. Routledge, 2008.
Stringer, C. *Homo Britannicus*. Penguin, 2006.
Stringer, C., Andrews, A., *Complete World of Human Evolution*. Thames & Hudson, 2005.
Stuart, A.J., *Life in the Ice Age*. Shire, Aylesbury, 1988.
Templeton, A., *Science* (1992) 255, 737. Human Origins and Mitochondrial DNA.

Neolithic and Bronze Ages

Barton, N., *Stone Age Britain*. Batsford/English Heritage, 1997.
Barber, M., *Bronze and the Bronze Age*. Tempus, 2003.

Bradley, R., *The Significance of Monuments*. Routledge.
Field, D., *Earthen Long Barrows*. Tempus, 2006.
Gibson, A., Simpson, D., *Prehistoric Ritual & Religion*. Sutton, 1998.
Harding, J., *Henge Monuments of the British Isles*. Tempus, 2003.
Laing, L., *Pottery in Britain, 4000BC to AD1900*. Greenlight, 2007.
Loveday, R., *Inscribed Across the Landscape; The Cursus Enigma*. Tempus, 2006.
Malone, C., *Neolithic Britain*. Tempus, 2000.
Parker-Pearson, M., *Bronze Age Britain*. English Heritage/Batsford, 1993.
Reid, M.L., *Prehistoric Houses in Britain*. Shire, Aylesbury, 1993.
Russell, M., *Flint Mines in Neolithic Britain*. Tempus, 2000.
Spindler, K., *Man in the Ice*. Weidenfeld & Nicholson, 1994.
Woodward, A., *British Barrows*. Tempus, 2000.

Iron Age

Creighton, J., *Coins & Power in Late Iron Age Britain*. Cambridge UP, 2000.
Dillon, M., Chadwick, N., *The Celtic Realms*. Cardinal, London, 1973.
Cunliffe, B., *Iron Age Communities in Britain*. Routledge, 2005.
Garrow, D., Gosden, C., Hill, J.D., *Rethinking Celtic Art*. Oxbow, 2008.
James, S., Rigby, V., *Britain and The Celtic Iron Age*. British Museum, 1997.
Miles, D., *The Tribes of Britain*. Weidenfeld & Nicholson, 2005.
Pryor, F., *Britain BC*. Harper Collins, 2005.
Puddle, R., Eyre, C., *Tribes & Coins of Celtic Britain*. Greenlight, 2006.
Ritchie, W.F., & J.N.G., *Celtic Warriors*. Shire, 1997.

Roman

Bédoyère, G de la., *Roman Britain: a New History*. Thames & Hudson, 2006.
Bédoyère, G de la., *Defying Rome; Rebels of Roman Britain*. Tempus.
Bidwell, P., *Roman Forts in Britain*. Tempus, 2008.
Clark, J., Cotton, J., et al., *Londinium and Beyond*. Council for British Archaeology, 2008.
Davies, H., *Roman Roads in Britain*. Shire, 2008.
Edmonde Cleary, A.S., *The Ending of Roman Britain*. Routledge, 2000.
Fleming, A., Hingley, R., *Prehistoric & Roman Landscapes*. Windgather, 2007.
Faulkner, N., *Decline and Fall of Roman Britain*. Tempus, 2000.
Kunzl, E., *Current Archaeology* (2008) 222, 22. Celtic Art.
Laycock, S., *Britannia: The Failed State*. Tempus, 2008.
Marsden, A., *Roman Coins found in Britain*. Greenlight, 2007.
Mills, N., *Celtic & Roman Artefacts*, Greenlight, 2007.
Ottaway, P.J., *A Victory Celebration*. Colchester Archeological Trust, 2007. [Colchester].
Rudling, D., *Ritual Landscapes in Roman South-east Britain*. Oxbow, 2007.

References

Abbeto, E, 1998. *Nature*, 393, 458. Eritrian Homo sapiens?

Adkins, P, Brown, N, et al, 1984. *Essex Archaeology & History*, 16, 94. Blackwater.

Aiello, L, Dean, C, 1990. *Human Evolutionary Anatomy*. Academic Press.

Aitken, MJ, 1990. *Science-based Dating in Archaeology*. Longman.

Aldhouse-Green, S, 2001. *British Archaeology*, 61, 20. Paviland Cave.

Aldhouse-Green, SHR, Pettit, PB, 1998. *Antiquity*, 72, 756. Paviland Cave.

Alexander JA et al, 1978. *Essex Archaeology & History*, 10, 189. Ambresbury Banks.

Allen, DF, 1944. *Archaeologia*, 90, 1. Belgic Dynasties and their Coins.

Allen, DF, 1975. *Britannia*, 6, 1. Cunobelin's Gold.

Allen, P, 1988. *Essex Journal*, 23(ii), 27. Chelmsford Mansio and Bath house.

Allen, RH, et al, 1980 in Buckley, D. *Archaeology in Essex to 1500*. CBA Res Rep 34, 1.

Andrews, DD, 1999. *Essex Archaeology & History* 30, 232. Tree-ring Dating.

Aston, M, 1985. *Interpreting the Landscape*. Batsford.

Aston, M, 2003. *British Archaeology* 70, 8. First Humans.

Atkins, L and R, 1982. *Handbook of British Archaeology*. David & Charles..

Atkinson, M, 1995. *Essex Archaeology & History*, 26, 1. Broomfield Enclosure.

Atkinson, M, Preston, S, 2001. *Essex Archaeology & History*, 32, 42. Maldon Elms Farm.

Austin, L, 1996. *Essex Archaeology & History*, 27, 304. Flint axe from Ingatestone.

Baker, JT, 2006. *Cultural Transition in the Chilterns & Essex 350 to 650 AD*. Hertfordshire UP.

Bahn, P, 2003. *British Archaeology*, 72, 8. Art of the Hunters.

Bailey, K, 1988. *Essex Journal*, 23(ii), 34. East Saxon Kings.

Barclay, GJ, Maxwell, GS, 1998. *Soc of Antiquaries of Scotland*, mono 13. Neolithic Monuments.

Barford, PM. 1988 in Bond, D, *East Anglian Archaeology*, 43, 37. Mucking North Ring.

Barford, PM, 2000. *Essex Archaeology & History*, 31, 276. Salt-licks.

Barford, PM, 2002. *East Anglian Archaeology*, 98, 188. Little Oakley Villa.

Barham, L, 1999. *British Archaeology*, 42, 8. African Homo.

Bartholomew, P, 1984. *Britannia*, 15, 169. Fourth Century Saxons.

Bartlett, R, 1987. *Essex Archaeology & History*, 18, 115. Harlow temple.

Barton, KJ, 1962. *Trans Essex Archaeological Society*, 1(ii), 77. Linford excavations.

Bassett, SR, 1989. *Studies in Early History of Britain*. Leicester.

Bassett, SR, 1989 (ed). *Origins of Anglo-Saxon Kingdoms*. Leicester, pp108,146.

Bassett, SR, 1997. *Landscape History*, p.25. The Rodings.

Bates, E, 2004. *East Anglian Archaeology*, occ paper 20. Roman Maltings.

Bédoyère, G de la, 1988. *Samian Ware.* Shire.

Bedwin, O, 1979. *Sussex Archaeological Collections*, 113, 225.

Bedwin, O, 1991. *Essex Archaeology & History*, 22, 13. Asheldham Iron Age Fort.

Bedwin, O, 1992. *Essex Archaeology & History*, 23,10. Early Iron Age Settlement at Maldon.

Black, EW, 1990. *Essex Archaeology & History*, 21, 6. Caesar's Second Invasion of Britain

Blake, BP, 1960. *Trans Essex Archaeological Society*, 25(ii), 344. Dedham barrow.

Bond, D, 1988. *East Anglian Archaeology*, 43. Mucking.

Boismer, W, 2002. *Current Archaeology*, 182, 53. Lynford.

Boulter, S, 2004. *Current Archaeology*, 187, 280. Wuffings.

Bowman, S, 1990. *Radiocarbon Dating.* British Museum.

Bradley, R, 1993. *Altering the Earth.* Society of Antiquaries of Scotland, monograph 8.

Bradley, R, 1996 in Bedwin, O. *Archaeology of Essex*, Essex Co Council, p41. Bronze Age.

Breeze, A, 2004. *Britannia*, 35, 228. God Callirius.

Brennard, M, Taylor, M, 2000. *Current Archaeology*, 167, 417. Seahenge.

Bridgland, DR, 1994. *Quarternary of the Thames.* Chapman & Hall.

Bridgland, DR, 1994 in Ashton, N. Stories in Stone. *Lithic Studies Soc*, occ paper 4, p28. Paleolithic of Thames.

Briscoe, G, 1957. *Proceedings of the Cambridge Antiquarian Society,* 50, 101. Swales Tumulus.

Brophy, K, 1999. *British Archaeology*, 44, 6. Neolithic Cursus.

Brooks, H, 2002. *Essex Archaeology & History*, 33, 54. Fingringhoe Frog Hall.

Brooks, H, 2008. *Colchester Archaeologist*, 21, 13. Coin Moulds.

Brooks, H, Bedwin, O, 1989. *Archaeology at the Airport.* English Heritage.

Brooks, H, Holloway, B, 2006. *Essex Archaeology & History*, 34, 14. Great Notley.

Brooks, RT, 1977. *Essex Journal*, 12(iii), pp50, 81. Abridge Roman Villa.

Brown, N, 1988. *Essex Archaeology & History*, 19, 1. Late Bronze Age Settlement.

Brown, N, 1988. *Proceedings of Prehistoric Society*, 54, 249. Lofts Farm, Gt Totham.

Brown, N, 1989. *Essex Archaeology & History*, 20, 147. Shoeburyness Pottery.

Brown, N, 1995 in Kinnes, I. *Unbaked Urns of Rudely Shape.* Oxbow monograph 55, p123.

Brown, N, in Bedwin, O, 1996. *Archaeology of Essex.* Essex Co Council, p26. 1500-500BC.

Brown, N, 1997 in Topping, P (ed). *Neolithic Landscapes.* Oxbow monograph 86, p87.

Brown, N, 1998. *Essex Archaeology & History*, 29, 1. Late Bronze Hoard from Vange.

Brown, N, 1998. *Essex Journal*, 33(i), 12. Archaeology of South-east Essex.

Brown, N, Bartlett, R, 1992. *Essex Archaeology & History*, 23, 114. Knife from Sheering.

Brown, N, Germany, M, 2002. *Essex Archaeology & History*, 33, 8. Cropmark Project.

Brown, N, Knopp, D, Strachan, D, 2002. *Landscape History, 24.* Stour Valley Cropmarks.

Brown, N, Lavender, N, 1991. *Essex Archaeology & History*, 22, 153. Great Baddow Manor.

Brown, N, Lavender, NJ, 1994. *Essex Archaeology & History*, 25, 10. Bronze Age in Chelmer.

Brown, N, Murphy, P, 2000, in Brown, N, et al, *East Anglian Archaeology*, occasional paper 8.

Brown, P, 1985. *Essex Journal*, 20, 42. Iron Age Hoard from Lofts Farm.

Brück, J, 1995. *Proceedings of the Prehistoric Society,* 61, 245. A Place for the Dead.

Buckley, DG, 1977. *Essex Archaeology & History*, 9, 60. Barling Magna.

Buckley, D, 1984. *Essex Archaeology & History*, 16, 134. Springfield Lyons.

Buckley, D, Brown, N, Greenwood, P, 1986. *Antiquaries Jnl*, 66(ii), 248. Bronze Age Hoards.

Buckley, DG, Hedges, JD, 1987. *Springfield Lyons*. Essex County Council occasional paper 5.

Buckley, DG, Hedges, JD, Brown, N, 2001. *Proc of Prehistoric Soc*, 67. Springfield Cursus.

Buckley, DG, Major, H, Milton, B, 1988. *Proceedings of Prehistoric Society*, 54, 77. Rivenhall.

Budd, P, 2000. *British Archaeology*, 55, 12. The Metal Makers.

Burgess, CB, 1969. *Archaeological Journal*, 125, 1. Later Bronze Age in the British Isles.

Burl, A, 1991. *Prehistoric Henges*. Shire.

Carbonelli, E, Jose, M, et al, 2008. *Nature*, 452, p465. The First Hominin.

Casey, PJ, 1980. *Roman Coinage in Britain*. Shire.

Chadburn, A, 1999 in Davies, J et al. *Land of the Iceni*. University of East Anglia.

Chadburn, A, 2006. *British Archaeology*, 87, 27. Currency of Kings.

Chadburn, A, 2008. *Current Archaeology*, 215, 12. Silbury Hill.

Chadwick, N, 1970. *The Celts*. Penguin, p264.

Chandler, RH, 1932. *Proceedings of the Prehistoric Society of East Anglia*, 6, 377. Hoxne.

Chapman, H, Johnson, T, 1973. *Trans London & Middlesex Arch Society*, 24. Aldgate.

Christie, M, Dalton, W, 1928. *Trans Essex Archaeological Society*, ns 18, 27. Red Hills.

Clark, AJ, 1993. *English Heritage Archaeology Rep* 20 vol 1. Mucking. (See Hamerow).

Clark, A, 1996. *Seeing Beneath the Soil*. Batsford.

Clark, JGD, 1954. *Excavations at Star Carr*. Cambridge University Press.

Clark, JGD, 1960. *Proceedings of the Prehistoric Society*, 26, 202. Mildenhall Hurst Fen.

Clark, P, 1997. *British Archaeology*, 24, 7. The Dover Boat.

Clark, P, 2004. *The Dover Bronze Age Boat*. English Heritage.

Clarke, C, 1991. *Current Archaeology*, 126, 272 Brightlingsea Bronze Age Cemetery.

Clarke, CP, 1988. *Essex Archaeology & History*, 19, 47. Roman Coggeshall.

Clarke, CP, 1998. *East Anglian Archaeology*, 83. Chignall Roman Villa.

Clarke, DL, 1970. *Beaker Pottery of Great Britain and Ireland*. Cambridge.

Clarke, F, et al, 1998. *Romano-British Settlement at Chigwell*. West Essex Arch Group.

Clarke, RR, 1963. *East Anglia*. Thames & Hudson.

Clarke, WG (ed), 1914. *Prehistoric Society of East Anglia Report* 1915. Grimes Graves.

Cleal, R, 2002. *British Archaeology*, 67, 22. Windmill Hill.

Coles, B, 1990. *Proceedings of the Prehistoric Society*, 56, 215. Anthropomorphic Figures.

Coles, BJ, 1998. *Proceedings of the Prehistoric Society*, 64, 45. Doggerland.

Collard, M, 2004. *Current Archaeology*, 195, 134. Ironworking.

Collis, J, 1984. *The European Iron Age*. Batsford.

Cooper-Reade, H, 1996. *Essex Archaeology & History*, 26, 268. Langford Bronze Age.

Cook, J, Ashton, N, 1991. *Current Archaeology*, 123, 132. High Lodge, Mildenhall.

Cooke, N, Brown, F, 2008. *Huntergatherers to Huntsmen, Stansted*. Framework Arch mono 2.

Couchman, CR, 1975. *Essex Archaeology & History*, 7, 14. Bronze Age, Ardleigh.

Couchman, C, 1976. *Essex Archaeology & History*, 8, 146. Little Baddow.

Couchman, CR, 1980 in Buckley, DG. *Archaeology in Essex to 1500*. CBA Res Rep 34, p40.

Crowe, K, 1984. *Southend Museum Report on Great Wakering*.

Crowe, KL, 1992. *Essex Archaeology & History*, 23, 1. Mesolthic Flints from South Benfleet.

Crowe, K, 2003. *Essex Archaeology & History*, 34, 1. Bronze Hoards.

Crummy, N, 1994. *Colchester Archaeological Reports*, 4. Coins from Colchester.

Crummy, P, 1977. *Essex Archaeology & History*, 9, 1. Chitts Hill, Colchester

Crummy, P, 1978. *Aerial Archaeology*, 4, 77. Crop marks at Gosbecks.

Crummy, P, 1993. *Current Archaeology*, 132, 492. Aristocratic Graves at Colchester.

Crummy, P, 1997. *Current Archaeology*, 153, 337. Stanway burials.

Crummy, P, 1997. *City of Victory*, Colchester Archaeological Trust.

Crummy, P, 2005. *Journal of Roman Archaelogfy*, 18, 267. Roman Circus.

Crummy, P, 2008. *Britannia*, 39, 15. Roman Circus at Colchester.

Cuddeford, MJ, Sealey, PR, 2000. *Essex Archaeology & History*, 31, 1. Hoard at High Easter.

Cunliffe, B, 1993. *Danebury*. London.

Cunliffe, B, 1995. *Iron Age Britain*. Batsford.

Curteis, M, 2006. *Essex Archaeology & History*, 37, 1. Iron Age Coinage.

Dale, R, Maynard, D, et al, 2005. *Essex Archaeology & History*, 36, 10. The A130 Bypass.

Dark, KR, 1994. *Civitas to Kingdom*. Leicester University.

Dark, K & P, 1997. *Landscape of Roman Britain*. Sutton.

Darvill, T, 1987. *Prehistoric Britain*. Batsford.

Davies, DG, 1979 in Burgess, C, et al. *British Archaeological Rep* 67. Bronze Hoards.

Davies, G, 1996. *A History of Money*. University of Wales, Cardiff.

Davies, GMR, 1992. *Archaeological Journal*, supplement. Prehistoric Colchester.

Davies, H, 2002. *British Archaeology*, 67, 8. Roman Roads.

Davies, W, 1874. *Catalogue of Pleistocene Vertebrae from Ilford*. [In Essex Record Office].

Day, MH, 1986. *Guide to Fossil Man*. Cassell.

De Brisay, K, 1978. *Antiquity Journal*, 58, 31. Red Hill at Peldon.

De Jersey, P, 1996. *Celtic Coinage in Britain*. Shire.

De Jersey, P, 2001. *Britannia*, 32, 1. Cunobelin's Silver.

Delderfield, RB, Rippon, S, 1996. *Essex Archaeology & History*, 27, 322. Thundersley.

Denison, S, 1999. *British Archaeology*, 46, 4. Thames Bridge.

Dennis, M, 2008. *Current Archaeology*, 217, 20. Silver of the Iceni.

Douglas, A, 2004. *Current Archaeology*, 193, 20. Shadwell.

Draper, J, 1985. *East Anglian Archaeology*, 25. Gestingthorpe.

Drury, PJ, 1972. *Essex Archaeology & History*, 4, 7. Roman Settlement at Chelmsford.

Drury, PJ, 1976. *Essex Archaeology & History*, 8, 121. Braintree Research.

Drury, PJ, 1977. *Essex Archaeology & History*, 9, 23. Excavations at Rawreth.

Drury, PJ, 1978. *Council for British Arch Res Rep* 26. Excavations at Little Waltham.

Drury, PJ, 1980 in Buckley, DG (ed). *Council for British Arch Research Report* 34, 52.

Drury, PJ, 1986. *Council for British Archaeology Research Report* 66. The Mansio, Caesaromagus.

Drury, PJ, Rodwell, 1973. *Essex Archaeology & History*, 5, 48. Gun Hill, West Tilbury.

Drury, PJ, Rodwell, WJ, 1978. *Antiquaries Journal* 58(i), 133. Asheldham.

Drury, P, Rodwell, W, 1980, in Buckley, D. *CBA Research Report* 34. Iron Age Settlement.

Drury, PJ, Wickenden, N, 1970. *Medieval Archaeology* 26, 1. Maldon Heybridge.

Dunnett, R, 1971. *Britannia*, 2, 27. Gosbecks theatre.

Dunnett, R, 1975. *The Trinovantes*. Duckworth.

Ecclestone, J, 1995. *Essex Archaeology & History*, 26, 24. Southend excavations.

Eddy, MR, 1982. *Kelvedon, Origins*. Essex Co Council occasional paper 3.

Eddy, M, 1986. *Essex Archaeology & History*, 14, 111. Osea Island.

Ellis, PB, 1991. *Celtic Remains in Britian*. Constable.

Ellis, PB, 1994. *Caesar's Invasion of Britain*. Constable.

Ennis, T, Foreman, S, 2002. *Essex Archaeology & History*, 33, 63. Kelvedon enclosure.

Erith, FH, 1968. *Colchester Archaeology Group Annual Bulletin*, 14, 38. Lawford Barrow.

Erith, FH, Holbert, PR, 1970. *Colchester Arch Gp Ann Bull*, 13(i), 7. Vinces Farm, Ardleigh.

Evans, C, forthcoming. *Proceedings of the Chelmsford Conference 2008*. Mucking.

Evans, JG, 1975. *The Environment of Early Man*. London.

Everson P, Williamson, T, 1998. *The Archaeology of Landscape*. Manchester University.

Evison, V, 1994. *Council for British Archaeology Res Rep* 91. Great Chesterford cemetery.

Fairclough, J, et al, 2000. *Proc Suffolk Inst Arch Hist*, 39(4), 419. Waltow.

Farrands, RH, 1958. *Colchester Archaeology Group Annual Bulletin*, 1(iv), 43. Little Oakley.

Fawn, AJ et al, 1990. *Colchester Archaeological Reports*. Red Hills of Essex.

Fitzpatrick, A, 2003. *Current Archaeology*, 184, 146. The Amesbury Archer.

Fleming, A, 1988. *The Dartmore Reaves*. Batsford.

Fleming, A, 1998, in Everson P, Williamson, T (eds). *Archaeology of Landscape*. Manchester.

France, NE, Goble, BM. 1985. *Temple at Harlow*. West Essex Archaeology Group.

Frere, SS, 1970. *Britannia*, i, 267. Votive from Witham.

Frere, SS, 1973. *Britannia*. Routledge Kegan Paul.

Frere, S, Fulford, M, 2001. *Britannia*, 32, 45. Roman Invasion AD 43.

Gaffney, V, 2007. *Curent Archaeology*, 207, 14. Doggerland.

Gardner, A, 2007. *The Archaeology of Identity*. Left Coast Press.

Garwood, A, 1998. *Essex Archaeology & History*, 29,33. Roman Great Sampford.

Gelling, M, Cole, A, 2000. *Landscape of Place-names*. Tyas, Stamford.

Germany, M, 2007. *East Anglian Archaeology*, 117. St. Osyth.

Gibbard, PL, 1994. *Pleistocene History of the Lower Thames Valley*. Cambridge.

Gobbold, S, 1996. *Essex Archaeology & History*, 27, 1. Writtle Enclosure.

Going, CJ, 1996 in Bedwin, O. *Archaeology of Essex*. Essex Co Cncl, p95. Roman Countryside.

Going, C, Plouviez, J, 2000 in Brown, N, et al, (ed). *East Anglian Archaeology*, occ paper 8, p19.

Gower, G, 1999. *London Archaeologist*, 9(iii), 90. Bronze Age Bridge at Vauxhall.

Green, HS, Stringer, CB, et al, 1981. *Nature*, 294, 707. Pontnewydd Cave.

Green, MJ, 1983. *Gods of Roman Britain*. Shire.

Green, MJ, 1992. *Celtic Myth & Legend*. Thames & Hudson, p120.

Greenwood, P, 1988. *Essex Journal*, 23, 19. Uphall Camp, Ilford.

Greenwood, P, 1989. *London Archaeologist*, 6, 94; (2001) 9, 207. Uphall Camp, Ilford.

Grinsell, L, 1979. *Barrows in England & Wales*. Shire.

Gurney, D, 1980. *Essex Archaeology & History*, 12, 207. Red Hills of the Dengie Peninsula.

Guttman, EBA, Last, J, 2000. *Proceedings of the Prehistoric Society*, 66, 319. Hornchurch.

Hamerow, H, 1993. *English Heritage Archaeological British Rep* 21. Mucking. (See Clark, AJ).

Haselgrove, C, 1979. *British Archaeological Reports*, 73, 197. Pre-Conquest Coinage.

Haselgrove, CC, 1989a. *Archaeological Journal*, 145, 99. Potin Coinage.

Haselgrove, CC, 1989b. *Oxford Journal of Archaeology*, 8, 73. Iron Age Deposition at Harlow.

Havis, R, 1993. *Essex Archaeology & History*, 24, 54. Roman Braintree.

Havis, R, Brooks, H, 2004. *East Anglian Archaeology*, 107. The Stansted Project 1985-91.

Hawkes, CFC, 1980 in Buckley, D. *CBA Research Report* 34, 57. Caesar to Claudius.

Hawkes, CFC, 1983. *Essex Archaeology & History*, 14, 3. Colchester before the Romans.

Hawkes, CFC, Smith, MA, 1975. *Antiquaries Journal*, 37, 161. Iron Age Buckets & Urns.

Healey, F, 1993. *Proceedings of the Prehistoric Society*, 59, 417. Excavations at Grimes Graves.

Hedges, JD, 1977. *Essex Archaeology & History*, 9, 75. Iron Age, Stock.

Hedges, JD, 1980 in Buckley, DG (ed). *CBA Research Report* no 34, p26. Essex Neolithic.

Hedges, JD, 1982. *Essex Archaeology & History*, 14, 114. Layer de la Haye Grimston bowl.

Hedges, JD, Buckley, D, 1978. *Proceedings of Prehistoric Society*, 44, 219. Orsett Enclosure.

Hedges, J, Buckley, D, 1981. *Springfield Cursus*. Essex Co Council occasional paper 1.

Herne, A, 1988, in Barrett, JC, Kinnes, IA (eds). *Archaeology of Context in Neolithic & Bronze Ages*. Sheffield Dept of Archaeolgy & Prehistory.

Higham, T, 2008. *Current Archaeology*, 214. 4. Paviland.

Hinchcliffe, J, 1981. *Colchester Archaeology Group Ann Bulletin*, 24, 2. Ardleigh Project.

Hingley, R, 1990. *Archaeological Journal*, 147. Currency Bars.

Hodder, IA, 1982. *Archaeology of the M11*, London. Wendens Ambo.

Hodder, IA and Halstead, P, 1982. *Archaeology of the M11*, vol 2, pp 4-64.

Holgate, R,. 1996, in Bedwin, O. *Archaeology of Essex*. Essex Co Council, p15. 4000-1500BC.

Hooper, B, 1967-71. *Essex Naturalist*, 32, 341. Burials at Great Chesterford

Hope, JH, 1978. *Essex Journal*, 13, 27. A Crop mark at Cressing.

Huggins, PJ, 1978. *Essex Archaeology & History*, 10, 110. Nazingbury.

Hull, MR, 1947, 1963. *Potters Kilns of Roman Colchester*. Society of Antiquaries Res Rep.

Hunter, J, 1993 in Andrews, DD. Cressing Temple, a Templar & Hospitaller Manor. EssexCC.

Hunter, J, 1999. *The Essex Landscape*. Essex County Council.

Hunter, J, 1999 in Green, S (ed). *The Essex Landscape*. Essex County Council, p 4.

Ireland, S, 1986. *Roman Britain, a Sourcebook*. Routledge.

Jacobi, RM, 1978, in Limbrey, S et al. *CBA Res Report* 21, 75. Effect of Man on the Landscape.

Jacobi, RM, 1980, in Buckley, DG. *Council for British Arch Research Report* 34, p12-25.

Jacobi, RM, 1996, in Bedwin, O (ed). *Archaeology of Essex*, Essex Co Council, p10. Mesolithic.

Jacobi, RM, 2004. *Proceedings of the Prehistoric Society*, 70,1. Cheddar.

Jacobi, RM, Martingell, HE, et al, 1978. *Essex Archaeology & History*, 10, 206. High Beech.

Johns, C, Bland, R, 1993. *Current Archaeology*, 136, 152. Hoxne.

Johnson, JS, 1979. *Roman Forts of the Saxon Shore*. P. Elek.

Johnson, T, 1975. *Trans London & Middlesex Archaeological Society*, 26, 278. Shadwell.

Jones, C, Bland, R, 1994. *Britannia* 25, 165. Hoxne hoard.

Jones, G, 1982. *Archaeology of the M11*, vol 2, London p50.

Jones, M, 1996. *British Archaeology*, 20, 8. The End of Roman Britain.

Jones, MU, 1978 in Bowen HC et al (eds). *British Archaeological Reps*, B 48. Mucking.

Jones, MU, 1978. *Panorama*, 21, 48. The Mucking Excavations.

Jones, MU, 1980 in Buckley, D (ed). *CBA Reseach Report* 34. Mucking, Saxon Cemeteries.

Jones, MU, Bond, D, 1980 in Barrett, J, Bradley, R. *British Archaeol Reps* 83, 437. Mucking.

Kemble, J, 1999. *The Tithe Place-names of Cressing Parish*. Essex Record Office.

Kemble, J, 2000. *Essex Journal*, 35(i), 19. Celtic Essex, Place-name Evidence.

Kemble, J, 2003. *Essex Archaeology & History*, 34, 157. 'Beorg' & Other Essex Mounds.

Kemble, J, 2007. *Essex Place-names, Places, Streets & People*. Historical Publications.

Kretz, R, 2000. *Numismatic Circular* 108(2), 49. Tasciovanus Coins.

Krings, M, Stone, A, Schmitz, R et al, 1977. *Cell*, 90, 19. Neanderthal DNA Sequences.

Lang, ATO, Keen, DH, 2005. *Proceedings of Prehistoric Soc*, 71, 63. Hominids in the Midlands.

Langton, B. et al, 1997. *Essex Archaeology & History*, 28, 12. Roman Heybridge.

Last, J, 1999. *Cursus Monuments of Britain & Ireland*. Neolithic Studies Gp Seminar paper 4.

Lavender, NJ, 1993. *Essex Archaeology & History*, 24, 1. Principia at Boreham.

Lavender, NJ, 1996. *Essex Archaeology & History*, 27, 266. Brightlingsea Ring-ditch.

Lavender, NJ, 1997. *Essex Archaeology & History*, 28, 47. Settlement at Great Dunmow.

Laver, H, 1889. *Transactions Essex Archaeological Society*, ns v, 33. Roman roads and fields.

Lawson, AK, 1986. *Britannia*, 17, 333. Bronze equine Statue from Ashill.

Lawson, AJ, Martin, EA, et al, 1981. *East Anglian Archaeology*, 12. Barrows in East Anglia.

Layard, N, 1920. *Proceedings of the Prehistoric Society*, 3(ii), 210. Stoke Tunnel, Ipswich.

Layard, N, 1927. *Antiquaries Journal*, 7, 500. Palaeolithic Settlement in the Colne Valley.

Legg, AJ, Rowley-Conwy, PA, 1988. *Star Carr Revisited*. London University.

Letch, A, 2005. *Essex Archaeology & History*, 36, 55. Jaywick, Clacton.

Lucy, G, 1999. *Essex Rock*. Essex Rock & Mineral Society.

Mack, RP, 1975. *Coinage of Ancient Britain*. Spink.

MacLeod, DG, 1971. *Southend Museum Publications*, 15. Prehistoric South-east Essex.

Major, HE, Eddy, MR, 1986. *Britannia*, 17, 355. Lead Objects of Christian Significance.

Manning, A, Moore, C, 2003. *Essex Archaeology & History*, 34, 19. Springfield.

Martingell, HE, Jacobi, RM, 1978. *Essex Archaeology & History*, 10, 233. Walton Bi-points.

Martingell, H, 1986. *Essex Archaeology & History*, 17, 141. Tranchet Axe from Ardleigh.

McMaster, I, 1982. *Colchester Archaeology Group Annual Bulletin*, 25, 6. Iron Age Pottery.

Meddens, F, 1995. *Current Archaeology*, 143, 412. Bronze Age Trackways.

Meddens, FM, 1995. *Essex Archaeology & History*, 26, 251 Iron Age & Roman Ilford.

Medlycott, M, 1994. *Essex Archaeology & History*, 25, 28. Roman Birchanger.

Medlycott, M, 2005. *Essex Archaeology & History*, 36, 1. Fieldwalking.

Medlycott, M, Germany, M, 1994. *Essex Archaeology & History*, 25, 14. Fieldwalking..

Meeks, ND, Varndell, GL, 1994. *Essex Archaeology & History*, 25, 1. Woodham Walter Torcs.

Mellars, P, 1998. *Nature*, 395, 539. Neandertal/sapiens contacts.

Mellars, P, 2004. *Nature*, 432, 461. Neanderthal Colonisation of Europe.

Mercer, N et al, 1991. *Nature* 351, 737. Dating of Neandertal Man.

Merrifield, R, 1983. *London City of the Romans*. London, p.l26.

Merriman, N, 1990. *Prehistoric London*. London.

Miles, D, 2008. *Current Archaeology*, 215, 21. Lasar Scanning.

Milton, B, 1984. *Essex Archaeology & History*, 16, 87. Orsett Cock Beaker Burial.

Milton, BH, 1986. *Essex Archaeology & History*, 17, 91. Excavations at Braintree.

Milton, B, 1987. *Essex Archaeology & History*, 18, 16. Excavations at Orsett Cock.

Mitchell, S, Reeds, B. 1997. *Coins of England*. Seaby.

Moore, IE, 1948. *Proceedings Suffolk Inst of Archaeology & History*, 24, 176. Corton station.

Moore, IE, 1988. *Archaeology of Roman Suffolk*. Suffolk Co Council.

Morris, J, 1995. *Arthurian Sources*, vol 4. Phillimore.

Morris, R, 1980, in Rodwell, W (ed). *Temples, Churches & Religion in Roman Britain*, i, 175.

Morris, S, Buckley, DG, 1978. *Essex Archaeology & History*, 10, 1. Excavations at Danbury.

Murphy, P, 1984, in Barringer, C (ed). *Aspects of East Anglian Prehistory*. Geo, Norwich.

Murphy, P, 1988, in Wilkinson, TJ. *East Anglian Archaeology*, 42. Environment in SE Essex.

Murphy, P, 1996, in Bedwin, O. *Archaeology of Essex.* Essex Co Council, p168. Environment.

Murphy, P, Brown, N, 1999, in Green, SA. *The Essex Landscape*. Essex Co Council, p11.

Myers, JNL, 1986. *The English Settlements*. Oxford.

Needham, SP, 1988. *East Anglian Archaeology*, 43. Excavation at Mucking North Ring.

Needham, SP, 1992 in Mordant, C (ed). *L'Age du Bronze*. Comité des Traveaux Historiques,
    4,39. Paris.

Oakley, K, Andrews, P, et al, 1977. *Proceedings of the Prehistoric Society*, 43, 13. Clacton.

O'Connor, B, 1976. *Essex Archaeology & History*, 8, 279. Nordic Socketed Axe.

O'Connor, B, 1980. *British Archaeol Rep*, international series 91. Cross Channel Relations.

Orton, C, 1998. *London Archaeologist*, 8(ix), 198. Thames Bridge.

Orchinnikoc, I, et al, 2000. *Nature*, 404, 490. Neandertal DNA.

Ovey, CD, 1964. *Royal Anthropological Institute*, occasional paper 21. The Swanscombe Skull.

Parfitt, K, 1993. *Current Archaeology*, 133, 4. The Dover Late Bronze Age Boat.

Parfitt, S, Barendregt, M et al, 2005. *Nature*, 438, 1008. Pakefield.

Parfitt, S, Stringer, C et al, 2006. *British Archaeology*, 80, p18-21. Pakefield.

Parfitt, S, et al, 2008. *Proc Suffolk Inst Arch Hist*, 41(4), 489. Paleolithic.

Pearson, A, 2002. *The Roman Shore Forts*. Tempus, Stroud.

Pettitt, P, 1999. *British Archaeology*, 45, 6. Largar Velho child.

Pettitt, P, Bahn, P, Ripoll, S, 2006. *Cave Art, Creswell*. Oxford University Press.

Philpott, R, 1991. *British Archaeological Reports* 219. Burial Practices in Roman Britain.

Pitts, M, 1980. *Later Stone Implements*. Shire, Aylesbury.

Pitts, M, Perring, D, 2006. *Britannia*, 37, 189. First Urban Landscapes.

Plunkett, S, 2005. *Suffolk in Anglo-Saxon Times*. Tempus, Stroud.

Priddy, D, 1982. *Essex Archaeology & History*, 14, 114. Wormingford cropmarks.

Pryor, F, 1998. *Farmers in Prehistoric Britain*. Tempus.

Rackham, O, 1986. *The Woods of South-east Essex*. Rochford District Council.

Rackham, O. 1987. *History of the Countryside*. JM Dent.

Rees, S, 1981. *Ancient Agricultural Implements*. Shire.

Reidy, K, 1997. *Essex Archaeology & History*, 28, 1. Bronze Age at Great Wakering.

Reynolds, PJ, 1979. *Iron Age Farm, the Butser Experiment*. British Museum.

Reynolds, P, 1987. *Ancient Farming*. Shire.

RIB. *Roman Inscriptions of Britain*. Frere, SS et al. 1990-4. A Sutton.

Richards, M, Hedges, R, et al, 2000. *Journal of Archaeological Science*, 27, 1. Gough's Cave.

Ripoll, S, Muñoz, P, et al, 2004. *Proceedings of Prehistoric Soc*, 70, 93. Creswell Engravings.

Rippon, S, 1991. *Essex Archaeology & History*, 22, 46. Landscapes in South-east Essex.

Rivett, ALF, Smith, C, 1979. *Place-Names of Roman Britain*. Batsford.

Roberts, M, 1994. *Nature*, 369, 311. A Hominid Tibia from Boxgrove.

Roberts, M, 1997. *Current Archaeology*, 153, 324. Boxgrove.

Roberts, W, 1982. *British Archaeological Reports*, 106. Romano-Saxon pottery..

Rodwell, KA, 1988. *Council for British Archaeology Research Report* 63. Kelvedon.

Rodwell, KA & WJ, 1975. *Current Archaeology*, 45, 25. Kelvedon.

Rodwell, W, 1970. *Antiquaries Journal*, 50, 262. Romano-Saxon pottery.

Rodwell, WJ, 1971. *South-east Essex in the Roman Period*. Southend Museum, publcn 16.

Rodwell, W & K, 1973. *Britannia*, iv, 115. Rivenhall Roman Villa.

Rodwell, W, 1975a in Rodwell & Rowley, RT. *British Archaeol Reps* 15,85. Trinovantian Towns.

Rodwell, W, 1975b. *Roman Essex*. Colchester Borough Council.

Rodwell, W, 1976. *Brit Archaeol Reps* suppl 11. Coinage, Oppida & the Rise of Belgic Power.

Rodwell, WJ, 1977. *Essex Archaeology & History*, 8, 234. Bradwell-on-Sea.

Rodwell, WJ, 1978a, in Bowen HC (ed). *British Archaeol Rep* 48, 89. Land Allotment.

Rodwell, WJ, 1978b in Todd, M (ed). *Studies in the Romano-British Villa*. Leicester, p29.

Rodwell, WJ, 1979 in Burnham, BC (ed). *British Archaeol Rep* 73, 133. Rome & Trinovantes.

Rodwell, WJ and KA, 1985, 1993. *Council for British Archaeol Res Rep* 55 & 80. Rivenhall.

Rodwell, W, 1993. *The Origins of Witham*. Oxbow Monograph 26.

Roe, DA, 1968. *Council for British Archaeology Research Report* 8. Paleolithic Sites.

Rudd, C. 2009. *Current Archaeology*, 227, 12. Wickham Market Coin Hoard.

Rudling, DR, 1990. *Essex Archaeology & History*, 21, 19. Roman Billericay.

Russell, M, 2000. *Flint Mines in Neolithic Britain*. Tempus.

St Joseph, JK, 1964. *Antiquity*, 38, 290. Aerial Photography.

Salter, AE, 1914. *Essex Natualist*, 17, 186. Sarsens.

Salway, P, 1981. *Roman Britain*. Oxford.

Scaife, R, 1988 in Wilkinson, TJ (ed). *East Anglian Archaeology*, 42, 109. Mar Dyke.

Sealey, PR, 1987. *Essex Archaeology & History*, 18, 7. Bronze Hoard from Fingringhoe.

Sealey, PR, 1991. *Essex Archaeology & History*, 22, 1. Bronze and Iron Finds in Essex.
Sealey, PR, 1995. *Essex Archaeology & History*, 26, 65. Salt Industry.
Sealey, PR, 1996 in Bedwin, O. *Archaeology of Essex*, Essex Co Council, p46. Iron Age.
Sealey, PR, 1997. *Essex Archaeology & History*, 28, pp270, 273. Bronze Hoards.
Sealey, PR, 1997. *The Boudican Revolt*. Shire.
Sealey, PR (forthcoming). *Proceedings of the Chelmsford Conference 2008.* Iron Age.
Shand, P, Hodder, I, et al, 1990. *Current Archaeology*, 118, 339. Haddenham Long Barrow.
Sharples, NM, 1991. *Maiden Castle*. London.
Singer, R, Wymer, JJ, et al, 1973. *Proceedings of Prehistoric Soc*, 39, 6. Clactonian Industry.
Sloane, B, Swain, H et al, 1995. *London Archaeologist*, 7(xiv), 359. Roman Westminster.
Smith, RA, 1925. *Antiquities of the Early Iron Age*. British Museum.
Smoothey, MD, 1989. *Essex Archaeology & History*, 20, 1. Roman Rayne.
Sollas, G, 1913. *Journal of the Royal Anthropological Institute*, 43. Paviland Cave.
Strachan, D, 1995. *Essex Journal*, 30(ii), 41. Aerial Survey.
Stead, IM, Bourke, JB, Brothwell, D, 1986. *Lindow Man*. British Museum.
Stringer, CB, 1996, in Gamble, CS, et al. *English Palaeolithic Reviewed*. Wessex Archaeol.
Stringer, C, 2006. *Homo Britannicus.* Penguin.
Stringer, C, Davies, W, 2001. *Nature*, 410, p791. Elusive Neanderthals.
Swanscombe Committee, 1937-38. *Journal of Royal Anthropological Institute* 67,339; 68,17.

Taylor, C, 1983. *Village and Farmstead.* Phillip, London.
Thomas, J, 2008. *Current Archaeology*, 216, 24. Bronze Age Monuments.
Thornton, P, 1976. *Archaeologia Cantiana*, 42, 119. Thames Ford Campaigns 54BC, AD43.
Timby, J, Brown, R et al, 2007. *Oxford Wessex Archaeol,* monograph 1. A120 Bypass.
Tobias, P, 1971. *The Brain of Hominid Evolution*. Columbia University Press, New York.
Tolan-Smith, C, 2000. *British Archaeology*, 56, 8. Hoxne.
Tonnochy, AB, Hawkes, CFC, 1931. *Antiquaries Jnl*, 11, 123. Roman Sacred Tree Motif.
Topping, P, 2003. *British Archaeology*, 72, 14. Grimes Graves.
Trinkaus, E, Shipman, P, 1993. *The Neandertals*. Cape.
Trump, D, 1993. *Essex Journal*, 28(ii), 40. Mistley church.
Turner, BRG, 1982. *Essex County Council, occasional paper*, 2. Ivy Chimneys, Witham.
Turner, R, 1999. *East Anglian Archaeology*, 88. Ivy Chimneys, Witham.
Tylecote, RF, 1978 in Drury, PJ (ed). *Council for British Arch Research Rep* 26, 115.
Tyler, S, 1984. *Essex Archaeology & History*, 16, 91. Possible Crop mark Long Barrows.
Tyler, S, 1996 in Bedwin, O (ed). *Archaeology of Essex*, Essex Co Council, p108. Saxon.

Van Arsdell, RD, 1989. *Celtic Coinage of Britain*. Spink, London.
Victoria County History of Essex (especially 1901, 1963, 1994) vols i, iii,and ix.
Victoria County History of Suffolk (1911) vol i.

Waite, GA, 1985. *British Archaeological Reports* 149. Ritual & Religion in Iron Age Britain.
Wallis, S, 1989. *Essex Journal*, 24(ii), 41. Great Totham site.
Wallis, S, Waughman, M, 1998. *East Anglian Archaeology*, 82. Landscape in the Blackwater.
Ward, R, Stringer, C, 1997. *Nature*, 388, 225. Neandertal DNA.

Wardill, R, 1997. *Great Chesterford Geophysical Survey Report*. Essex County Council.

Warren, SH, 1909-11. *Essex Naturalist*, 16, 265. Hullbridge.

Waughman, M, 1989. *Essex Journal*, 24(i), 15. Chigborough Farm, Goldhanger.

Webster, G, 1993. *Boudica*. Batsford.

Weller, SGP, Westley, B, Myers, JNL, 1974. *Antiquaries Journal*, 54, 282. Billericay.

West, SE, 1976. *East Anglian Archaeology*, 3, 63. Icklingham.

White, M, 2003. *Current Archaeology*, 44, 598. Levallois.

White, M, Jacobi, R, 2002. *Oxford Journal of Archaeology*, 21(2), 109. Bout Coupé Axes.

White, M, Schreve, DC, 2000. *Proceedings of the Prehistoric Society*, 66, 1. Island Britain.

Whittle, AWR, 1978. *Antiquity*, 52, 34. Population in the British Neolithic.

Whittle, AWR, 1985. *Neolithic Europe*. Cambridge.

Wickenden, NP, 1986. *Britannica*, 17, 348. Votives from Chelmsford.

Wickenden, NP, 1988. *East Anglian Archaeology*, 41. Great Dunmow.

Wickenden, NP, 1990. *Essex Journal*, 25(iii), 58. Caesaromagus.

Wickenden, N, 1991. *Caesaromagus*. Chelmsford Museum Service.

Wickenden, NP, 1996 in Bedwin, O. *Archaeology of Essex*. EssexCC, p76. Roman Towns.

Wilkinson, P, 1978. *Essex Archaeology & History*, 10, 220. Uphall Camp, Ilford.

Wilkinson, TJ, 1987. *Essex Journal*, 22(ii), 29. The Hullbridge Project.

Wilkinson, TJ, 1988. *East Anglian Archaeology*, 42,101. Environment in South Essex.

Wilkinson, TJ, Murphy, P, 1995. *East Anglian Archaeology*, 71. Archaeology of the Coast.

Williams, J, 2007. *Britannia*, 38, 1. Latin in Pre-Conquest Britain.

Williams, JH (ed), 2007. *Archaeology of Kent to AD 800*. Kent County Council, p.189.

Williamson, T, 1984. *Britannia*, 15, 225. The Roman Countryside in NW Essex.

Williamson, T, 1986. *Essex Archaeology & History*, 17,120. Field Survey of NW Essex.

Williamson, T, 1986. *Jnl Hist Geography*, 12, 241. Parish Boundaries & Early Fields.

Williamson, T, 1987. *Proceedings of the Prehistoric Society*, 53, 419. Field Systems.

Williamson, T, 1987. *New Scientist*, 19th March. A Sense of Direction for Dowsers.

Wiltshire, P, Murphy, P, 1988 in Wallis, S. *East Anglian Archaeology*, 82, 117. Blackwater.

Winterbottom, M, 1978. *Gildas - Arthurian Period Sources*. Phillimore.

Wright, AG, 1923. *Trans Essex Archaeological Society*, ns 16, 288. Dagenham Idol.

Wymer, JJ, 1977. *CBA Research Rep* 22. Mesolithic Sites. Geo Abstracts, Norwich.

Wymer, JJ, 1984 in Barringer, C (ed). *Aspects of East Anglian Archaeology*. Geo, Norwich, p31.

Wymer, J, 1985. *Prehistoric Sites in East Anglia*. Geo Books, Norwich.

Wymer, J, 1991. *Mesolithic Britain*. Shire.

Wymer, JJ, 1996, in Bedwin, O (ed). *Archaeology of Essex*. Essex Co Council, p1. Paleolithic.

Wymer, J, 1999. *The Lower Palaeolithic Occupation of Britain*. English Heritage.

Wymer, JJ and Brown, N, 1995. *East Anglian Archaeology*, 75, 142. North Shoebury.

Wymer, J, Robins, P, 2006. *Current Archaeology*, 201, 458. Earliest Britons.

Yorke, B, 1985. *Anglo-Saxon England*, 14, 1. Kingdom of the East Saxons.

Yorke, B, 1990. *Kings & Kingdoms of Early Anglo-Saxon England*. Routledge.

Index

217